Becoming Mariposa

Hope Emerges from a Dark Chrysalis

A Memoir of Mental and Spiritual Healing

ELIZABETH LEONE GONZALEZ

SILVERSMITH
PRESS

Published by Silversmith Press–Houston, Texas
www.silversmithpress.com

ISBN 978-1-967386-40-6 (Softcover Book)
ISBN 978-1-967386-41-3 (eBook)
ISBN 978-1-967386-42-0 (Hardcover Book)

Cover art and illustrations by Elizabeth Gonzalez

DISCLAIMER
This is a memoir. It reflects my personal memories, perceptions, and experiences as I recall them. Memory is a fickle friend, and while I have done my best
to recount events faithfully, some details may be blurred by time, perspective, or
emotion. Dialogue and events are reconstructed to the best of my ability but may
not be verbatim.

The names and identifying details of most individuals have been changed to
protect their privacy. Any resemblance to actual people, living or dead, is coinciden-
tal and unintentional, except where explicitly stated.

This book is not intended to malign any individual, group, or organization. The
opinions expressed are solely my own. Others may remember events differently, and
I respect their right to their own perspectives.

The content of this memoir is not intended as a substitute for professional
advice, diagnosis, or treatment. If you are affected by any of the issues discussed,
please seek appropriate support.

DEDICATIONS

To my brothers, Finn and Patrick—"The Powers," whom I treasure immensely as bright spots growing up. Thank you for loving me steadfastly. Laughing with you has been a refuge. Thank you, Finn, for encouraging me to tell my stories.

To my caring stepsisters, Rebecca and Agnes, and to the tías—Bellis, Carol, Lisy, and Elia—who have shown me what loving sisterhood looks like.

To my dear Martha—now you are truly free.

To my "frister" Vanessa, who knows the painful process of healing from childhood wounds.

To my mothers—GG, Nani, Bellis and Maggie—who have shown me unconditional love and generosity.

Thank you, friends—Julie K., Abby, Angie, Kristen, Hannah, Jessica and Inez—for making me laugh and bringing me joy.

Thank you to my beta readers—Finn, Zev, Bellis, Papa, Lynn, Vanessa, Jessica, Julie L., Hannah and June—for your support and valuable insights.

To Joanna Hunt, my amazing publisher and editing coach—your talent and encouragement were vital to birthing this book! I'm deeply grateful to you.

Most of all, to my husband Henry, who has fiercely loved me from a hot mess into the butterfly. You are my best friend, my forever love, my heart.

CONTENTS

INTRODUCTION

The beautiful butterfly—once a stubby caterpillar devouring everything in sight—her voracious appetite had one purpose: to fuel a fierce transformation.

She begins by spinning a silk chrysalis that will completely envelop her in a temporary home of protection. Suspended upside down, she waits for an excruciating change—requiring intense fortification. Her entire being becomes liquefied, totally undone and rebuilt. Dissolving everything within, her body digests itself from the inside out. Her old form is broken down into remnants that will shape her wings, legs, antennae, and new body.

A couple of days before emerging, her chrysalis changes color. What will emerge—her patterns and pigment—become visible through the transparent cocoon.

At the right time, the butterfly breaks free from her protective chrysalis. She pushes her body out with great effort, and her struggle is crucial—it builds muscles she will need to fly. Clutching firmly to the remains of her chrysalis, she waits several hours while blood pumps into her freshly formed wings. Then, with untried legs, she walks, probing her habitat for food. Silently roving, she opens and closes her wings slowly, repeatedly. When the moment arrives that she has readied herself—the butterfly flies away with her new form, and her new life.

No one can improve upon the glory of the butterfly. The vibrant patterns and colors that contour her shape delight the eye and for many, evoke joy in the heart. Even the gloomiest souls are brightened by the playful gentleness and fluttery excitement of her flight. When we happen to encounter one, the whimsy of this winged wonder holds us captive as she dances with ease and then flits away in her own pleasurable ballet, her beauty hinting at a deeper transformation.

The butterfly's journey, with its painful unraveling and costly rebirth, echoes my own path through shadowed struggles and restless seeking. I wandered through many gardens, drawn to warmth that sometimes deceived, and shelter that sometimes stung. But the chrysalis held me, even when I didn't yet know I was *Becoming Mariposa*.

Hope emerged from that dark chrysalis, lifting me toward a light I had yet to understand.

PART ONE

The Caterpillar

"We're all vulnerable. Mix the wrong feelings together, the right kind of bad with the wrong kind of good, and you'll wind up with a total breakdown."
—The Caterpillar from *Alice in Wonderland*

ONE

Uprooted

Time was running out. It was the middle of the pandemic, and our landlord was pressuring us to leave our home of twelve years. Given two months to vacate and find a place to live, we felt a terrible strain, especially since we were months removed from a severe family health crisis.

Forced to uproot during a brutal housing market, properties in Tucson were selling within hours of listing and rising by nearly $10,000 every week. We watched this hyper-inflated market bloat before our very eyes and as intimidating as this was, there was no sign of it slowing down. This kept pushing the boundaries of what we could pay for, making it hard to relax until we were able to find some-thing affordable for our family of three—my husband and me with our 14-year-old son. So far, we attempted to put in offers on two ideal homes, but each sold within the time it took to put an offer together.

We pulled up to another house—it had just listed the night before. We almost didn't make it here this morning. Hoping to put a salve on my stress level, I woke up ill from drinking mere sips of wine. *I am such a lightweight.* Nursing a migraine, I mustered up the strength to go, even though photos of the house were not impressive, which raised some red flags.

Our real estate agent Ed, an old friend of my husband's, was running late. The window of time to view this home we were parked in front of was also dwindling. Mounting tension was making it hard to unwind for even a breath of reprieve. Each minute of delay seemed like an eternity considering how hot this seller's market was.

Opening the car window, I noticed the lure of this cottage-looking property. Relaxing the weight of my jaw into a cupped hand, I surveyed the yard's show of nature. Upon my brow, a soft breeze blew while enchanting plants swayed to its rhythm. The resonance of a wind chime soothed my mind as it twirled below the house trim. I recognized the warm woody scent of a sage bush tipped with purple blooms. More than a couple of butterflies flit into my view and hovered all around the flowers. As I stared at them playfully resist drifts of air, a familiar rest of peace washed over me. My next breaths were full and restorative—like a brief respite from the past month.

A growing anticipation for this home came over me. Could this be the treasure we get to unearth at the end of this trying season? It felt like hope—hope which I reeled in rapidly like a fisherman winding his line at the first hint of a fish's nibble.

Cool your jets.

There have been so many setbacks.

Chill out!

I had become weary of being let down by these listings. Life had taught me to expect that obstacles were lurking around every corner. At the same time, as the youngest of four siblings, I had a strong inclination to express exhilaration over potential joys on the horizon. I have depended upon my husband Henry to pull me out of the frustration caused by this wildly divergent fear of disappointment on the one hand and dreamy optimism on the other. He has always been the level-headed one, content in most situations and helping redirect my attention. I turned to him and said, "I hope we are not disappointed by the inside because the outside is really cute." With patient resolve, he held back any first impressions.

At the time, Henry and I would have described the rental home we had been living in as adequate. Accustomed to low-cost rent and the complacent inertia of the status quo, we settled there for more than a decade. With constant dimness from lack of natural light, it was gloomy, oddly designed and horribly outdated—the sort of home that perpetually lacked an inviting feel. But because we built a life there, raising our son and my stepdaughter, we intended to buy and renovate it with all our dream plans.

It was time for us to leave, however. Situated in the migratory pattern of scorpions, we experienced anxious encounters with those miniature monsters. The park across the street which had been a refuge for our autistic son Elisha was now occupied by a couple of kids who began to bully him, and he struggled to communicate it to us. We needed this push from our landlord really—just to release the clenches of our own stubborn lethargy for change. But—*not this way!* Not in the middle of a pandemic in a crazy housing market with almost no notice, and a hard deadline!

Ed pulled up. By this time, I was coming out of my skin to view this place. Quickly, I got out of the car, crossed the threshold of the home and scanned the entryway. Mesmerized by soaring vaulted ceilings, I stood astounded with fizzing elation. My eyes registered an abundance of natural light which glowed from two large bay windows. A warm sense of renewal and welcome filled my heart. Wooden floors graced the entryway and through to the kitchen contrasted by cool sage walls. Struck by how open the floorplan was, my astonishment continued to balloon. Could this be our new home? My heart was beating out of my chest! I noticed more details—elegant white trim, decorative edgings, crown molding and marble-topped vanities. *This house is beautiful!* I thought. Truly, it was something special. Henry stood dumbfounded at the entrance for a few moments, until he finally breathed out, "Wow!"

Then suddenly I remembered what I considered was a red flag after seeing the listing. It was the master bedroom—in the photos it looked compact and even claustrophobic. When I got to the room, I stopped in my tracks. *Yes! This is a perfect size!* I ran back to Henry. "Behb!"—as we affectionately call each other, "Come and see! There are no red flags!" When Henry saw it, he said, "Oh wow, I see what you mean. This is really nice!" It looked like something out of *Pride and Prejudice*. Dreamy shades were drawn from an ornate valance revealing backyard foliage bathed by the sun. This felt like a redemptive home of built-in beauty which we lacked for so many years in the rental home. With minimal needed updates, it was brimming with charm and move-in ready! My stomach began to lift into my heart. Would a contract on this home go through for us?

There was still another area worth seeing. I darted out back to look at the garden. At first glimpse, I covered my open mouth and began to cry. This was stunning! Unlike anything in the harsh Sonoran Desert, this backyard splendor was teeming with plants, flowers, greenery and the fragrance of sweet, earthy aromas. A set of young pine trees first stole my gaze. I had sorely missed the texture and smell of evergreens. Framed by a merlot-covered arch, a stone crafted staircase was adorned with flowering pots. Ivy and fig vines wrapped around a sloping rock backdrop, bordering the yard with wonderful surfaces of green. A grand canopy of shade given by a large African Sumac tree created dazzling speckles of light, highlighting vibrant plants nestled just below it. All I saw was life, nature, reflected gleams and bursts of pretty color everywhere—a feast for my teary eyes! And how can it be? There was even a dedicated butterfly garden. *A butterfly garden*? This area was the most magical to me—glistening with a vivid palette of blooms that specifically attract butterflies. Even while we were standing there, monarchs and queens fluttered all around us. It was like a dream!

Henry and I looked at each other. Nothing needed to be said or discussed. He saw how the dread of the past four weeks had shifted into jubilant tears on my face. Henry told Ed to put in an offer of $5000 over the asking price—a wise gesture, just to be sure. But nothing was certain in this market. I hated this next phase—I braced myself for it. This was the unavoidable part of yet another roller coaster ride of a potential letdown. My mind leapt to the sensation of being fastened inside an amusement park car, steadily moving higher on the tracks. Tuning to the click-click-click-click-click sound while scanning below to harrowing heights, knowing we were about to reach the top, crown the inevitable summit and plummet with a harrowing scream. This was worth it, even if we had to suffer yet another rejection. There was no turning back now—*Ahhhh!* Everything about this home was beyond anything we had hoped for.

Though it's ridiculous to purchase a house because of a backyard, it was like tasting supremely delicious icing upon an incredible cake. And really, it has a garden dedicated to butterflies? I couldn't get over the meaning this held for me. We would have to wait and see what providence had for us. Before we headed out, I scurried to the backyard once more.

As I watched them effortlessly flutter from flower to flower, I longed to perceive life as these butterflies did. Their movements were seamless and untroubled. With paper-thin vulnerable wings, they seemed to play with the wind, responding with a joyful retort to life. I have spent years now thinking about them. And of course, I imagined myself resting in this garden area dedicated to the butterfly—or *la mariposa* as it is called in Spanish. The fear of disappointment gripped me as I gave a few final glances back at the garden. We would have to see if our offer would be enough—if our family could in fact, move here and I could take further refuge in this sanctuary. I longed for my own completed metamorphosis, and could this, *would* this home be a part of that transformation?

TWO

Mystic Feast

Behold the eating machine. First, chomping its way out of an egg, the newly appearing caterpillar gorges straightaway on its host plant. Sentient only to available grub, it consumes until it expands one hundred times in size. The caterpillar has no imagination for the hero's journey to come. Its beginnings obscure any future hope. It doesn't dream of anything but food.

PARANORMAL SEARCH

At thirteen, I sat perched in a healer's special room filled with angel statues wondering, *How many actual angels are present right here, right now?* Especially hypnotized by smaller figurines balanced on the windowsill, I pondered, *Are they talking to me?* I strained to see if I could hear a word they were saying. At one point I asked her, "Do they talk to you?" She replied, "Yes, they do sometimes." We traveled a fair distance just to visit this "angel healer's" home. I tried to perceive another dimension there—one that I desperately wanted access to. Earnestly, I sought a magical solution. The visit typified what came to be a carousel of mystical things my mother and I pursued over the years that fed my longing for something beyond the visible.

My search for paranormal answers began with my mother's book collection. When I turned ten, she began treasuring self-help New Age volumes that opened a gateway for her into the metaphysical world of self-realization. Her eyes sparkled with excited passion as she told me mysterious truths that only she and a "select few people on the planet" had discovered. Because she was my mother, I was highly receptive to her influence. After growing up a devout Catholic and following religious tenets for years, my mother suddenly became intoxicated by psychic fairs, crystals, reincarnation, tarot cards and spiritual "healers."

Up to that point, I knew the holy hush of Catholic ritual and staring at crucifixion scenes strewn across stained-glass windows. Never receiving answers that satisfied, I tuned out during mass. In communion class I asked one of the nuns, "Does the communion wafer really, I mean *really* turn into the body and blood of Christ?" The sister deflected my question once, and then twice when, determined to know the truth, I asked her again. When it was my first time to "confess to the priest," I could not recall anything, so in a tizzy—I fibbed about treating our pet fish badly. Next, I asked for forgiveness for lying because at that moment I had lied about the fish! The truth is our cat "Mackie" had recently left an intact fish skeleton next to his food bowl. So, it was not really my confession to make—I had confessed for Mackie, who was probably not Catholic anyway.

The last time my mother and I attended mass, I endured weighty drowsiness just to stay awake during the midnight Christmas service. On the way home, just as we spoke about all the pretty poinsettias lining the church altar, we were rear-ended by another vehicle. The accident was so startling to my mother that she saw it as a sign to stop being Catholic. After that night, my hunger for New Age spiritual things began to mirror my mother's. Like the voracious caterpillar, this time in my young life roused a growing appetite for the spirit world.

So, here we were at the affluent home of the angel healer. None other than the color white was visible in her monochrome hearth, and I wasn't sure if it reminded me of purity or hollowness. We lay down on her massage table while she supposedly communed with angels to channel their angel healing—cleansing our bodies of negative energies. The funny thing, and she informed us prior to our sessions, she belched loudly when she helped to release energy. I have vivid memories of listening to her let rip obnoxious burps! While this woman was very serious about noises she believed were a byproduct of true healing, she didn't scold me for my uncontrollable giggling.

My mother and I managed to convince ourselves that we felt some kind of "release" in our souls, so we reserved more sessions with the angel healer. We also traveled to psychic fairs to consult with psychics and astrologers. I was told things which enticed my naïve, suggestible ears—things like, "People will think you are very young, but you will always be smarter than you look—they will underestimate you." As the youngest of four siblings, this was music to my ears! Like the hungry caterpillar, I ate everything my mother put in front of me, eager to fill a growing emptiness inside.

SELF-HELP

Especially affected by my mother's fascination, I was introduced to various concepts such as "healing yourself" or believing you can transcend your own psychology with metaphysical spirituality. True potential can be unlocked using tools such as—master and cleanse your chakras, learn yoga, manifest the destiny you want, surround yourself with high energy crystals, see this guru, meditate, go to this retreat, speak this mantra, think positive thoughts, travel to this sacred place, travel, open your heart, be free, be you. I grew up in Northern California, where many non-religious people lived their own paths to become their best selves.

Once my mother embarked on her master's in counseling degree, I learned firsthand the language of psychotherapy and was exposed to hypnosis, personality assessments, "working on yourself," introspection, and using "I statements" ad nauseum. Because I was pre-pubescent while she was in the thick of her studies, this time is marked for me when my personality began to shift. While I had been a light-hearted, playful, spontaneous kid, I began to overthink and overanalyze everything. I also started adopting aspects of my mother's thinking such as obsessively caring about what others thought of me, adapting my speech to be pleasing, and developing paranoias about how I might be perceived. This was when my mother imparted how to become as perfectionistic as she was—molding me into her "idyllic" image.

In an effort to free myself from these warring mental constructs, I started giving myself tarot card readings. During college, I read *Tao De Ching* and *The Way of the Yogi*, practiced Aikido martial arts, hung out at metaphysical bookstores and like many of my friends, we smudged with sage. Sometimes I would meditate for hours in front of an altar—though unbeknownst to me, I spent that time dissociating from reality.

Desperately, I searched for something tangible that might help me transcend my own psychology. But striving to rise above mental constructions just led to more annoying self-analysis. So, when my sister invited me and my mom to the International Spiritual Ascension Festival in May 1994, I was enticed by the prospect of being mentally free. This is when it all got more intense!

THE ASCENSION FESTIVAL

At Mount Shasta, we convened with international spiritual enthusiasts to "master the spiritual, psychological and physical aspects of self." At the time, this path was heralded as a "balanced approach to self-realization" seemed perfectly logical to me. The occult world had been tickling my ears, and I arrived hopeful for transformation.

We were led into a weekend of meditations, encouragements, "accelerations" and channelings "from another spiritual realm." Throughout the conference, I sat on the tip of my chair, completely engaged, and most impressed by the palpably heavy sensations I felt. True as anything I knew at the time, I was wholly mesmerized by otherworldly energy. Lorelei Schook, one of the Ascension leaders, channeled the "divine mother." She had sparkly eyes, and her thin lips framed a charismatic smile. I was riveted by her nurturing words. In just a few years, she would become the most influential person in my life. Though we were primarily there to receive a "channeled message from the ascended masters," a conversation I had with an Australian woman who started the "Breatharian" movement made me chuckle inside.

"So, you have lived on light for a whole year?" I asked.

"Yes, I have lived off my own prana life force," she replied.

"Can I ask how it is that you haven't become anorexic?"

She responded, "I just tell myself what weight I want to be, and I don't go below that. I control it all with my mind."

Wow. I wasn't entirely sure about all that. While I was a vegetarian in college, that did not stop me from walking across campus to sneak in an extra-large turkey sandwich—so I wasn't convinced.

There was a booth on "aura" light photography. It was so mysterious. The cost was $20 for a single Polaroid photo, and there was no question, it was worth every penny. I had to see who I was and how spiritual I was! As an artist, I was also interested in which colors would choose to rest on my face. My photo showed red and yellow, but there wasn't much information given about what that actually meant.

THE BANQUET

I left the Ascension Festival without a tangible guide to feel freer, but I gained a hopeful answer to how to eventually fix my frustrating internal landscape. The weekend caused me to focus on spiritual endeavors as the greatest priority in my life, and it was the start of obsessing about ascension spirituality including its leaders, books and the prospect of "spiritual advancement."

I was about to become a very fat caterpillar, having just crawled up the table legs to the top, overlooking the grandest feast I had ever laid my eyes upon. As a result of attending the first and then second annual Ascension Festival, I met two influential characters who would become my guru "masters" long into my twenties.

In all honesty, my quest for spiritual enlightenment was not born out of some noble sense to evolve into a higher consciousness—it was wrought out of a desperate need for wholeness and self-worth.

Sure, it was easier to buy into an elevated sense of self by seeking "enlightenment" rather than have to deal with my handicaps and brokenness. But essentially, I was a truth seeker. I needed to unearth the truth about my own identity and who truly loved me. By now I felt trapped in a large web of coping mechanisms, developed for reasons I did not yet understand, and I could not see past them to know who I really was. A glutton for mystical experiences, I truly believed spiritual endeavors could release me from this confusion. Resolute to fill internal voids, I devoured otherworldly escapes until they disappointed.

So, to understand what fed my insatiable appetite for spiritual growth, let me introduce you to "Little Bethy."

THREE

Little Bethy

Scampering down the hallway, I fell onto the living room carpet in a howl of laughter. My brother Finn tickled me mercilessly so that I couldn't catch my breath between uncontrollable laughs. Arresting me with playfulness, he cried out, "Say it! Say it again Bethy!" We had recently watched *The Attack of the Killer Tomatoes*, and his tickling hands would not cease until I delivered his favorite comical phrase. Wildly amused with stretched cheeks of joy, I couldn't get a word out! Finally, in between squeals, I emitted the words in a cute growl just like those dreaded tomatoes—"Dub-bah, Dub-bah, Dub-bah." As soon as Finn heard my impersonation, he cracked up until his whole body was in stitches, and he couldn't help but release me from his tickling hold. *Oh, how I loved to laugh with him!*

As a child, I was joyful, ebullient and I loved to chuckle—I still do. Grandma said that I giggled in my sleep, and Mom recounted that I was a "lover of life." I recall the excited rush of tricycle racing through the house. With my tiny red vehicle, I relentlessly peeled around corners without care of tipping over—a perma-smile covered most of my face and a measure of adrenaline coursed through my little body. On summer days, I splashed about in my plastic turtle pool, and during bath time, I was content to sing passionately behind faux glass doors. Precociously, I pretended to read words inside greeting cards before I even knew the alphabet. On most days, I was satisfied with art supplies or singing to my favorite Disney records.

I was such a free-spirited, happy kid that it was unsettling to learn I had repressed many bad memories, leaving me with a mixed bag of recalls. Mostly I remember in vivid detail the enjoyable times, and my favorite recollections of childhood were during the holidays—bright, chaotic and strangely comforting.

TIMELY TURKEY

My mother laid our Thanksgiving bird into the oven, encased in an oven bag and bordered by full-size carrots. With the promise of a scrumptious meal, she drove two grown teenagers and me, age eight, to the Modesto Reservoir. I was thrilled to be with my oldest brother Patrick—I didn't see him often and I trusted in his tender heart and filter-less candor. While my mother dozed off, we had the entire lake to ourselves.

Patrick found a branch in shallow waters. Holding it high like a famed superhero, he exclaimed with a powerful rush of hilarity, "I AM THE POWER!" I followed in suit with my own stick held high, retorting with equal enthusiasm—"No, I AM THE POWER!" We burst out laughing while finding bulkier sticks to proudly declare to the world—

"WE ARE THE POWER!"

Apparently, this was the catch phrase of "He-Man," but we were very entertained to obnoxiously shout it as the water clapped our skin.

Patrick then dragged the heaviest, most massive branch to announce that he really was *THE* Power. He mustered up the strength to lift it for a few seconds—before it hysterically tumbled into the water with a grand splash. As we laughed aloud, Patrick looked over at me with eyes that said—*You are funny my beloved little sister!* To this day, we affectionately call each other "the Powers."

Well, time flies when—you aren't really paying attention. The turkey bag instructions described three hours of cooking. *Oops!* We had been gone six. Heading back, we kids joked about arriving home to a charred turkey in our house of flames. My mother stepped up her slug-paced driving into a racetrack pace. Though my tomato-red cheeks began to sting, the memories I made were worth acquiring sunburnt-scorches comparable to our imagined turkey.

Once home, we ran inside to discover a faint smoke coming from the oven, but nothing that warranted our dire predictions. In fact, when we carved into our poultry beauty, it was juicy with a thin layer of crunchy skin—the perfect combination. As we devoured it, our mouths declared the glory of this turkey, "Wow!" "Yum!" and "Oh man!" And though we scurried home to an imagined Thanksgiving disaster, our over-cooked bird had burnt to a surprisingly delicious crisp! I've honestly never tasted better.

HOLIDAY TREASURES

Perched upon a highchair, my legs kicking with excitement, I gazed at our dining room table adorned with charming glitter, a heart-shaped cake and red foil hearts. Twirling a chocolate sucker in my mouth, I fell in love with Valentine's Day. A few weeks later, I ogled over my mother's homemade Easter Bunny cake with colored coconut and Juju-be eyes. Each of our treasure-packed baskets were hidden in clever spots, and I squealed with delight looking for mine.

Because Cecile Ann made sure every celebration was exceptional for her four children, I liken my mother to "Martha Stewart during the holidays." She divorced my father when I was nine months old, and mostly had custody of me and my sister, while my older brothers Patrick and Finn—nine and eight years older than I—were eventually sent to live with my dad. In the unrest of transferring siblings, I greatly anticipated times when we were all together.

OUR CHRISTMAS STORY

Christmas was magical for me, perhaps because my mother believed it actually was. Fragranced by orange-clove potpourri simmering on the stove, our December home was adorned with poinsettias, ribboned garlands, and a bountiful wreath hanging on the front door. Every winter, she bought a cord of wood to be kindled during cold evenings—the aroma of pine infused the area where it lay stacked. I loved to sit on our fireplace mantle and stare into the blue-highlighted flames until the heat approached a searing intensity on my skin. In early December, she drove us to chop down a tree, which always ended up looking like a "Charlie Brown Special" once in the stand. I relished trimming it and then staring at the one flashing pink bulb randomly inserted into our light set—it made its own unique twinkle.

On Christmas morning, Mom had us open one present at a time—she wanted to hear us appreciate each hand-picked gift. Even though we were trained to be patient for it, amongst four siblings, the process was slow. But stocking time was free for all—a Christmas finale of ravaging through paper-wrapped toys, candies and a new toothbrush. As we popped chocolate sweeties into our mouths, a colorful mess of shredded paper crinkled beneath us long into the morning.

Through super eight movie reels from my childhood Christmases, you would view us in a chaotic ham fest of wide-open smiles and expressive faces. Once the camera rolled, on cue my siblings and I spazzed out with funny antics. Though we didn't own a VCR, I fondly remember viewing these silent retro reels as a family. We munched on buttery popcorn while projected images illuminated our eyes. Our imaginations filled in the loud gestures, jokes and poking at each other which we knew in real time had been great fun!

We laughed as Finn acted out savoring his holiday favorite—dried apricots with a hilarious expression. After tucking a napkin into his shirt, he pierced each fruit delicacy with a fork, lifting them singularly to his mouth like an English gentleman. In the next moment, Patrick took over the screen, raising his shirt and proudly pounding on his chest like King Kong. Emilia popped bubbles from an extra-large wad of gum gathered in her mouth, and I entered the scene with a chocolate-stained smile. Every time my own face showed up on the screen, I felt a happy zing within—"That's me!" It reminded me that this is my family, that I belong to them. Although memories of these scenes are only part of our story as a family, they are my most beloved, pleasant part of it.

What was not captured on those super eights was the sugar crash of energy that came when we were tired from spending heightened time together, or from underlying power issues which sparked some kind of outburst. We were Irish–Italian kids with passionate fuses and strong personalities. It was the flip side of the Lupone family and certainly my least preferred part.

I have a vivid memory of one such morning from my highchair vantage. Picture a beautiful holiday with all the trimmings—a cheerful tablecloth with white scalloped trim, orange juice in glass goblets and a breakfast made for young kings and queens. At this table of perfection, we settled in at first until my siblings turned on each other. It was as if their genuine sentiments could not be contained within the idealism my mother wanted to project, and in fact, probably made it worse. I watched the back of Patrick's 70's hair as he stormed away from the table. Emilia, Em for short, chimed in, "Mom did all of this for us and you are acting like such a jerk!" Everyone abruptly left the decorated table and slammed their bedroom doors. My face looked down. I remember it was a pivotal time when Mom was getting ready to kick my brother Patrick out of the house and send him to my dad's. As an empathetic child, I was uneasy that everyone was upset.

Of course, there was always an expectation of perfection on days like this, as my mother is a classical idealist. There wasn't room for discord or interruption of her plan for us, and how we acted she seemed to take as a personal affront to her view of her own parenting. But what an outburst between the three teenagers! It was like dogs from *The Christmas Story* ran into our home, ravaged our perfect meal, pillaged presents and destroyed all hope for a lovely day.

ROSE-COLORED GLASSES

During their high school years, my brothers mostly lived with my dad and our stepfamily. When either one or both of them stayed with us, sounds of aggression were pervasive and largely instigated by my sister. Between brief times of boisterous banter, there was a constant clash of will among my older siblings with some particularly obnoxious fights.

I tensely witnessed my sister and one of my brothers fuming to the point of house damage. Em ran after my brother to punch him, while he closed himself behind the laundry room door. He pummeled the wall in frustration, leaving a gaping hole. Then, I watched one of them furiously slam an entire bottle of laundry detergent into the other. Neon-blue liquid smacked across their reddened faces and arced onto the floor. The aftermath of this epic battle left a soap stain that never quite came out.

Though I wish this were the only traumatic brawl I saw, there was more than one trip to the emergency department due to a racket to the face, a pencil lodged into the skull, and blood dripping from the head. Multiple babysitters resigned from the shock of my mother's neglect and the chaos of taking care of the Lupones.

Sometimes, while they escalated and clashed, I stood in the middle of my siblings. Plugging my ears, half their height, I screamed at them—"Stop, you guys—STOP!" I remember how they turned back at me briefly with fire in their eyes—like a slow-motion reaction to a momentary distraction. *Nice try little one.* Though I believed in the power of my baby-in-the-family cuteness to alter the course of their feuds, I just wanted there to be peace between us, and I had the young heart to hold onto good times when we just laughed hard together. Those occasions were when I felt most like myself—when we were most like a normal family. And though more the exception than the rule, they are my fondest memories.

Through it all, my mother chose to live in her own delusion, refusing to acknowledge there was disunity among us—or any imperfection whatsoever. Perpetually donning rose-colored glasses, her children's needs were left unmet. Determined to have her own identity apart from motherhood, she met with varied groups after work, went on trips with boyfriends and hosted singles gatherings while we kids were hushed into the back of the house. Sadly, after both my brothers were sent to live with my dad, I was the one holding the short end of the stick. Put daily in the care of my older sister until late at night, I was usually in bed when my mother arrived home.

BIG EM

The day was no different than most. Em blazed at me with a bone-chilling look. Dread engulfed me and I took off running. I knew she was in the mood to put someone down, and that someone *was me!* My heart raced with a frenzied beat, and I could not grip the floor with my feet fast enough. Her malicious tone resounded behind me like a hundred subwoofers—"Oh, go run and hide! You're such a scaredy cat!" At six years younger than her, I pushed out panicked breaths. *Where do I go? There is no safe place to hide!* But it was too late. She had cornered me in the living room. Imprisoned by the snare of her larger body, she gloated with a menacing smile, "You can't get away from me! Don't even try!" My face was flush with frustration—*No! No! Not this again!* I knew not to punch my way out because I would get flogged back. And as much as I struggled away from her smothering arms holding me in place, I just couldn't release myself. My body stiffened in exasperation, and I turned my head to avoid her gloating expression. Within minutes, I grew jaded trying to outmatch her strength. Leaning against the wall, I slumped to the ground and erupted into tears. Just like abundant times before, Em had trapped me—until she broke me.

When I was around six years old, my older sister began to terrorize me. Towering over me, she bullied me with her imposing full-frame and vexed me with emotional manipulation. Em created immense confusion within me. With a dichotomous flip of a switch, she was at once gregarious, protective, and fun to be around and in the next instant moody, accusing and hostile.

Even at a young age, I could tell that jealousy drove her aggression towards me. Any hint of my success was only acceptable if she had a hand in it. For example, my emerging talent as an artist was, according to her, likely because she taught me how to draw the sun, the clouds and rainbows. I was elected vice president of my elementary school *obviously* because of the speech she helped me write, and of course I won a poetry contest because of how she helped me rhyme one set of words. When I began achieving without her help, it grew worse. She had no part in me excelling at schoolwork, entering the gifted program and medaling in speech contests. And it made her seethe. This is something I sensed and internally adjusted my "shininess" because I didn't want to risk angering her by twinkling brighter than she did.

CONTROL

Though the distress of the abuse was severe enough for my subconscious to suppress scores of memories, enough of them have recently resurfaced. I have diminished recollections of my sister punching me, slapping me and locking me into closets, small spaces and the outside garage for what seemed like hours. This happened frequently enough to cause great fear to arise in me. No matter how much I tried to fight back, I was pushed and thrown into confined areas of our home for as long as she wanted me to stay there. Once, she shoved me into my mother's closet and the back of my head struck a low closet dowel. Even as I cried out in pain, she didn't let me out right away.

When she locked me in a room or small closet, I could tell she received some kind of vile rush from my distress, as she boasted that she had power over me. Repeatedly, I screamed for what appeared like forever trying to get free from my forced confinement. Efforts to loosen myself were fruitless, and she laughed behind the door at my attempts—making me feel belittled, powerless and demoralized.

One of Em's favorite tactics was threatening to ruin my favorite toys if I told Mom what she was doing to me. Her words echo within my scant remembrance—"If you tell Mom, I will punch you so hard!"

Other times, she would pull my hair, ordering me, "I said come here!" Her jealousy-induced abuse grew over the years, even though I tried to put it under wraps for her benefit, or so I wouldn't have to fear her. I was acutely aware of what she didn't like and what might set her off. I knew she didn't like to be wrong or told she doesn't know something, and I walked on thin ice to appease her. Em held up a façade as my chief-protector, cheerleader and principal role model until resentment built within her, and she burst into an explosion of frustration.

My standing memories are composites of threats mingled with impressions of sudden fright as I would run to get away from her, and the maddening awareness of being locked out of the house, or trapped in rooms, closets and corners. Placed alone for hours with her in charge, she was so much stronger than me, and I felt defense-less. The misery of being at the mercy of her swinging moods left me feeling battered by her control, stiffened by her threats to hit me and depleted of dignity.

Em did punch me, but more often her hand was opened with slaps upon my scalp. She also thumped me repeatedly on my skull while snapping "Think, think, think!" or "Stupid, stupid!" Sometimes she delivered a more forceful pound upon my head, the kind that made me wince, taking my breath away. She did a lot of pushing me away and grabbing both my arms with a firm grip asserting, "You will do what I say." This made me believe it was normal to be con-trolled by others. As years passed, she hit harder with an obvious greater strength behind her hand until the time I was eleven, and she was seventeen.

Because her moods were wavering, the bullied state I experi-enced was not continuous. But my intense fixation upon her was relentless because at any moment, she could make a massive swing from affection to terror. This sudden change in her made my whole body dreadfully tense up. While her physical abuse seldom left bruises, it was the persistent threat of intimidation that left me in a constant state of uncertainty. I was hypervigilant—diligently reading her moods, trying to pick up on her nonverbal cues and nuances. My eyes would follow her—wherever she was, making it difficult to relax. Warnings that she was about to dominate or slug me were unremitting, so much that her body language and threatening words were the most terrifying part of the abuse. It got to the point that I remember thinking,

Just do it already! I wish you would just punch me so hard all over my body! Then I could show Mom the bruises and she would have to believe me!

When I searched deeply to remember, one remembrance of her control came to the surface, and it felt like an overlay of thousands just like it.

THE RENOVATED BATHROOM

I heard Em's surly laugh through the door—"Now what? What are you going to do, Bethy?" With both my tiny hands, I tightly gripped and turned the handle while pushing hard against my only escape. The struggle to move the doorknob even a centimeter was exasperating. Today, Em pushed me into the hallway bathroom and kept me there while she gloried in my failed attempts to get free. For an instant, I was able to turn the knob slightly in my favor. But she reinforced her will by pushing harder against the door with her considerable body. She mocked, "You're not getting out Bethy! Don't even try!" I had no words to express my swelling frustration, only a visceral response to this repeated entrapment that she enjoyed. The only armament I had was screams to beat upon her ears like high-pitched intolerable alarms.

So, I screamed. I screeched as loudly as I could muster from my little lungs. Banging on the door, I roared, "GET ME OUT OF HERE! OPEN THE DOOR! GET ME OUT OF HERE!" I wasn't just crying out to get her attention, the rage within my soul from being trapped by her—yet again—was mounting into a monstrous fight within. This fight felt like eternity while she taunted me from the other side, "Ha haaa! Keep crying out to Mommy, she is not here. No one is coming for you! It's only me!"

I really didn't understand why she kept me imprisoned in here—I didn't understand *why* she enjoyed this power over me. It severely confused me. My whole body began to shake with a trembling frustration, an inner rage of imprisonment. This was certainly not the first time this week—the other day she had confined me in a different way, yanking me by the hair some distance, enforcing her will—by trying to break mine.

I screamed louder. This time I clenched with my entire frame, whatever helped the volume of my scream—"LET! ME! OUT! OF! HERE!" I shrieked until I coughed. Breathless, I wacked the door harder. With as much force as I could harness, I kicked it until she barked back with a sardonic-punitive tone, "You're going to ruin the door Bethy! Stop that!" I yelled back, "THEN GET ME OUT OF HERE!" Then I punched vigorously until my fists began to hurt. Shifting to open palms, I beat upon the door until the slapping force stung. Though I was getting tired, I was willing to put up a fight for a good while because it took that long for me to accept that *I was getting nowhere.*

Then it came. After what felt like twenty minutes of fighting against her, I gave up. Leaning against the wall, I slumped to my knees on the floor and loudly sobbed. At first, they were angry cries and then unceasing tears down my face. She may have stepped away from the door, but I didn't care anymore. I had spiraled far away from the joy I felt earlier that day. Now I was back to where I landed by the end of most days with her—with a defeated spirit, as if the state I was now in was what I really fought against. *No, no, no! Not this crushing feeling again!*

With soaked eyes, I gazed at the khaki patterned wallpaper of this bathroom. Spaces of white between the green were nearly unnoticeable until you studied it closely, and I counted how many times the pattern repeated on the wall. The linoleum tile was uncomfortable on my butt, but at least I was alone now. Here in my weeping, I believe

I was comforted by another being, an angel perhaps. I succumbed to this time, it was when I made the decision to forget—to put this aside in a hidden compartment. My surroundings became glazed all around me, and I stared off as if I wasn't even there—as if none of this happened. Checking out, I dissociated from the pain.

Shortly thereafter, Em said smugly, "You can come out now!" When she opened the door, I rose up slowly and walked out with low countenance. Shutting my bedroom door, I did not lock it behind me—she would have bullied me to let her in, and I loathed the sounds of her temper. I was too worn-out to determine a new plan anyway.

Some years later, my mother hired a designer to make an 80's uplift to our home. She spent her entire inheritance from my grand-mother's passing on an inlaid living room bookcase, chair rails, new wallpaper, new paint—and an update to this bathroom. Before it was redecorated, I remember what the designer said about it, "We need to warm this room up, there's a dreadful feeling in here." Perhaps she perceived the cold chill from what had been done to me repeatedly in this bathroom. My mother never knew the history that took place there or in any of these other renovated rooms or closets, and I prob-ably just told her I liked the changes so she would feel better about spending tens of thousands of dollars.

IT'S NOT THAT BIG OF A DEAL

Memories of my own screams are most deafening to my ears when I remember how Em temporarily suffocated me with a pillow. While she firmly held me down, I frantically struggled to thrash my body free from her restraints. My dampened screeches broadcasted to nowhere beneath a smothering cushion. Just to recount the memory of it and the terror I felt is disgusting. While I don't believe she had it in her heart to actually snuff out my life, she enjoyed the power that surged within her and relished the intimidation she held over me. Perhaps she felt so powerless that she had an overwhelming need to control me—but this is not her story.

To add insult to injury, after she released the pillow, and I was visibly distressed by her asphyxiation attempts, she made light of my frightful response—"Oh shut up Bethy, it's not that big of a deal!" It doesn't matter if she never intended more than a provisional threat, even a moment of it left a mark on my psyche—even a second of it was cruel. I think she subjected me to this pillow smothering two or three more times and then no more—maybe it freaked her out. Nonetheless, she certainly enjoyed feeling powerful, and in turn, I learned to feel I was powerless against her and against others.

From that day forward, whenever I would hear the high-pitched sound of a child screaming in exasperation, I was reminded of the oppressive desperation I felt, and its grating memory stopped me in my tracks. I also felt anxiety rise when people would inadvertently block the doorway of a room I was in.

I DO THINGS THE WAY SHE TELLS ME

It is amazing to me the love of a child. Enduringly optimistic and willing to forgive almost anything, children are vulnerable and look for who they can depend upon to keep them secure. My sister stood large and in charge over me, but her same imposing body was soft like a teddy bear that I leaned into to feel safe. She was the most consistent presence I knew—the person who cared for me, and I pined for her affection. Ironically, she felt *safe* to me—the one constant that my heart leaned upon. This is only because I blocked out painful memories of her long into my adult years. After every trauma rendered through her, I forgot that she was my greatest threat and instead willed myself to believe that she was my sincerest ally. Determined to hold onto the reality I needed, I overlooked everything other than continuing to trust in her to keep me safe.

The most painful part was feeling the disdain that dripped from her lips and the push-pull of her affection. Within her prickly words was an unspoken threat that she could withdraw fondness and instead heap contempt upon me. I panicked that she would withdraw her approval from me, and inwardly, I obsessed over it. She controlled me with this fear of her rejection, ultimately conveying that she was the one who decided what I do, what I think—*I do things the way she tells me.* Paralleling the cornering and abuse, the derision in her voice drove further into my psyche that I was annoying, or a brat—that she despised me.

That small, I was defenseless against her belittling remarks. I second guessed myself because she was the one raising me, and my mom never said anything to the contrary, so I thought, *Maybe Em is right.* Her words permeated my psyche and made me very anxious about the intentions of others, especially women.

In the aftermath of her emotional or physical bullying, her taunt was always the same—"C'mon Bethy, you know you want to smile! C'mon, smile!" Soon after, I released my furrowed brow, freely forgave, repressed the injury and moved on with the smile she coaxed out of me because, of course, it was always much better to be in her favor than to be her victim. She knew this—that I could easily be swayed back to trust her, and this allowed her to flip the script back to "happy Em." But these were never apologies because the pattern continued. Instead, I was treated like her favorite but battered rag doll—back and forth, loved and then dragged into the mud—always with her forceful grip upon my arm.

No child is meant to be raised by another child. It is concerning when parents are negligent, and children are forced to raise younger siblings. Even when the older child is kind, problems will arise, but especially if the older child is openly mean. I can only imagine that Em felt victimized by what Mom asked her to do in taking care of me during her own childhood, and she in turn victimized me for all those years. But the fact that she damaged me remains. You could chalk it up to her not knowing better, but her pattern of manipulating family members with emotional bullying has persisted.

IS EVERYTHING OK?

As children, my stepsisters Agnes, Rebecca and stepbrother Blake were averse to Em's domineering nature. When we stayed at my stepfamily's house, Agnes hated that she had to share a room with her. My older stepsister Rebecca made every effort to show affection to me by taking me on bike rides and treating me to Slurpee's or popcorn at K-Mart. Em was habitually jealous of her fondness of me. If Em were merely protective, this would have been understandable, however she would hover over me, possessively clutching me close to her. I sensed her ill response to others who treated me well.

My stepsisters tried to give me a safe harbor from her stifling behavior. Rebecca pulled me aside when I was a young child, looked straight into my eyes and asked, "Is everything ok with you at home, Elizabeth?" I responded with a detached gaze, "Yes, it's ok." Sincerely, she continued, "You know I am always here if you want to talk about anything, anything at all." Had we spent more time with my stepfamily, I would have greatly benefited from their protection, however, weekend trips to their home ended when I was around seven years old.

Though Em wanted to control me as a child, the love she offered as a reverse switch to years of harm she trivialized was like sand slipping between her fingers. Without a speck of remorse, she could never hold onto me as she once imagined. Some doors are meant to be shut for the mental health of survivors.

MOODY POWER

During her last two years of high school, the hitting and entrapment stopped because Em had her sights on more than power struggles with me. We had fun making up dances, playing goofy dress up, and having bellyaching laughs. But I continued to walk on eggshells around her because she was easily agitated and I was easily manipulated by her moods. Good interactions were always met with a pendulum swing of strife, and our painful clashes left me reeling with a bruised ego. When she came to charm me again, I relented—I always let it go because I loved her.

As I grew older, my furrowed brow set deeper. The pattern of fighting and "making up," because Em suddenly felt better, was not okay for me anymore. I still remember the day in college when I held off from relenting—the first time I didn't give her the satisfaction of prompt forgiveness for spewing me with searing, blameful blasts. Even without conscious memories, I was wary of my gut reactions to her—hints of stored pain from our buried past. Her love would always have a stipulation—that I allow her to control the relationship. But eventually, suppressed memories began to surface, and my heart could no longer bear quashing them again just for a temporary swing of her affection.

FOUR

Gaslit

"Mom?" "What Beth?" She straightened the crease of her newspaper and didn't look away from it. At age eight, I was smart enough to realize this was my chance—Em was outside with a friend. Gently, I tugged at her arm, "Mom!" She turned to face me. "What?" "Emilia is bad to me, Mom." I spoke the rest quickly before she didn't want to hear anymore—"She says she'll break all my toys. She is so mean, Mom—she hurts my arms and pulls at my hair and locks me in your closet and the bathroom, for a long time, Mom!" I didn't dare mention about the hitting. I was afraid Em would do something really bad to me. She heard my words, and I watched as shock registered on my mother's face. For a second, I even felt hope that she was going to save me. But, just as quickly, she composed herself. Her open mouth of disbelief morphed into an aloof, disingenuous smile. With a patronizing tone she closed the door on our conversation, "Oh, honey. Emilia is doing her best and she doesn't really mean any of it. She would never hurt you."

Whenever hope is snatched away like that, it makes you heartsick. And I was heartsick. I was counting on my mom to rescue me, or at the very least, to be concerned about what Em was doing to me. Instead, I watched her coldly reject the truth.

I remember my mother as a calm, patient woman. She gave me a contrast from my volatile sister, and I loved that about her. Still, her pleasantries were not enough—her coolness did not keep me secure like I imagined. A mother needs to know when to protect her child, but I never saw her shielding instinct. She was averse to rising up and advocating for me. It was exasperating and only intensified the dread

I felt while imprisoned by my sister. On more than one occasion I tried to tell her, but always with the same result, eventually, I stopped hoping she would care.

Her utter lack of compassion was detrimental to my soul—more traumatizing than my sister's abuse. Stubbornly refusing to conceive that her life choices had negative consequences for her children, she completely gaslit me to continue her illusory freedom from parenthood.

The fact that I couldn't rely upon her to see my affliction and guard me from Em crippled me psychologically. This reality was not lost on Em who often taunted—"Go ahead, tell Mom. She won't listen to you anyway!" What Em spoke to me became ingrained recordings that played on repeat in my heart—*No one believes me, no one hears me.* In the place of trusting love, I learned that my mother *doesn't care* and that *I'm not worth protecting.*

This was a bitter pill to swallow. She abandoned me to my own defenses. Sensations of fight or flight ran unceasingly through my veins. I never felt safe. Without an adult to run to, I survived independently as a child. To engender my own sense of safety and dignity, I created paralyzing mental-emotional mechanisms. Deprived of someone defending me, my boundaries became porous, my identity diffuse without confident borders. Instead, I learned to parrot my mother's and sister's opinions of what did or didn't matter. And to them, what never mattered was me.

SEEKING SANCTUARY

Frozen in fear, I lay arrested in bed, my shoulders tight from nervous, shallow breathing. Desperate to feel comfort, I mustered up strength to walk through the dark hallway lit solely by a smoke detector. Quietly, I opened my mother's bedroom door and slipped into her king-size bed just so I could feel the safety of her presence. A heavy weight continued to grip my little chest. I heard the sheets rustling as my mother turned towards me. She whispered,

"You can stay here, Beth, but don't stir. I need my sleep." With eyes wide open, I noticed how lights from her alarm clock shrouded the room in faint red. Anxiously craving assurance, I remained motionless, holding even my breath so my body wouldn't move. I didn't want her to kick me out of her bed like she had done before from excessive fidgeting.

It took a lot of courage for me to walk to her engulfed by apprehension in the thick of night. Though I craved to be held and for her to ask me what was wrong, to pull me out of what was tightly bound inside my heart—my mom never wanted to comfort me. The presence of a parent gave me some assurance, but I yearned to know her love when Em's voice could not overpower my own. So, I lay there stiffly, my body tight with an exaggerated stillness. This was the only sanctuary I knew.

While my mother valued me for my talents and strengths, I was a victim of what she refused to acknowledge—abuse happening right under her roof—a terror really. I knew she prized me as her special girl, and part of me didn't want to disrupt that idealistic vision she had of me, especially since scripts of being Em's "brat" had already begun to settle into my mind. Time and again, I was reluctant to tell her the extent of it all because she was disinterested and because of countless threats made by Em if I did.

Whenever I pleaded my case in my less impactful kid voice, Em always had a way of convincing Mom that I was lying or exaggerating, and of course, she denied everything—"Oh shut up Bethy, you're so annoying!" Even if she spoke this directly in front of Mom, she did not stand up to Em, which would have helped prevent Em's words from settling deeply in my spirit. Instead, she responded indifferently to our disputes, dispassionately denying responsibility to protect me.

Her injected narrative about Em made me question if what I was experiencing was even happening, and it caused me to betray my own suffering. Really, my mother taught me to dissociate to the point of a severe identity disorder. I learned from her that if I negated things enough, then I can pretend none of it ever happened. As a true narcissist, she was able to do this effectively. But to me, her daughter, denying my own affliction and hiding it even from myself, caused a huge chasm of emotional scarring.

My mother removed all my familial defenses so that I was completely vulnerable. My brothers and my father would never have tolerated Em's treatment of me. Certainly, they would have kept Em in check! My brothers were disheartened to hear in recent years that my unlocked memories revealed abuses that were more pervasive than they ever knew.

For Cecile Anne, it was all about appearances—a perfect cake, a perfect table setting, a perfect family trip. The truth is, her parenting rarely involved personal sacrifice, nurturing or compassion, which caused me and my siblings to grow up love starved. Other clues point to an embedded narcissism within my mother.

My father married my stepmother "GG" when I was close to 18 months old, and my stepsisters remember how my development was delayed in stark contrast to their half-brother Joel, who was the same age as me. They understood I was not reaching milestones. What caused me to be delayed? I believe my mother lacked maternal attentiveness and did not bond with me the way I needed. My brother Finn said my mom gave me over to my sister's care at a very young age—as young as two. And consistent with Cecile's tendencies, she was willing to be done parenting me when I was 16 years old, leaving me to be fostered by another while she began her new dream life elsewhere.

My stepmother GG, on the other hand, gave me a contrasting picture of what a mother could be. In a home full of children, I observed her care for her children and for all of us Lupone kids as well. Whereas my mom did not send me with a brush or my favorite toys, GG made sure I had toiletries of my very own tucked away in a drawer. She engaged me with activities like baking cookies and thoughtfully ensured that as the youngest, I was well taken care of. Always showing concern, to this day, she has never stopped loving me.

BOXES OF UNSTABLE POTENTIAL

I never knew how dysfunctional we Lupones were. Our loud out-bursts and darker dramas seemed normal until I was exposed to more secure families. Every family suffers from some form of dysfunction, even though not all rise to the level of abuse. And because brokenness exists in every home, there is room for healing within everyone.

Instability became the only constant for me as a child. Struggling to secure myself in sinking sand, my mom gaslit my pain and did nothing to stop my sister's repeated injury. The coping mechanisms I created were not meant to help me function as an adult, only as a child suffering from neglect and abuse. By the time I reached adult-hood, I was a shell of myself—wrapped up in hundreds of tiny boxes of unstable potential in my mind.

A FLAWED CHOICE

In college, I took baby steps to make sense of my "spacey" exis-tence and the negative emotions I experienced for no apparent reason. In my freshman year, I saw a therapist on campus, but I evaded her questions as an unconscious defense against painful recalls, and after three sessions, she told me she could not help me.

Soon after, I made a flawed choice to seek help from my mother who was now a licensed marriage, family and child psychotherapist. During a visit, I asked her, "Mom, can you do hypnotherapy on me?" Impatiently, I was eager to get to the heart of myself—to understand my 'core issues'. Perhaps I could just unlock my heart and crank it wide open? Initially, she refused, "No, Beth. It's a conflict of interest." But I watched as her eyes changed focus all over the room. I knew she was actually considering it when she said, with soft-spoken hes-itancy, "I can't because you are my daughter." So, I pressed more, "But Mom, please, I need to understand myself. It's driving me nuts! I just know this will help me. Plus, you know it's going to be all about

Dad!" I had just spoken the magic words that would spark her interest, though with unfailing conviction, I did believe that what would surface would be about my father. After all, she had told me my whole life that every mental-emotional difficulty I'd experienced had to do with my father's 'abandonment'. She finally relented—even though she seemed apprehensive about it.

Leading me under hypnosis, she began directing the session, "Talk to your inner child; ask what you want from her."

Speaking directly, I said, "Show me my core issues!"

Surprisingly, what immediately surfaced was very dark feelings and fears regarding my sister and mother. In glimpses of submerged trauma, I experienced impressions of torment, painful punching, yelling and screaming while drawn to dark shadows covering a massive, heavy door at the end of a hallway. In this vision from my psyche, my mother shut the door in my face while I stood there panicking for her to let me in, to escape from a dark figure that had formed from the shadows. But she never opened the door to let me in. I was confounded by these images, enough that I couldn't speak them aloud. Baffled, I uttered quietly, "What? How can that be?" She asked, "What do you see, Beth?" While under hypnosis, I recalled to her exactly what I saw and felt.

This made her so uncomfortable! Even with my eyes closed, I heard the nervous nuance of her voice—the squirming inside her spirit. Ignoring the contents of my vision, she changed the direction of the session. "Now Beth, do you see your father? Is he the dark shadow you see? Look closer at the shadow. Isn't that your father?" Her words irritated me! "No, Mom! You don't know what I am seeing!" She pressed, "Were you panicking that I couldn't protect you from your father? I am so sorry that I couldn't protect you from him." My brow furrowed, "No! It's not my dad! It looks like Em. This is from inside me—and you don't see what I see! It's not Dad, so stop saying that it was!"

While under a vulnerable hypnotic state, she "assisted" the

session—reinforcing her deceptions about my father instead of following the leading of my subconscious. And she kept adding to it, "Beth, I am so sorry that he was not there for you as a child. His abandonment must have been so painful." Her attempt to obfuscate my hidden feelings just added fuel to feelings of deep neglect I already knew from her subconsciously as a child, and I responded in anger. "No! You are changing things, Mom! I don't see anything about Dad, only about you and Em!" The session became aggravating for me—probably even damaging as I pushed myself out of hypnosis without her guidance to return to present awareness.

Under hypnotherapy, my subconscious had made one final attempt to cry out to her—"*Are you going to listen to me now? Pay attention to what really happened?*" Sadly, she refused to hear once again, and in doing so, she may have messed things up for me on a deep subconscious level. No wonder I was ticked off as I came out of hypnosis. I wanted to see the truth and instead, she manipulated my psyche. I left that session more confused than ever—and more alone.

Over the following weeks, I couldn't put my finger on why my "core issues" had nothing to do with my father but instead pointed entirely to Em and my mom. It was overwhelming to think that everyone who raised me caused me such confusion. So, soon after, I buried my own experience and questioned my memories even more, suppressing them further. Instead, I returned to the familiar narrative I had long held—that my deepest wounds stemmed from my father's supposed neglect, and that the absence of a consistent father figure was the root of my emotional struggles.

FIVE

My Father and The Guru

At around two years old, I remember walking barefoot on the carpet of my stepfamily's home. A sharp object in the hallway grazed the bottom of my foot and I screamed out in pain. Without a moment's hesitation, I heard the pounding reverberation of my dad's footsteps rushing to where I was. The hallway was dark, and I saw him looking for the sound of my voice. Swiftly, he lifted me high into his arms. "It's ok, Little Bit, I've got you," he said. He held me close, and I was reassured by him as my loving father. Nestled in his broad shoulders and chest, I felt safe. From the height of his embrace, I stared into his soft brown eyes and memorized them, trusting in his gesture of concern. I thought, *I am very special to him.*

In this one moment, I knew my dad cared for me and sought to protect me. He was a big man, with a large belly, who I can mostly picture lying on the floor or falling asleep in front of the TV. But on that day, he somehow defied the laws of physics as I understood them at that age, got up immediately and even came running towards me just to ensure I was comforted and removed from harm.

I didn't know how much my father loved me until he was close to passing. Growing up, I felt he didn't care, mostly because of narratives I heard from my mom about what he should have done to reach out to me. Incessantly she voiced spiteful rhetoric—"He just doesn't care. You just have to realize who your dad is . . . He only cares about himself." Not only did these injunctions cement themselves within me as the truth of the way my dad felt about me—they grew into a chiasmic hole of rejection.

From the time I was a toddler until I was six, I stayed with my father every other weekend. My earliest memories are how he affectionately nicknamed me "Little Bit," how he gazed at me with beaming gentle smiles and how his whole face filled my view. He got down on the floor beside me to play with toys, and I knew he was gratified just to be with me.

During my grade school years, when my dad was in his fifties, he lived alone in Riverside and Fresno. My brothers intermittently resided with him while they finished high school. On the weekends, Dad would travel to see our stepmother, GG. He remained living away from her while fruitlessly struggling to gain employment as a "hatchet-man." It was his job to take financial control of dwindling companies, disassemble them and sell them off for profit—costing many people their jobs. Not surprisingly, his profession did not win him friends or a solid network to gain new employment.

SUMMERS WITH DAD

Even though his faltering job situation consumed him with depression, he was protective of his time with Em and me during holidays and for month-long periods of summer. This was when we experienced the misery that was eating away at him. I can picture him regularly lying in front of the TV, while eating entire boxes of donuts—donuts he refused to share. Years later, I found out he suffered from manic depression, which explains his gloomy, temperamental behavior.

My dad's Riverside address offered a nearby pool, but the Fresno one provided limited recreation. One summer, out of sheer boredom, Em and I entertained ourselves by making cookie dough and repeatedly listening to the one cassette tape by *Bananarama* that our brother Finn left behind for the summer. From that album, we wailed aloud with funny animated faces, the track "It's a Cruel, Cruel Summer." By the time the song ended, we were cracking up because it was all too real for us.

Sometimes we begged Dad to take us to Disneyland or go out

for a McDonald's 25-cent soft-serve ice cream. Eventually he would relent, and this was the extent of our summer adventures with him. He was a film buff and would either play slap-stick parodies like *Death Race 2000* or shoosh us away to our room while he watched rated R films. When I was eight, he took me to see the Jaws 3-D opening. I was terrified at the floating detached body parts and the great white shark which leapt out of the screen with 20 feet of pointed teeth just to eat me! *Ahhh!* I pretended to be brave for Dad and for Em, but the movie freaked me out.

My father had a large intimidating presence in both size and animation—factors which favored him to become the middle-weight boxing champion at his university. I have memories which caused me to literally fear him. By far the worst was when I witnessed him punch my brother Patrick with a scary and devastating hit. Afterwards, he apologized to my sister and me as we sat holding each other crying in the upstairs room.

When Dad drove us to and from Modesto, CA, his right arm lay outstretched behind the front seat next to him as he zipped on the freeway up to 100 mph. While Em and I braced ourselves in the back seat, I was frightened by his driving but simultaneously soothed by the Windham Hill instrumental cassettes he blasted in the car.

We stopped staying with Dad during summers at a certain point, and I rarely saw him during my junior high and high school years. Once Em went to college, Mom said I had a choice whether to visit my dad, but by then, she impressed upon me fear of being around him without the "protection" of Em. The irony is, when we stayed with him as kids, Em did not afflict me. Instead, she was humbled by Dad's potential temper and by leeriness our mother had instilled in us about him. Memories with Dad are therefore clear because I didn't need to dissociate from her.

As a child, I rarely experienced my dad's charming, soft-hearted, gregarious nature, because it was a hard time in his life. The temper, the walking on eggshells, the manic-depression, the loner tendencies—these were idiosyncrasies I observed in him. Unfairly, my mother took these traits to the extreme, brainwashing us to believe that he was essentially a bad man who didn't care about us. But though Dad was not perfect, he was not the monster she made him out to be.

What remained hidden in my heart was that when he ran to me as a toddler, I received a foundation of love from my father. I knew he loved me and would never harm me. Could he have fought for more time with me and reached out more often in my life? Sure, but he was consumed with battling his own demons.

DIRECT VIOLATION

When I was in first grade, my mother took us to live in Sarasota, Florida at my grandmother's. Her health was deteriorating, and Mom planned for us to move there when grandma passed. For several months, I attended Catholic school, watched *Buck Rogers* on the television and tried to catch little lizards. Sometimes, while swimming at the country club, my sister and I were showered by warm Florida rains. I loved how it felt to have two different temperature waters on my skin, even though we didn't know the danger of swimming during these storms. One day a Floridian rushed us out of the pool while short bursts of lightning flashed all around us.

Years later, I learned from my stepmom that by leaving the state with us kids, my mother had violated a court order. Moreover, she planned to move us there without informing my father. Evidently, my dad hired a private investigator and lawyer to bring us back to California because he didn't even know where we were. That process took a great financial toll upon him, and his family. My stepsiblings all recall making sacrifices for us to be brought back into the state. This is not what I was told. I never knew the truth.

For part of the time we were in Florida, my mom was back in California supposedly "selling our belongings" while Em and I stayed at the home of our Catholic school's secretary. The reality is my mother returned to address leaving the state with us in direct violation of the court order.

Em and I were miserable at the secretary's home. She and her spouse regularly fought, and I slept in the nursery with an infant they never consoled. My mother's time away from us kept extending. Memories of this time are vivid because Em probably felt afraid to be without our mother while I was used to my mother's neglect, so it was not an exceptional trauma. A couple of months passed when my mother arranged for us to fly as unaccompanied minors back to California. When we got off the plane she explained, "Grandma told us to move back." Of course, this was a lie.

I would have wanted to know then that my dad had been *fighting for me!* He made financial, personal and family sacrifices just to find me and get me home to California. The loving, tender story I heard from GG was that my dad was a wreck trying to get us back into the state!

I was blinded to the love my father had for me all along. I never knew his heart towards me and that not having us near was a source of great disquiet and sadness. After he passed, I more fully grasped that he was afraid to share with us how he truly felt. He knew we were sold out to Cecile's narrative about him, and he was respectful enough to not come between our relationship with our mother.

A SUBTLE SHIFT

In spite of all his eccentricities and faults, at a certain point my father had a transformation of sorts. He finally came to terms with his inability to gain employment and even made steps toward becoming a deacon in the Catholic church.

When I lived with my mother's best friend Maggie for the last two years of high school, my father was upset to hear that my mom had left me. He made offers to take me in and care for me, offers which my mother mocked. Apparently, my stepsister Rebecca asked Joel her half-brother to look for me at football games and see if I was ok. Because he lived closest to where I was, when he did track me down at games, I felt cared for—he happened to be my only nearby family connection. Once they discovered my address, my father came to visit me.

During their visit, Dad and GG were kindhearted; they did not speak angrily about my mother leaving me. I could tell they genuinely just wanted to see me. My father was there for every one of my graduations, including from nursing school years later. When we all celebrated together, my mom was overtly annoyed with my dad while he was the model of graciousness towards her. He overlooked her reactiveness.

Before this subtle change in my father, the uneasiness I felt about him could be typified by a multi-media piece I painted in high school.

AFFECTING ME MORE THAN IT SHOULD

I let out a big sigh, it was finally fourth period. My shoulders dropped. I had the entire art room filled with weathered brushes, wooden easels and creative supplies to myself. Noticing my talent, my art teacher Miss Gibson granted me access to an independent studio art class. She set expectations for me to be prolific, explore my abilities and develop my portfolio. However, I squandered this period as a break from striving toward straight A's and big high school emotions.

This was my junior year, right after my mother left me while I chose to finish high school in Modesto, California—a choice I shouldn't have been given at that age. I was just trying to be brave. Repeatedly, I shoved the substance of my true grief away and said to myself—*This is no big deal. I am very independent. College is only two years away.*

Clipping a Walkman to my shorts, I played my Red-Hot Chili Peppers tape. Their music felt like organized raucous with textured words and confidence. Layered sounds drowned out my own voices and woke up my senses. Even still, complicated feelings clouded all inspiration. Imagination had left me like an exhale that never quite returned.

Also, I wasn't thinking about painting at all. My art teacher Miss Gibson figured it out. She was a short, bold to-the-point young woman who passionately imparted, "Don't waste your future on a boy. And don't let thinking about one keep you from your gifts and goals, ok?" Really, how did she know? As a teenage girl, of course I pined for male attention, but I was not some sort of floozie—I just wanted to be noticed.

In the bedroom Maggie loaned to me, a separate land line was installed just for my use. Earlier that week, and for several months, I talked with a particular boy, Luis, on my blue rotary phone late into the night. We didn't hang out at school together, but we were a bit more than friends, and publicly we kept it platonic. In our beginning art class, he said of my drawn self-portrait, "That is really good, but you are much prettier than that." Luis was the first one to pay attention to me—I felt seen by him. Though he was known to have a jerky bad-boy front and was never "boyfriend" material for me, I knew he was genuine at heart.

One time at a party, I experienced aggressive behavior from a popular sophomore who attempted to sexually assault me. Luis heard about it and threatened the boy on my behalf. This made me feel protected—a new sensation for me. It bonded me to him, perhaps more than it should have. The conversations we had late at night staved off a depression within me. I was willing to sacrifice rest I needed for an important exam or water polo game I had the next day because these were drops of fondness, I was desperate to consume.

On several late nights, Luis knocked on my window, and I escaped from the house through it to go on walks with him. Maggie, bless her heart, found out about it the wrong way. Apparently, the sprinkler below my windowsill broke because I fell on it jumping from the window. She confronted me one day, "Beth, I know that you leave at night. Can you just use the front door, and tell me when you leave?" Maggie was awesome!

One evening long past midnight, Luis knocked on my window

to say that he went on a date with "the most amazing girl"—a girl he would eventually marry. "I'm going to ask her out again," he said, "so let's hang out tonight." Though my heart sank about the other girl, it also fluttered to be near him. I crept outside the front door without telling Maggie who was already asleep. We walked towards Luis' gold mustang, and he said, "Let's go for a drive." The door creaked as I opened it. With anxious butterflies in my stomach, my legs stuck to his leather seat. Luis said that the attention he gave me would have to stop so he could pursue this girl, but tonight we could be close one last time. He parked in a vacant field. We got in the backseat and made out. I stayed and talked with him until just before daybreak, all the while thoughts raced within me. *This can't be it. Will he really stop talking to me?*

I knew the girl he dated earlier that night. Five years back, we hammed it up together as the stepsisters in a grade school production of "Cinderella." I really liked her, which is why this hurt more. *Why is he letting me go? Why is she so much better?*

He dropped me off a little down the street so Maggie wouldn't hear his rumbling mustang. Silently, I entered the house and walked to my room in tears. *This is confusing, and affecting me more than it should!* Though I never considered a future with Luis, the rejection stung. At seventeen, I craved physical touch—because I had no parental contact, no one to receive affection from. I missed out on Dad's hugs, and as a child, I used to engage my mom in long conversations, just to prolong her soft caress on my back when she came home late. When Luis was near me or we hugged or kissed, it was intoxicating. Now his tangible touch was gone.

I didn't actually think he would stop talking with me—but he did. Though I was aware my needy emotions were magnified by living without parents, it was painful to surrender the current of comfort that hearing his voice late in the night supplied me. It took many months for me to let him go.

So, when Miss Gibson saw me wrap my identity in sadness over

Luis, she spoke to me intensely with a penetrating gaze. "Beth, who are *you*?" she said, "Use this time to paint who you are. What are you all about? Do not sacrifice your talents for him, focus on you!" I told her, "But I don't really know what to paint!" She replied, "Paint a self-portrait." "Hmmm, ok," I replied, even though I wasn't so sure about the assignment. How could I even view myself while I felt so numb? All I felt was the sting of lack. *Why was I not enough for Luis? Why is he ok with suddenly shutting me out? I thought we were still friends, but he doesn't want to see me anymore. Why does everybody leave me?* Then I thought of my dad. *Am I not enough for him?*

THE MONEY TIE

Latching onto the self-portrait idea that Miss Gibson gave me, I sifted through photos and found a print of me as a little girl that I loved. In it my long brown hair shaped rosy cheeks while my blue eyes pierced through with an honest look. It was then I decided I would paint this photo, but with the added lens of how I perceived myself—like a disconnected young child floating in outer space. I might have chuckled at the sci-fi goofy thought of it, but my hovering self would convey the unrelenting feelings of separation I knew.

A familiar passion began to rise—a stirring need to express. In painting, I had an outlet that I didn't need for others to understand. With an unhurried breath, I took a moment to unlock myself in this protected time.

I knew my portrait would be in the background, but because I felt disconnected, I thought, *Who do I feel separate from? Who do I put in the foreground?* Freshly losing the comfort of a boy's attention made me acutely aware of my father's absence.

Holding a photo of him standing assuredly in a brown business suit, I sketched Dad's bust as the prominent figure of my canvas with a sharply pointed chunk of graphite. His square glasses I marked out with dark thick frames, his eyes focused but assured, pointing away from my portrait in the upper left. I defined his strong Lupone jaw-line, and drew in his broad shoulders, barrel chest and frame, filling in his suit to a tailor's perfection. His form was confident, sharp, loud and proud—how I perceived him to be—his identity wrapped beyond anything else in his work. I decided I would specifically exaggerate my father's tie into a relief made of money by covering tie-shaped foam with play cash.

To the left of my father, I drew a portrait of my face and upper torso which receded into the background. My hair draped beneath my own Lupone jaw like a protective cloak, extending into a flowy end below my face.

I squeezed a bit of each pigment onto my palette, relishing these first applications of color. Dipping my brush into the paint and gliding onto textured canvas feels like a visceral flow of creative passion. My spirit becomes very quiet and upon the blank note before me begins to manifest depths that I could never speak into actual words.

Beginning with the background, I layered hues of ultramarine blue with orange to create a warm but unsettled feel. When finished it had a disturbing depth to it—a dissonance that never resolved. I felt the gravity of what I was painting, and cathartic tears welled up in my eyes.

Using Prussian blue, crimson, red ochre and warm white, I con-toured his suit and the soft shadows of our features. Then with del-icate strokes, I filled in our eyes, lips and highlights. Between broad sweeps and fine detail, I moved quickly until I could no longer blend through fast-drying acrylic paint. If both the rhythm and effect of painting colors were typified by a music genre, for me it is like jazz with highlighting solos—a brassy trumpet blasting a colorful note here, a lone sax improvising across the octaves in frenzied but skillful layers of color there, and an upright bass grounding the entire piece with deep resonance.

While painting, I feel the heat of an impatient zeal, quenched only by resolving tensions I see on the canvas. Finally, both my father and my form came alive, bearing emotions I wanted to capture. My father looked focused, but disengaged from me with his face turned away, while my own childhood gaze penetrated forward past the viewer.

The glaze produced a reflection, giving a lustrous sheen to the money tie, and its tangible presence formed a smooth lump that I could move my fingers over. Stepping back, I asked myself, *Why did I really paint my father's tie into a rounded relief of paper mâché money?* It was then I realized, *This is how I feel about him as a businessman focused on money.* Struggling with Dad's seeming lack of generosity, I believed he was distant from me because—he loved money more than me.

But the sad irony is that it was my mother who did things to indicate she loved money more than she loved me. Cecile pocketed child support money from my dad while Maggie took care of me, and she stole my inheritance from Grandma Betty. Still, it was too devastating to believe that both my parents had a greater affection for money than they had for me. And it was the memories of my father's volatility that caused me to believe one over the other.

MONEY MACHINE

For one week every summer from when I was seven until I was sixteen, I attended my beloved summer camp nestled in Sierra Nevada's foothills. It cost $150 which at the time was not an insignificant amount of money. My mother made me call my dad to ask him for the means to attend. This was an annual nerve-wracking phone call for me. Before I dialed him, Cecile first wrote out all she wanted me to ask him for which included other items like summer clothes and always mentioned an exact sum requested. One time, as I read to my father what she wrote, he probably sensed I was being prodded by her to ask for additional needs. He yelled back at me, "What am I? A god damned money machine to you?"

His words were like a dagger to my heart. They reverberated

inside of me and added to tiles of fear I felt. I broke down in tears and truly believed he didn't care about me—just like my mother said. In that moment, I surrendered to all her deceit about my dad. This only served to cause a deep well of pain within me, and a desperate need to relieve the heartache of his rejection. As I sobbed, my mother attempted to comfort me, but there was a sick look of vindication on her face—like she tried unsuccessfully to hold back a gloating smile. It was clear she was ecstatic that I finally accepted her conclusions about my dad. I felt alone in my pain, and I knew she actually relished how deeply this upset me. But she was all I had, so I had to believe that it was the best of her intentions to console me. Nonetheless, it was these kinds of stressful money-centric interactions that empha- sized to me my dad loved money more than me, in exactly the manner I had rendered it in the painting.

SHOWING DAD

When I found out Dad was about to visit me at Maggie's house, I was anxious about whether to show him my self-portrait. Maggie encouraged me, "Yes, why not? It is of you both together. I think he will really like it, Beth." I had made a statement I wasn't sure he would really understand. But when I showed him, I was shocked by his response. Maybe the tie was right in his face, but he was either oblivious to any implied meaning, or he genuinely wanted to just connect. He loved the painting and praised my talents, he was sincerely proud of me as a growing artist.

As he commented on the true likeness of our faces and the money tie, I realized he may have never known how harsh memories about money had stained my perception of him. His uncomplicated pleasant reaction began to grab my soul's attention. Perhaps I had it wrong about how he really felt about me because here he was— reaching out to me.

But as much as I wanted to believe I had been wrong about my dad, I was afraid to change my perception. I had learned to approach him through tainted lens and especially after he yelled at me over the phone, I came to fear him and fear more rejection from him. My soul was open and eager to fill an empty cavity that grew inside of me and during my college years, I was about to discover what I thought was the perfect answer.

THE GURU

It was the second annual Ascension Festival in 1995. Posters of the "ascended masters" covered walls of the conference. I noticed a new addition—an enlightened master that was actually living. As soon as I found out about Sai Baba, I became determined to see him. *Wow, he is alive now—I have to see him!* Someone at the Ascension Festival told me he had many followers, and that there was probably a local gathering I could join. Excitedly, I researched that next week, and attended my first Sai Baba gathering in Santa Cruz, CA, where I attended college. Straightaway, my exhilaration swelled about all things Baba, and I wondered when I would get the chance to see him in India where he lived.

In the meantime, I joined weekly Sai Baba meetings, resumed meditation, attended a Yogi ashram, visited a large Buddhist temple deep in the Santa Cruz redwood forest, and continued to practice Aikido Martial Arts. With a friend, I also visited a cult leader who lived with more than a dozen women and spoke to visiting crowds. He was strange and I saw through him. The whole time I tried to telepathically communicate to him that he was a fraud because he was not Sai Baba. He gave me an interesting stare-down because I was not buying his scam.

To say I was fanatical about Sai Baba would be an under-statement. I instantly believed his own claim about himself—that he was "god in human form." Since I had been looking for god, this seemed legitimate to me, as if a signpost pointing to him was made just for me. I was told Sai Baba's presence was like having someone like Buddha or Jesus walking on the earth *right now*. With devotees all over the world, I simply had to do everything in my power to visit him, worship him, give my all to him. This hole within me would be satisfied with nothing less. And I felt special to have discovered him. Just a couple of years later I found myself in India fulfilling my dream to see him.

SIX

Puttaparthi

With dreamy disposition, I gazed from my window into the atmosphere on a flight to India, imagining my first encounter with Sai Baba. Soaring thoughts filled my head. *I can't believe I am going to meet him—the one who created me.*

It was the summer of 1997, and I was twenty-two. I traveled to Puttaparthi, India with twelve fellow American devotees to attend the International Sai Baba Youth Conference. I was beyond ecstatic to be a part of this world event to celebrate "Swami" as we adoringly called him. Devotees from many countries had compiled a book with poems and artwork to honor him. A vivid watercolor I painted of him adorned the final page—his distinctive afro and fiery gaze captured in brushstrokes I was proud to contribute.

Beholding skies beyond my airplane window, I pondered in awe that soon I would be at Prashanti Nilayam, the Sai Baba ashram—the "abode of the highest peace." Because of basic finances, many are unable to travel to India, but, in my case, a devotee in America had graciously helped pay my way.

Packed within my suitcase, I had five beautiful saris to wear. Indian women had patiently taught me how to wear them, and I practiced the folds and safety pin placement until I got it right. The previous two years, I was exposed to traditional Indian customs at Sai Baba meetings, and my tastebuds were accustomed to spicy curries, dahls, and samosas. I was thrilled to immerse myself in this entirely different culture and travel outside of the United States. But more than anything, I was bursting with anticipation to meet Swami.

Before this flight to India, I found comfort in weekly Sai Baba meetings and meditating before his portrait, confiding in his reassuring eyes. I longed to become "one with the divine." Though I wasn't ever sure what this really meant, I wanted it, even if it merely helped me escape my own brokenness.

Now, traveling to India, I didn't need to wonder anymore about a personal connection with him. Inciting my heart with great expectation, I delighted to think about being face to face with the incarnation of god. To see god and be seen by god—this was an all-or-nothing kind of hope. It ignited a passion within me to finally feel loved. All my emotions, sentiments and soul were susceptible on the brink of my visit with him.

FINALLY IN INDIA

When we first entered the airport in Bangalore, India, I was shocked by dimly lit sodium lights and the glaring odor of musky oil and sweat. A chaotic press of bodies surged around me. Seasoned devotees in our group shouted directions—"Come! This way! THIS WAY!"—guiding us safely through the frenzy. It was late, and I was grateful for their leadership. They arranged for us to stay the night at a devotee's home and travel to Puttaparthi the next day. But we hardly slept—our senses were heightened, and we mostly gasped at different sounds and giggled at unfamiliar shadows.

The next morning as we drove through streets near the ashram, I looked for signs that the townspeople also loved Sai Baba. I saw locals busy selling items while rickshaw carts pulled by young Indian men on foot transported people wherever they wanted to go. With focused demeanors, they darted off so fast, as if their own eyeballs steered their carted carriages. Only a few motorized vehicles were in the road zooming past them.

When we entered the gates of the ashram, my face brightened with exhilaration. *Yes! We are finally here!* As our sandals met the sandy base of the ashram, a few of us shrieked with jubilation.

We rolled our suitcases to our assigned room. I was housed with my friend Heather and several others. Floor mats awaited us, but to our surprise, there were bathroom toilets—a recent upgrade to the ashram. I thought to myself, *Wow, how are six girls going to share that teeny mirror?* But the rest felt like camping, and I was content with the amenities.

HE IS COMING!

The anticipation to see him had welled up so considerably inside me—that a permanent grin raised the apples of my cheeks. We waited in the Southern India desert for over two hours as I wondered, *Will he give me a look? Will he notice me? Does he know I came all this way to see him?*

Pressed against several Indian women, I quickly learned their sense of personal space differed from mine. My bare feet were lodged into the small of the woman's back in front of me, while others' toes pressed into my back and sides. The flies were incessant, but I mustered every bit of self-control to resist swatting them away. Instead, I challenged myself to ignore their itchy annoyance. In smug comparison with others swatting flies around me, I thought to myself, *All those hours of meditation are paying off.* My face and arms grew damp with humidity while I looked around me.

The ashram arena was grand in scale and opulence—even ostentatious with inlaid gold, huge lion statues, and a great high ceiling. Holding thousands of souls, this main room was open on all sides supported by ornate pillars. Birds flew in and out, soothing my mind with the white noise of flapping wings and tranquil coos. Men sat to the left, women to the right. In front of all seated devotees, a walkway was present, leading to a lavish gathering area where Sai Baba would meet select individuals. Although we were heartened to trust whatever interaction he wanted to have with us, I was jealous to have a personal encounter with him. *I hope while I am here, he calls me into that small room. I want to get near him.*

Hearing squeals in the distance, I gasped. *He is coming!* I turned to see faces bathed in sunset light, eyes wide with awe. Sai Baba entered in his bright orange robe. A hush fell over the crowd. From the eleventh row, I caught my first glimpse. For a moment, it seemed he looked my way. My heart fluttered.

With a slow and graceful pace, he walked forward along the front veranda, making gestures in the air as if he was manifesting something or "praying." I had seen these motions in videos. Sometimes he paused to look at certain people, but mostly he walked from side to side before completing his procession.

Once his appearance was complete, all devotees stood to their feet. I found my American friends, and together we searched amongst a colorful pile of shoes until we located our sandals. Walking back to our rooms, we giggled in delight that we were finally here. For days, we pinched ourselves to make sure this wasn't just a dream.

THE CONFERENCE

The conference lasted two weeks, filled with Sai Baba's appearances, teachings by the Sai Baba organization, and youth-led bhajan or worship singing. Sizeable flags from around the world waved in the desert breeze, and in true Indian fashion, lively colorful parades with symbols of Sai Baba's tenets preceded the worship sessions. The energy was vibrant, and I was elated to be part of it.

One day, I was seated with other female bhajan leaders. Because we led songs for the conference, Sai Baba approached our small group. For three seconds, he unmistakenly looked directly at me. The moment stood still, as this was all I had been longing for. Though I didn't feel a particular burst of love, I certainly felt noticed by him.

My brother Finn recounts how a photograph capturing this moment still haunts him to this day. The photo was taken by my fellow youth group member. Finn described it as an image of me staring at Sai Baba who stood in front of me. He said I had fiery eyes, an open smile, and a glossy, glazed cast on my face. Certainly, I was intensely fixated on Baba, a moment which would have been evocative to see.

After a few days of the conference, Heather and I became very ill—so ill that we could not leave our room for three days. With dehydrated bodies, we dragged ourselves to the ashram booths, where young men chopped open green coconuts and handed them to us with straws. For a few rupees, fresh coconut juice did wonders to revive us and it was the finest, most refreshing drink I've tasted in any hot desert.

Eventually, we returned to the conference for more Swami appearances, bhajan singing, and teachings about how Sai Baba united all religions. After the conference ended, Heather stayed an extra week. American friends offered to let me stay as much as *five weeks longer* in one of their rented rooms. While I was sad to part with Heather, I had nothing else planned for the summer. And graciously, I was given an open return ticket. There were plenty of unspent rupees in my purse, and when would I get this chance again? I remained a total of two months in India! It was the summer of my fourth year of college, and I just wanted to stay—stay with god.

A RUSH OF SIGNIFICANCE

For a few days following my decision, I marveled at where I was on the earth. Assured that I could linger here for a while, I settled in, exploring the ashram and surrounding Puttaparthi. The vibrant fabrics of Indian culture colored everywhere my eyes scanned. Masses of people walked in saris, sandals and flowy clothing, and collectively they kicked up finely sifted dirt—wafting musky earth into the air. Mingled with Indian spices and burning incense, these distinctive aromas reminded me that I was on the far side of the world.

Nights were especially beautiful with warm air, and I loved Southern India monsoons which suddenly deluged warm showers. When I didn't run to take cover, I received funny looks from natives, nonetheless I enjoyed being cleansed from hours of sitting in the ashram. Because of the monsoon, this desert had silkier sand than I have ever felt touching the soles of my feet.

Each day revolved around Sai Baba's morning and evening strolls. At 4 a.m., we sat in orderly lines, drawing numbers to determine how close we'd sit. One day, my group drew row one. When Sai Baba walked directly in front of me, I perceived a deafening silence, affecting even the pressure of the air around me. I had read about this "hush" feeling when you meet him. He did briefly look at me, and I interpreted it however I wanted to. Apparently, what I experienced was not memorable.

He often looked down at specific people and glanced far out into the sea of faces. It was considered love from him that he saw you, noticed you. Because we believed he was god, of course to experience him looking at you was a big deal. Certainly, you instantly felt a rush of significance.

THE MEETING ROOM

It was time for me to meet him in person.

The week before, I had been granted a rare opportunity with other young adults to kiss Sai Baba's feet. As he walked in front of me, I struggled to fold myself into a bowing position while wearing a sari, and it didn't turn out well. I was barely able to reach, let alone kiss his feet, and I heard him sneer as he stood hovering above me. In that moment, I told myself I hadn't heard this from him because it would have been too painful to believe. Needless to say, this fortuitous occasion was not enlightening or enjoyable, and I was not easy on myself about it.

During my first month in India, Sai Baba asked to see Americans who remained following the conference. Within minutes of being told of this, we swiftly sat at the front of the veranda. Staring at gold filagree tile below my feet, I was overwhelmed with the magnitude of this moment.

But while waiting to be ushered into his inner room, I started to feel suffocating pressure on my chest. And I could not shake it. Distressing thoughts began to surface,

Why do I feel a heavy force all around me? Am I anxious? But this is coming from outside of me—like a crushing gravity. It shouldn't be like this. Woah, I am a little scared.

Increasingly disoriented, I whispered to one of the other young adults in my group, "Do you feel weird also? What is happening?" Several of them shushed me, "Be quiet!" I wondered if they felt similarly strange or if they just accepted whatever this unnerving sensation was.

Soon after, we were quickly escorted into Baba's tiny inner room. Ten of us crouched down, and we struggled to fit. He walked in and took his seat on an ornate chair. At first, he looked around at us a bit but said very little. I stared at his face only five feet away. Suddenly more of that inexplicable, severe, heavy weight came over me. My mind became disorganized and foggy—like a drowsy stupor. Perceiving a cloud of smoke entering the room, I felt lightheaded and out of my body. Though my eyelids were heavy with the burden of sedation, I endeavored to stay alert, noticing other devotees similarly struggled to remain awake. I watched as their postures limped downward in a stupefied daze.

It was then I became conscious enough to remember this was a chance encounter with Sai Baba, so I deliberately jarred myself just to ask him a question. I don't remember what I asked, but he talked about my question with someone sitting nearer to him. In all of this, he never looked at me.

I walked away from the encounter confused. Our group was called into his inner room one other time during my visit. Both times were foggy, heavy occurrences, and it was hard for me to stay present. Either the space was highly concentrated with "spiritual energy" or I was beginning to suspect that the hazy substance I saw in the room was some kind of drug. These disconnected experiences with a possible drug-induced euphoria only magnified my dissociative tendencies and made me anxious. During the second encounter with Sai Baba in this room, I watched as he took an adolescent boy into a smaller, private room for more than a few minutes. The young man returned pale and wide-eyed—like he had seen a ghost! Though I shoved away the thought, it nagged—*Things just don't seem right.*

After being wholly in his presence, I did not feel peace, love or transcendence—instead I felt literally drugged. Deeply affected by my time close to him, I analyzed that Baba didn't look at or speak to me directly because *maybe it's me, keeping him at arm's length?* And I told myself to just try harder as his devotee.

For two months, I waited hours to see Baba and received a few glances and looks I knew were right at me. Being seen is a big deal for human beings. Being seen by a being who you believe is god is a sensation on another level. But by the end of my trip, the glances were not enough for me. Many devotees experienced Sai Baba in their dreams, and I had a few of those as well, but they did nothing to bond me to him. Far more than fleeting introductions, my soul craved a close relationship with god.

THE REALITY OF INDIA

During my second month there, the reality of his indifference hit me, and I cried myself to sleep most nights. When I became tired of crying, I tried to leave my body to get ahold of Baba's consciousness, like a daughter peeking inside god's room to get his attention. Sounds strange, but I always had a huge imagination. Desperate to be free from this pain, transporting myself somewhere else was a form of dissociation that had worked in my life before.

I was confused that my god did not want to see or speak with me. I had come all this way and was losing perspective that he was even aware of me. I internalized to the deepest, most aching parts of my psyche—

Does he love me?

Does he care?

Does he even notice me?

Does he want me to stay?

It tore me apart. For all I knew, my eternal dad was residing hundreds of feet away from me and—couldn't I just go and be with him? Over the weeks, it became obvious he didn't want me to. He stopped walking towards me, and I was seated further and further away from him. I realized he had a protocol, a cold order to how he related with us, and this was who he was. Maybe this process was acceptable to those who enjoy keeping a distance from god, but my soul wasn't satisfied with any of it.

SAD END

A strained relationship with American citizens deepened my grief. With an open return ticket, I planned to travel home once my rupees ran out. The family who graciously offered to shelter me roomed me with a girl who was about to marry into their family. While initially friendly, she began to overtly judge my sorrowful nature. Focused on impressing her new family, cuttingly she told me, "You are bringing me down spiritually."

At first, the woman who was to become her mother-in-law was affectionate towards me, but one mistake on my part changed her whole demeanor. Apparently one evening, they accused me of somehow locking them all in their apartment, and as a result they missed Sai Baba's sunset appearance. I have no idea how that would be possible let alone that I did it, but she never let me know the end of how I had hurt her family that night. For the last three weeks of my stay, I received obvious judgement from them. They left me completely on my own, and my broken heart became sullener.

For nearly a month in this foreign country, I ate alone, waited in Sai Baba lines alone, left his appearances alone—I kept my own company. I missed my friends I traveled here with. Rejected by this family who originally welcomed me, no matter how much I apologized, I was no longer invited. I was holding them back from their spiritual enlightenment, and though it seemed disingenuous, it reinforced injuries of scorn I knew from my sister. I should have left India much earlier than I did, but persistently, I held out hope for more of a connection with Sai Baba.

BACK HOME

I returned to the States with a parting hole in my heart. To say I was disappointed would be an understatement. My faith in him was severely shaken. I did not experience evidence that he loved or even knew me at all—and it broke me. He was not the god of love I had been seeking, or the fulfillment of hope I desperately needed.

During my first several weeks back, I stayed with my mom in Pacific Grove, California. One day, despairing to feel better, I threw out all my high school yearbooks and old pictures, discarding any-thing that caused an emotional reaction in me. Flinging picture after picture into the trash, I determined to "detach" from it all—a teaching I learned from Sai Baba and New Age circles. My sister happened to be there, and she injected her own disappointment, telling me not to throw memories away. I argued she didn't understand how I needed to disengage from my past. Frustrated with inner conflict, I was willing to try anything, anything to free me from this unwanted pain that appeared immovable, like an obstinate boulder resting comfortably inside my chest.

As a Sai Baba follower herself, my mother would remember this time very differently. She loved it when I shared how "auspicious" my time in India was during Sai Baba gatherings we both attended. Other devotees were in awe that I had spent so much time at the ashram, and my mother loved riding the coattails of her daughter's newfound celebrity.

When I returned to college for my fifth year, at least four friends said to me, "What is wrong Beth? You don't seem like yourself." In response, I put up the same front to them about what an amazing summer I had in India. I outright denied how distressing it was to stay there so long and rarely interact with him. Using my preferred coping mechanism, I negated the reality of India even to myself.

Because I surrendered to Sai Baba and was subject to his ideology, I continued to follow him. While staring at his photo during devotional meetings, subconscious thoughts surfaced, *There must be something really wrong with me—because he rejected me.* Worsening fractures already in my mind, I could not separate a father's rejection from a spiritual father's rejection, and something in my psyche broke. My perspective became even more torn about my identity with god, and I spiraled into a heavy depression.

Over the months following my return, I was persistently uneasy, nervous and progressively fatigued. I developed an arresting anxiety that made my insides quiver with a constant, grating frequency. Exasperated with sensations I was powerless to address, impassively I threw myself into striving hard at college.

DENSE SENSATION

That next year I traveled with a group four hours to one of several supposed "Sai Baba miracle houses." Entering the home, I smelled curried dahl stirred by Indian women in the kitchen. With the procession of tourists, I strolled past exhibitions of "miraculous honey" and "vibhuti" or ash manifestations which oozed and trickled from statues aligning the walls. Sai Baba was known to "miraculously produce" ash with the wave of his hand. Covered by plexiglass, these displays appeared natural. Even still, I doubted their authenticity. At the far end of the home, we entered a big altar room and sat quietly in meditative style, facing an altar of Shiva, Kali and photos of Sai Baba. I clearly remember the well-acquainted weight of heaviness as I sat down, accustomed to what I felt in India. The pressure upon me was similarly stifling, and I felt short of breath.

As an empathetic "feeler" type person, an artist who paints with inspired passion, it is undeniable that I sensed something spiritual in India and at this "miracle home." However, the familiar emptiness accompanied by that dense sensation did not elevate or encourage me. It was mystical for sure—but devoid of love, lightness or warmth. I was still desperately seeking unrequited spiritual love, so I sat lingering in that weighted feeling—despairing to sense God.

There comes a point where you are so hungry that even drops of feeling what is bitter is better than sensing nothing at all. I knew that Eastern Mysticism was "so mysterious," and I was taught to not expect palpable love but instead "feel its spiritual mystery." So yeah, *I felt that*—in India and at this place. But that was not enough for me. I wanted and needed *love*. I never felt love in India or in anything related to Sai Baba.

Sai Baba is no longer alive. In fact, he died seven years short of the age at which he prophesized he would die. It is reported that leaders of his ashram preserved his body on ice until Easter to tell his devotees that he had died on an "auspicious" day.

Shortly after returning from India, I received another lifeline and transferred my devotion to someone else.

NEW HOPE

When my sister, my mother and I attended the second annual Ascension Festival in Mt. Shasta in May 1995, it was like a "spiritual family reunion." This time, we made a strong link to Lorelei Schook—the Ascension conference leader who channeled the "divine mother." She approached Em and me during the conference and invited us to her hotel room. There, she curiously recognized a unique spiritual connection between us and her and gave us ways to contact her any time we wanted.

From that point forward, I emailed Lorelei frequently during my third through fifth year of college, and my esteem for her guidance grew in intensity. In these emails, she asked me to call her anytime I wanted to reach out. It was an open invitation for spiritual direction, and I held back the opportunity with respect until I truly needed it.

During my final two weeks in India, at the point of my greatest desperation, I called her. Her loving tone immediately soothed and stilled my anxious mind like all those years in college. It was incredibly reassuring to hear Lorelei's warm acceptance from across the world! She would be waiting to carry me through the next phase of my spiritual journey.

SEVEN

Too Young to Cry

Peering from windows wrapped around my backyard rental cottage, my eyes held a soft gaze on different shadows of green. Like a typical day in Santa Cruz, it was drizzling with bulbous beads plummeting from saturated skies. Drops fell onto broad-sloped calla lily leaves, and my ears heeded to the rain's rhythmic *tud-tud, tud-tud,* as if nature was performing a pleasing drum concert just for me. Snuggled behind a yurt, a few baby redwoods remained steadfast in the face of every storm I watched from here, and I wish I could feel their soundness of being.

The downpour intensified. Syncopated beats blended into a constant rushing of water while bright tones resonated inside my cottage—tat-tat, Tat-Tat-Tat! The sound of this rain orchestra overtook the disquiet within me. I was sitting at my oak desk covered with opened chemistry books soaking in the reprieve, interrupted by my next thought—*I should go inside the house and make myself a sandwich.*

During my last three years of college, I lived with several fun-loving adults, but I didn't want to run into them right now. I told myself, *Just hold off a little longer, I can wait. Besides I will get totally soaked on the way there!*

Rainy days gave me cause to stay tucked inside my bungalow, and today my mood was enveloped in the imagined safety of seclusion. Here I could suspend annoying mental conflicts and feel safe from the threat of anything distracting.

Placing my elbow on the desk, I rested my chin on an open palm and let out a sigh. I knew the skies would part at some point—and my excuses to not go on a bike ride, see the beach or visit with friends would leave me as quickly as this rain had intensified. On this day and most days during this time, I was pretty hard on myself. Striving did not leave room for leisure, nor for failure.

I don't have time for distractions! I have to make perfect grades and reach my goals. Ignore this chaos inside! Just get this done already! I need to accomplish something great and move past all this confusion!

In my fifth year of college, I became zealously engrossed in my future. It seemed the only way I could escape the chaos of my own disillusionment was to focus on tangible achievements. Plus, nothing else worked.

My trip to India was a total letdown and made me feel unworthy of love. Lonely and confused, I felt fully disconnected from myself. With nagging numbness, I constantly tried to escape my reality, but I didn't know why, nor why I had very little sense of who I was. I felt that the only way I could be worthy of being loved, or at least be acknowledged, was to become a success. Relentlessly striving, impatience became amplified within me. I resolved, *If I achieve something impressive, I will finally be valued enough to be seen!*

I had already tried going in the opposite direction early in my college years, throwing myself completely in frivolity. Hoping to discover a semblance of wholeness, I sought ways to express myself and find meaning. Tucked to my desk, I rubbed my sore eyes. Strained from concentrating so hard, I took a break to reminisce about these more carefree times.

NATURE FROLIC

My cheeks felt the stretch of my smile as wind from the open bus windows blew against my sun-blushed face. Our UC Santa Cruz recreation vehicle moved at an easygoing pace, holding ten of us college freshmen. My beloved roommate Claudia and I had signed up for a long weekend's backpacking excursion to Yosemite with some of our charismatic friends. Just the four-hour journey there was a relaxing escape from staring at schoolbooks. Instead, we viewed scenic terrain from the car and kicked up our hairy legs. Yes, hairy. Eventually over time growing it out, it became soft and bleached by the sun. All of us had all adopted a hippie lifestyle typical of Santa Cruz which included sporting Birkenstocks, wearing little or no makeup, and eating vegetarian. We wailed aloud to a Crosby, Stills and Nash cassette that played on repeat. For this trip, we seemed to be of one mind—a nature-loving, free-spirited group of young adults who were particularly enjoying new freedoms.

Before we got to our campsite, we stopped to explore a wide-open field of Yosemite Valley. Standing below the majestic Half-Dome, it was exhilarating just to breathe. My lungs swelled in response to the crisp, oxygen-rich air. Before us, a mellow breeze caused sun-soaked grass to sway in a slow waltz, and its lulling motion appeared serene as in any dreamy landscape. Apart from our group, there was no one around, and we were all itching to run free and frolic.

One of the men in our group took off his shirt. What followed was definitely rated PG-13. We all stared as he just as suddenly removed his belt and took off his pants. Then came his underpants until he was in his birthday suit! Looking at each other, we shrugged our shoulders and immediately thought this was a terrific idea! Without a word or even a gesture of awkward hesitation, we all followed his bold spontaneity. Hurriedly we removed our clothes and began to run through open fields of nature's gold! Shouting with jubilation as we lept through it all, we felt no shame—everyone here had been exposed to skinny-dipping beaches along Santa Cruz shores. Cavorting care-free, skipping through Yosemite's glory, we couldn't help but crack up with hilarity at what we were doing, and our gleeful giggling was intoxicating. We weren't paying attention to each other or thinking about pretense at all. Instead, we felt waves of innocence wash over us and abandoned any other boring notions about it. I had not laughed so hard in years!

The rhythm of the rain on the roof pulled me back, and the memory of streaking through Yosemite made me chuckle. Though it was exceedingly joyful, it was one of many uplifting adventures whose freedom was never enough to shake me out of my own uncertainty. Life always brought me back to reality, and nothing changed inside of me.

Through my window, I saw evergreens swaying gently to the storm, reminding me how I used to immerse myself in nature for longer periods of time. During the summer of my junior year, I took a six-week backpacking environmental studies course in the New Mexico and Colorado country.

WILDERNESS

One frosty morning near Durango, several of us rose at three am to hike to a peak of the San Juan Colorado mountains. Even though it was uncomfortable to leave our toasty sleeping bags and get ready in the nippy night, we wanted to watch the sunrise over the mountains. After hiking for three hours uphill in the chill, we arrived at the most breathtaking view I had ever seen. Before me lay an entire panorama of majestic Rocky Mountain peaks. Entranced, I gawked at them for over an hour, while waiting for daybreak. At 14,000 feet, this was the closest I had been to the clouds. Embraced by incredible stillness, I heard my own breath as in an echo chamber. Turning to my side, I saw plumes of fog leave my friend's mouth as she said what we were all thinking, "Wow. So glad we made it here in time."

A spot of morning glory pierced my eyes. Exhilarated by its appearance, I was filled with gratitude for being here to see this splendorous view of the wild. The sun swelled over the horizon, and the east side of every peak shimmered with warmth. Shadows sandwiched between the mountains shifted to deep purple blue. Overwhelmed by radiant color and light transformations, this stunning scene stirred the deepest part of me to want to come alive—to soar! The illumination of the sun penetrated the entire landscape below me, as if it ascended just to bathe in these glorious mountains.

I could hear whispered "wows" and delighted gasps. My face was befriended by warm sunshine, and a soothing calm washed over me. I told myself—*This is so spiritual. I wish I could connect with the source of so much beauty.* Desiring to hold this euphoric moment for the rest of my life, I made sure to mentally record every detail so I could treasure it forever.

The mountain light dimmed in memory, and the soft gray of the Santa Cruz sky reclaimed my gaze. I pondered that though my wilderness experiences were sincerely meaningful, they did not lend themselves to wholeness, nor was I able to soothe my frenzied psychology by trekking through pristine forests or resting in the tranquility of back woods.

Even my old standby—art—left me wanting for self-expression, despite having a couple of gallery exhibitions. As a promising creative venture, I participated in a whacky live art installation.

MUD PEOPLE

I watched as the first brave people dipped into full-sized trashcans full of soupy mud. My artsy friends had gathered us all here at a downtown park to collectively dunk into sludge. Once we were all slathered, we were going to walk across town carrying goofy expressions as a gathering of "mud people." *What?* This required a great deal of boldness on my part, but I loved tactile experiences, and I loved fun. So, after an awkward moment of hesitation, I stepped into one of the troughs.

As soon as the cool, oozing mire surrounded my frame, it felt pleasing to my skin. Having sculpted before, the sensation was like being enveloped in my own clay statue. I decided I could be a transient ridiculous art piece! Man, this was weird, but it was also hysterical.

Before we started our mud walk, one of the leaders really got into it saying, "Don't say a word! Just make scary, grunting expressions and noises as you look straight at people and keep walking contortedly like a mud person, ok? Oh—and don't break out of character!" Already chuckling to myself, I thought, *This is too funny. How am I supposed to stay in character?*

Up to our eyeballs in mud, we paraded through downtown, and we were quite a sight. *Only in Santa Cruz!* I thought. People were shocked by our sudden presence, but when we came up close to them with wild expressions, they laughed aloud with open smiles, staring at our nutty performance. There was no stated purpose for it all except that it was totally bizarre and greatly amusing. And just as I thought, I couldn't stop cracking up at what we were doing, especially when my artsy friends stared into me with ridiculous expressions.

As the mud caked on our bodies, we became increasingly anxious for the beach water finish line. Our entire group sprinted into the ocean with thunderous elation—"*Waaaaah!*" Thrilled to have fun with this silly ensemble, in the end, I was so glad I did it. It was no doubt the messiest, most nonsensical and outrageous thing I ever did in Santa Cruz.

Just because it was so foolish, this happy diversion to express myself briefly took me out of my existential funk. But alas, in zany mud art or even in painting, though I was looking for a way to break out of emotional paralysis, I never discovered anything but a temporary release. Art therapy did not bring lasting joy or a sense of completeness. I stood up from my desk chair. Stretching wide my arms, I recalled taking a more altruistic approach.

CUTTING ONIONS

Bicycling across Santa Cruz to different jobs and locations, I met transient folks and gave them what I had to give—whatever happened to be in my backpack. At a homeless garden project, I helped make floral wreaths and tended vegetables alongside transients. There, I learned to listen to the plights of others.

While working at a local vegan brownie shop, for many weeks, I brought unsold brownies to a particular homeless woman at her abandoned shop front corner spot. At our first meeting I asked her, "Hi, I brought you some brownies. Can I sit with you?" "Yeah, that's fine," she said. I sat down on the sidewalk in front of her. While unwrapping the dessert and handing it to her, she told me, "You know, NASA stole my invention. I am really very smart." I said, "Oh, wow. What invention did they steal?" She answered, "I created a time travel device. It was like an antenna that fits on your head. Mmmm, this cake is good. I like this one. What kind is it?" "It's raspberry chocolate," I replied. "The other one is mint chip—hope you like them." She said, "Yes, thanks. I do."

She paused briefly, and then continued, "I was an engineer at NASA and they stole my time travel device. Now they are making money off my invention." I really wanted to believe her, if for no other reason than that she felt like someone was listening. But every time I visited her, she kept returning to that magnificent story, and I knew she was probably lonely. Like her, I understood loneliness of mind. I kept bringing her brownies until I could no longer find her resting at her typical shelter. Who knows, maybe she traveled to a better time with her antenna contraption?

During summers, I found a local Meals on Wheels to volunteer my time, knowing it would lift my spirits to be doing something good. One day, I was asked to chop a few pails of onions, and my eyes began to water profusely. Along with tears of cutting onions, I added my own tears of sadness over the break-up of a summer boyfriend. Thinking I could hide my misty face, the older woman I worked with figured it out, "Honey, are you crying? Honey—you're too young to cry!" Having gone volunteering just to feel better, I ended up purged from repressed emotion, and hey—buckets of onions were prepped for nutritious meals.

I opened the window. The smell of fresh rain filled my cottage room. I remembered it did feel good to try to ease the burdens of others. But despite attempts to reach outside myself, bottled-up anguish over my own worth continued to fester within me. I really wanted it to work, but no amount of service would fundamentally change who I was or help me find completeness.

Feeling my cheeks blush, I remembered one more thing I attempted—a chemical approach to escape mental and emotional bondage.

YEP, EVEN THAT!

In typical Santa Cruz hippy fashion, marijuana was part of the college experience. However, I quickly found out I couldn't share this part of my friends' gatherings. I knew better anyway. Years prior, I was kicked out of an art camp for inhaling one puff of marijuana. It caused such a bad physical and psychological trip that I believed it had been laced with some sort of hallucinogenic drug.

In my first few months of college, I tried pot again for the first and last time. My dear friend Zahira carried me through the whole night. Hoping the art camp experience was an anomaly, I took a hit and immediately suffered the same bad reaction while we walked from a party across many acres of UCSC terrain. Zahira and I ended up getting lost circling the entire campus a few times. She stayed with me when I saw delusions and needed to just close my eyes and freak out. Back in my dorm room, I kept hearing a mania of voices long into the night.

I figured out I had a different reaction than friends to drugs and alcohol. Marijuana magnified the paranoia of my fragile psychology and intensified dissociative voices that began to proliferate within me at this time. And with alcohol, because of my easily affected nature, I got tipsy on just a few sips. Friends thought I had drunk more than I had and wanted to engage me with other drugs. My friend Mara made a funny request, "I want to shroom with you so bad Beth!" Like me, Mara could be a joyful spaz, and she thought shrooms could free up some of my mental frustrations. But if just one of my internal references felt powerless, it generated chaos and delirium within me. I responded to her with a hearty chuckle, "Nah, that probably wouldn't be good for me Mara!"

From that point on, I never smoked pot while many around me continued to do so at parties. Still, friends would laugh at my goofy, laid-back manner saying, "Man you are so wasted!" But I never was. I was just giddy on very little of anything, and I enjoyed loose environments which removed my usual uneasiness.

The haze of those nights cleared, and the scent of wet earth through the open window brought me back. Not only did drugs not work, but they made things worse. Mind altering substances were definitely not an option for me.

CROSSROADS

I reclined on my bed and listened to the symphony of the rain. Recalling all of these different attempts at self-discovery helped me realize I really did try everything to escape my hidden reality so I could feel whole, or even normal.

And as much freedom as I gained from gaiety and light-hearted adventures, that didn't help me now. I was frantic about something different. My psychology was complicated, all bound up within me. I needed something far-reaching and permanent towards wholeness. Was this a hopeless desire within me? All my trying had left me weary. Troubled by noxious anxiety, I focused again on my future. *I can get this right. I am smart and creative—I can be successful!*

I believed that if I chose the right career, did what I was destined to do and fulfilled my purpose, I could transcend all inner obstacles. But because I struggled to know who I was apart from how I was raised to see myself, figuring out my chosen career was a battle. A deep identity crisis lay dormant inside, and I fought to grasp what I truly valued. Vacillating between two of my passions for most of my college years, it came down to pursuing art or biology.

STRESSED OUT

In the end I went with studying medicine, partially because when I applied for the art major, I was told that I "lacked a defining point of view." And yeah, of course—that was the problem. I sought hard to find my own voice, but apart from my mother and sister's influence, and a flurry of echoes parroting them inside of me, I really didn't have one.

So, it was decided. I was going to throw myself entirely into being accepted into medical school. I would fix my eyes on succeeding in the grandest career I could conceive. Both my fascination for science and my desire to earn my mom's admiration won the "what is my purpose" contest. Even in my favorite childhood game of "Life," becoming a doctor was the ultimate career card you could pick. As an added bonus, I knew this would make me untouchable to my sister. If I could succeed at becoming a physician, there was nothing she could say about me.

The problem with endeavoring towards medical school was that I didn't know when to stop. Every moment I was not studying, memorizing, and reading the material, I would hastily return. Consumed, I lacked an internal gauge to know when to take a break or unwind. My sense of self was buried by striving, and any readiness I had for companionship I would willingly starve to commit every moment to my goal.

And it was working. I was constantly achieving top grades in all my prerequisites for medical school and on track to being accepted. Overworked for sure, but I had to stay focused. The artist-playful part of myself was on a long vacation. Meditating nightly in front of my Sai Baba altar, I awoke to more studying. Withdrawn, I was thirsty for connection and relaxation.

In May 1998, my classes were finished, and I was about to take final boards to complete a combined Biology/Environmental Studies major. But when the requirement suddenly changed to finalize my degree—I froze in my momentum. Apparently, I had to pass a 200-question monster exam covering every detail of every upper division biology course from molecular biochemistry to genetics to zoology. Confidence drained from my body as if it were sucked out by a giant leech. Extremely overwhelmed, I was too weary to begin preparing for this final exit exam.

The finish line was imminently within my grasp, but I was fraught with mental and emotional fatigue. I needed a repose, not another massive test which would take countless hours to study for, perhaps another semester to ensure success! My brain was fried. Yes, just like a couple of eggs in a searing skillet. Adding the pressure of these boards didn't make sense to me—as if my mind were at capacity and already taking a detour.

The thought of more rigor to pass my boards, take the MCATS and then work to get accepted into medical school was backbreaking! The pressures I imposed on myself were also aggravated by a nagging spiritual and emotional crisis within me. I had been singularly focused on seeing my goals through, but now I found myself petrified with dysfunction. Exhausted from my efforts and following typical dissociative tendencies, I required an escape!

Every fiber of my being needed an adventure. Desperately, I lacked the cheerfulness of youth felt during my early college years. I didn't reach out to my family because I knew they would nudge me to push to the end, and I only wanted to hear what "the universe" thought was best for me. Though logic said I *should* complete my degree and keep my head forward, I knew that if I kept ploughing, I would have a total mental breakdown. Frozen in overwhelm, I realized I just couldn't go forward with any of it.

With tight shoulders and furrowed brows, I was incredibly stressed out and desperate about what to do. One night in early March 1998, my struggle of striving met an impossible decision. I needed help—I needed spiritual direction. I decided to call Lorelei Schook, the Ascension spiritual leader who appeased all my anxiety when I called her from India less than a year ago. With that one phone call, she had calmed the storm within me. Somehow, I knew she could do it again.

"Hello?" she answered after the second ring.

"Lorelei? This is Elizabeth."

"Oh, Hi!" Her voice raised with apparent joy, "I was just thinking about you!"

"You were??" I replied, astonished.

"Yes, I was thinking, 'Elizabeth is going to call me soon!'" Then she had a great big laugh.

"But . . . how did you know?" I asked.

She kept laughing in response, as if to say she really was aware I was going to call her.

Feeling the urgency of my troubles, I got right to it, "Lorelei, I was hoping to talk with you about something."

She replied attentively, "Yes, how are you doing right now?"

"Oh, I'm not doing very well," I said.

"What is going on?" she asked.

I told her all I was facing—my boards, then the MCATS, then medical school and how I didn't know how I could go on. I really needed a break. With clenched jaw and near tears, I vented how anxious I was to hear what was right for me to do. Even as I heard myself speak it out loud to her, my cheeks turned beet red because I felt cornered with only two choices—quit or keep going.

Then, unexpectedly she answered, "It's so funny you should tell me all this! Now I know why you have called me!"

"What?" I reacted, surprised that apart from soothing words of comfort she would have any real solution to my predicament.

"Do you know where I am right now?" Lorelei said.

"No, where are you?" I asked.

Excitedly, she answered, "I am living in Arizona on some beautiful land, with some great friends. We are starting something big out here, and I want you to be a part of it." She proceeded to tell me about the property, the animals and how enjoyable it was to all be together. She invited me to come live with them in rural Dragoon, Arizona.

My mind was captivated by this out-of-the-blue offer. "Wow! Really?? But wait, what about my big exit exam?"

She answered, "Just like you said—you need a break! Come out to be with us this summer to relax, take a load off, feel the warm air. We can enjoy being together! I would really love to have you out here!"

"What? Wait . . . so just for the summer?" I was getting excited. This seemed a real answer to all my tensions.

She replied, "Yes! You can return refreshed from the summer and complete all that you have set out to do. Medical school, finish your college degree, all of it. What do you think?"

"I think . . . wow! That sounds awesome and this is an amazing offer! I feel such peace about this, as if, this feels right . . . Yes! Yes, I would love to go out for the summer! Wow, I didn't expect this at all!"

We both squealed with delight. I was elated! And apparently so was she that I would join her.

She said, "Yay! This is so exciting! Ok, so call me back in April because, can you come out when we celebrate the Ascension Festival here in Arizona at the end of May?"

"Umm, yes, I can! My last classes will be done by then!" I replied.

"Wonderful! OK, then wonderful! I will email you the details. I am so excited you are coming! So, do you feel better now?" she asked.

I said, "Yes, I do! I can hardly contain myself! Thank you so much for this offer! I wasn't expecting this. Yes, I feel so much better now!"

Lorelei replied, "Good! I am so very glad you called me! I love you!"

"I love you too! Thank you, Lorelei!" I said.

"Talk to you soon!" she said. With a melodic inflection to her voice, I could tell she was smiling as she said, "Bye-bye!"

Calming me with her uplifting laughter, she offered me an out which lent so much serenity. She invited me to press the pause button on all the stress I had been experiencing—or better yet—she was pressing it for me. And there was no commitment to press it indefinitely. It was like a lifeline for me, and I truly believed it was the right way to go at this major crossroads. After all, Lorelei's invitation was *just for the summer.*

EIGHT

The Divine Mother

Greeted by the sun piercing through mini blinds, I opened my eyes to the morning light and rolled to one side of my futon bed. I pondered the whole new spin my life would take that summer. *Woah, what a detour. But I need this breather!* Lorelei's offer yesterday seemed a heroic gesture to save me from capsizing within my own sea storm. My face cracked a smile, a smile which I held—up until the moment I overthought it all—and my eyes returned to a pensive stare. This opportunity thrilled me exceedingly, even though just considering it placed me at a major junction. *Is it worth halting the momentum of my career goals to follow after healing I need?* The only thing I knew for sure was everything motivating me and everything about me needed to cease.

Weighing my new trajectory, I was faced with the same defining moment realized by the caterpillar. Continuing to gorge on food and inch through life, she searches for an eventual haven—a hidden place, away from wasps and other predators—a place to begin chrysalis formation and bring to fruition her final form. She may not know she will transform into an entirely different creature, but she knows some kind of change is imminent. Purposefully looking for *where* she will weave herself with silk to a structure, I was likewise choosing *where* to shift my surroundings—even if it was for a short time.

In only two months, after I finish my last semester at UCSC, I will be on a parcel of land with Lorelei and new friends. Coming from California's congested towns, the wide-open spaces of the Arizona desert enticed me. I wanted to know the stillness of sweeping panoramas and feel arid winds blowing across my face. Comforting myself that it was just for the summer allowed me to still hold onto a promising future in medical school and eventually complete my degree. Giddy for this journey, my heart soared thinking about being close to Lorelei. She had poised assurance in who I could become, and I knew she could lead me into wholeness. Through calming emails or calls, she had lent me confidence that she could help me heal.

Now it would not only be occasional words from her, or a chance moment with her at a spiritual conference. I would be living with her, and I saw this as an invitation of honor. I already trusted in her affection, and there was a new promise—come learn directly from her. Feeling rejected by Sai Baba last summer, Lorelei invited me with open arms.

ARIZONA

I left for my trip to Arizona in May 1998 at the age of twenty-three. Weary from enduring a lengthy collegial trek, I was eager to become part of something new. As my beloved housemate Martin drove me to the airport, he remarked, "I'm happy for you, Elizabeth. You have always been on your own spiritual path so I'm glad you are doing this. At my age, I should have reached enlightenment by this time—Ha ha ha." I bid Martin a grateful goodbye, got on the plane and finally felt I was not a slave to my own striving.

Lorelei's friend Charlotte picked me up from Tucson's airport wearing a black cowboy hat. Charlotte appeared to be a practical down-to-earth woman of few words. She had a deep-lined weathered face, the first of many I would see in Arizona among locals who don't give a second thought how face-slapping winds and blistering sun toughens the skin. In an open jeep, she drove us 90 minutes from Tucson to the remote Dragoon mountains, and the wind that beat upon my body felt like newness for all my senses. My heart swelled with anticipation as I beheld the limitless landscapes I had been craving to see.

When I first stepped onto the property, the sun was beginning its descent on a warm, spring afternoon. I walked into the spacious main house where Lorelei gave me an invigorating welcome. Dressed in a flowy, ethereal outfit, she stood confidently and called out to me, "Elizabeth! Look at you! You are already glowing! Come here!" She embraced me and introduced me to the other members of her household—Zev and Ray, two men in their mid-thirties to early forties. They were working on the house, constructing large wooden beams to reinforce the living room. I liked their outgoing personalities immediately. I watched them happily work together as brothers and their sincerity put me at ease.

After dinner, we all sat on the porch as the tip of the sun set, and I was able to catch my first glimpse of a spectacular Arizona evening. Breathing in crisp desert air, I had never before seen such brilliant orange and pink hues arranged within a sunset. The warm night was a perfect temperature to wear my summer garb. I relished the light breeze which blew through it. This was nothing like moisture-chilled Santa Cruz evenings, and tonight I preferred the balmy twilight here. Being in Arizona was immediately grounding. The vast panorama signaled repose to my eyes—they could now relax from laser focus and effortlessly rest.

We talked into the night, or rather I listened as a curious new participant. Lorelei, Zev and Ray bantered with each other warmly, and their hearty laughs were infectious. Lorelei poked, "Oh Ray, I know you miss eating veggie patties and beans every night like before we came here." Ray retorted with a laugh, "Naaaah, you are a much better cook. Plus, you cook us meat. I like meat!" Being with them felt like home to me, having just left Santa Cruz where my housemates were all ten to twenty years older. I listened to their amusement and settled in, instantly feeling I fit in. Because Lorelei had welcomed me here, it was easy for me to trust Zev and Ray who seemed exuberant with strong constitutions. All three were enlivened to be a part of what was taking place, and perceptive to me that first night, things certainly felt electric.

When it got late, I wondered where I would stay among several bedrooms in the big house. Ray said to me, "I hope you don't mind, we set you up in the RV tonight until we get things cleaned up in here." "Oh, no that's great, thanks," I replied. In the RV, I stared at a flickering candle left for me and had trouble falling asleep until hours later. Ever at the mercy of stowed emotions, I woke up the next day already in a mental-emotional funk. Tears coated my cheeks. *Not this again!* I thought. *Not here!* Still overwhelmed by my own dysfunction, I was now sensing an added spiritual weight that hovered over the property.

Embarrassed by my own confusion, I sucked it up, and kicked into familiar gear wanting to help, grateful for my new community who were housing and feeding me for free. After years of struggling to make it on student loans, hearing from Lorelei I would be fully taken care of was a current of comfort to my ears.

From that first morning and for several weeks, there was a flurry of activity. Quickly I pieced together the purpose of our community. This picturesque land was to become a spiritual retreat center. With construction plans led by Lorelei and the "ascended masters" she channeled, the men were expertly skilled in their trades to carry them out. As the architect, Zev had been a general contractor, in charge of overseeing construction projects in the nearby town of Sierra Vista for the last ten years. Ray was a gifted metal worker who made parts for engineering and aviation companies. I was riveted by both their abilities to carry out designed projects with craftsmanship. And in large part because of their dedicated efforts, I was certain Lorelei's plans would manifest.

I loved being a part of the activity, the plans, the doing. I was all too happy to complete whatever was needed. Apply wax to an entire new linoleum floor? Yes, great—happy to contribute. Paint the trim of installed windowsills? I would love to! Help in the machinery shop with Ray? Yes please. I also helped clean, organize and assisted whoever was cooking meals. There was plenty to do, and I was eager to prove my usefulness.

We did not work hard every day though. "Ok, we're all going for ice cream," Lorelei would say. Even in the middle of nowhere Dragoon, AZ there was a Dairy Queen within fifteen minutes that we frequented on a whim. Sometimes we all drove into Tucson to get needed supplies at Home Depot, dining out along the way. This time with Lorelei, Ray and Zev lulled my mind away from its usual turmoil. Instead, I enjoyed harmonious repartee with my new friends. It didn't matter to me what we did together, I knew I belonged. By this time, I slept in the middle room of the big house, and in the evening, we watched movies in the living room or hung out on the porch.

Lorelei and the guys quickly learned how strongly nature appealed to me here in Southern Arizona. I appreciated being on the property's scenic 40 acres we referred to as "the land," and we also explored the surrounding area.

One day we traveled to Roper Lake near Willcox. Wading to the center of the lake, Ray showed me how nearby hot springs change the lake's buoyancy, so your body becomes featherlike in the water. "See, just stretch out and look up at the sky," he said. "You will float, I promise. Look, even I do," he said with a laugh. When I tried this myself, it became one of my favorite memories that summer. With outstretched arms, I drifted on the lake while looking into the infinite sky. The wind caused my body to glide upon the water, and I could only hear my own breath. With the perfect temperature of freshwater and pleasant weather on my skin, the experience was euphoric, and the closest to peace I had felt in a while.

THE MISSION

In those early days, apart from making improvements on the property, there was growing anticipation to hear about "the mission" for this land—a mission given by multiple divine personalities who collectively called themselves "the council of ascended masters." Lorelei had mannerisms with her eyes which would roll backwards a bit as she spoke, and it seemed she was checking in with this council of beings she channeled. She would allude to what "the mission" was but evade details about it—like throwing out a fly-fishing lure with a charming tease. She declared, "The masters have a very specific and powerful use for this land. You will all see." We were certainly baited and curious. I'm not sure if Lorelei herself had the whole picture, but we trusted her implicitly and followed through with her instructions.

A couple of weeks after my arrival, Lorelei called Ray and Zev for an important meeting. She told them her name was now "Lilith" and that she was a "walk-in" and a "light bearer." I remember how after their private talk, her behavior shifted subtly, and I couldn't understand why. Soon after, Zev took me aside and explained with bright eyes, "Ok so listen, we were just told that Lorelei is now Lilith. Lilith is a higher vibrational being who has "walked in" Lorelei's consciousness. Everything has changed now. We not only have the ascended masters talking to her, but now we have Lilith, an enlightened one who came here just to fulfill this mission. These are exciting times!"

As unusual as that sounded, it made sense because of all the ways Lorelei was involved in the hierarchy of the New Age movement. Apparently, Lorelei had surrendered to "Lilith" for her to "walk in," accomplish the mission here and "help raise the consciousness of the planet." It was like having the embodiment of the divine mother herself on the land. My excitement for being here transitioned to a whole new level. I couldn't believe I had been chosen for this spiritual awakening. This "consciousness shift" was akin to something I read about for years in New Age books, and here it was coming to life before me.

THE TRIANGLE

Within a few weeks of my arrival, Lilith called Zev, Ray and myself to the living room. On a poster board in front of her, Lilith drew a triangle with her name at the top point, Zev and Ray's name at the bottom two points. She said, "This is a triad. Together we are this triad." With narrowed eyes, and pointing back to the triangle, she emphasized the significance of the two men holding her up, saying, "I don't know if you understand the gravity of all that will take place here. And the enormity of both your roles to protect me, to shield me, is very great. I will be vulnerable during this mission. And your gifts will make a way for the mission to take place."

It made me intensely curious why she had invited me to this meeting, and what my role could be amongst these three. It made me want to be a part of this "triad"—*like badly*. Lilith continued, "There will be great shifts in the universe coming soon and this land will become a major center for spiritual transformation on the planet." I pinched my thigh and could not believe that I was here! I felt very important, and I wanted to get in on the inside. I would be crazy to not take advantage of this opportunity. Impulsively and naively, I felt willing to put all my hard-earned goals in the backseat.

She looked over at me, as if she could see the wheels in my head turn. Lorelei now Lilith was a major leader of this international New Age movement. How she saw me involved with "the triad" was burning inside until I could no longer wait for her to say. Adjusting myself high in my seat, I asked her if I was somewhere in that triangle diagram? With an engaging smile, she said, "You are here just to love me and be my handmaiden." *Be her handmaiden?* Oh, how this enthused my eager-to-please ears. I could be her helper—she could rely on me! My eyes opened in wonder, and my mouth stretched into a sparkly grin. She smiled at my expression and ended the meeting.

I was hooked! Even beyond what she said was my purpose here, I had this chance to learn directly from her. How could I miss out on this kind of "enlightenment?" I believed that being close to her would spark the transformation I was seeking. All of this was like being charmed by a promising hope towards all I had ever sought.

IMMERSED IN EFFERVESCENT WATERS

The following day, Lilith called me to sit with her on the back porch. Her attention was intoxicating. With diffuse boundaries and skewed self-awareness, her affection gave me a sense of identity. She started to ask me questions, "So, what did your mother say about you pausing your goals to come out here?" My eyes trailed to the ground as I answered, "I don't think she really cares to be honest. I told her I was coming here for a few months, but I didn't tell her about not finishing my graduation exam." Lilith probed curiously, "Why didn't you tell her? Don't you think she has your best interests at heart?" I gave a great sigh, "Hmm, not really." I paused and then, feeling myself disconnecting I said, "Do you know she left me in high school?" Tightening her lips and subtly shaking her head, she said, "Hmmm, that makes sense." I asked her, "What do you mean?" Lilith replied, "It's just that, well I noticed something about your mom when I met her—but I won't say it. I want you to come to your own conclusions."

Curiously, I sat there wondering, *What does she mean?* I valued her every word—I wanted to know just what she thought.

For a moment, I dropped my conjecture and soaked in the presence of the "divine mother" next to me. Just sitting near her felt like being immersed in effervescent, cool waters which soothed my chaffed collected wounds. She seemed to revive my soul which was scorched by hot winds of self-effacement. I didn't understand how she had this effect on me.

Musing more what she meant about my mother, I just had to know—*What conclusions does she already know about her?* Sharply, I began to contrast the two of them, wondering why I was so pulled towards Lilith who was so different from my mom. I felt my eyes turn vacant as I recalled events that made me want to lean into Lilith more. I remembered the pain I felt at my mother's indifference when she announced she was leaving.

THIS IS MY HOUSE!

"Beth, my 'financial guidance counselor' recommends I sell the house. She advised me now is the time to sell," my mother said with a honeyed intensity. "What? No! There must be another way for us to keep the house!" I protested. *But I have lived here since I was a baby!* My breaths turned shallow. She continued, "No, not according to the financial counselor. And Beth, I know deeply within I need to not only sell the house but take this chance to move to the coast where I have always dreamt of living." In disbelief, my eyes widened and began to water. She went on, "Beth, I need to move for my highest spiritual growth and so I can establish clients with my new counseling license in the place I want to be. This is my time, a time like I've never been given before."

At sixteen years old, she had sat me down at my favorite fast-food place just to drop this bombshell on me. Choking back tears, I slowly popped a warm crispy spud into my mouth. I recalled how she had been trying to "manifest" moving to the coast with a "vision board" she created several years back. And I realized my mom planned this long before our Foster Farms date.

"The exciting thing is, you have a choice," she explained. "You can move with me three hours away or stay here with Maggie and Summer until you go to college." She did not plead for me to journey with her. "Beth, you are bright, independent, and strong, and I know you will get into the college you want—I am not worried about you either way," she said. While finishing my meal, I quickly resolved to stay in Modesto. I knew that Maggie and her daughter Summer would love me as I loved them.

Deep within, I did not believe she wanted me to go with her, nor did I feel wanted. There was no "financial counselor" advising her to move—no, this was a lie. Because I was a minor, I was in the way of her "manifested" destiny. And so, she found a way around it. It was her excuse to stop being a parent and chase after her dreams.

Before she moved, when it was time to leave my childhood home, something broke in me. Standing in the laundry room with the real estate agent, my mom made last handshakes and turned to me with a smile of relief saying, "Ok. Beth. It's time to leave the house." My mother's sweet girl, usually amiable, bendable and accommodating, became undone. My knees buckled, and I fell to the floor while leaning against the clothes washer. From deep within, I cried out—"No! I don't want to leave!" My mom covered her mouth. She looked at the agent and said, "Beth, where is this coming from?" I cried out again and ran to the back of the house where my bedroom had been. I overheard her saying to the agent, "This isn't like her. She just needs a few minutes."

Running to the farthest closet of the house, I thought, *Maybe I can lock myself inside. No! I can't leave! But—there's no way out of this!* I couldn't escape this moment like I had been able to tune out from so many other hard times in this house. Memories flooded my heart and head. I was angry and couldn't grasp why we had to leave my home. *My whole life has been here!* In a moment of panic, I determined to carve my mark. I picked up a safety pin from the floor and feverishly scratched an expressive phrase behind the doorpost of my bedroom closet. With frenzied panic and tear-moistened cheeks, I scraped into the painted wood the most obvious sentiment which burned within me—*"This is MY house! -Beth"*

My foundations and my childhood were ending, I could never return. Our family home, where my siblings and I gathered to laugh and live, was being ripped from me forever. Even though, hidden behind walls of dissociation, lurked memories of terror I suffered here, all I knew was—*This is home to me.* In its place, halfway through high school, I would be fostered by a family friend.

My eyes trailed back to the beauty of the back porch, and I recounted to Lilith a little more of the story. Tears rolled down to my chin, and I brushed them away. Lilith sighed and said to me, "See, if I were your mother, I would have waited until you were done with high school, or I would have made you move with me so I could watch over you. I don't understand a mother who wouldn't!" Sobbing quietly, I was grateful Lilith was there. She was willing to take me in this summer, and she wanted me close, totally different from how easy it was for my mom to let me go.

Once Lilith spoke those words, it validated my pain and helped me understand my mother was not a normal mother. Stinging memories of grief she caused reminded me why I needed to remain close to the divine mother to heal. Just seconds before, Lilith looked into my eyes and did not evade my gaze with evidence of manipulation. She spoke directly to me with ease of plain speech—so I trusted in what she said. In that moment, I remembered a very different experience I had with my mother.

WHY DID SHE DESERVE TIME?

It was December of my high school junior year. I was flying out to see my mom. She had been begging me to come stay with her for winter break, but I almost didn't come. My friend Roger was leaving from Modesto a few days after Christmas for his 2-year Mormon mission, and I didn't want to miss seeing him off. Mom dangled it like a carrot to get me to come to see her. She promised me many times that I could return after the holidays to give him a final goodbye.

On the plane, I thought, *I'm excited to see Roger again, and oh how I will miss him!* My endearing artist friend was one of the few things that made high school separate from family bearable. He lived close to Maggie's house, visited me frequently and always had a way of getting me to laugh and lift my spirits. With his goofy and animating nature, I considered him a close friend during this time when I felt very alone.

When I got off the plane, my mother greeted me and said, "Oh, it's so good to see you darling! I need you to know I will not allow you to go back to say goodbye to Roger after Christmas. I'm your mother, and I deserve to have you with me the full two weeks." Confronting her was futile—she lacked concern for my feelings anyway.

I roared at her—"How could you?!" and I took off running. With my backpack style luggage, I bolted far away from her in the airport, fuming with disgust. Thoughts screamed within me, *How could she lie to me? She promised me over and over—just so I would come at all! She knows Roger is important to me!*

Dropping my heavy luggage, I found a place to release a storm of pent-up emotions. Because I had distanced myself so far from my mother, I was called repeatedly over the airport loudspeaker. Paralyzed by my own fury, I did not budge when I heard my name. In a hidden refuge tucked tightly behind a column, I sat on the carpeted floor as waterworks spilled from my eyes. Crushed over years of disappointment, I never wept so furiously. I did not know how deeply those caverns of mistrust ran. My face drenched in tears, my body trembled in exasperation over being let down once again—entirely broken by her lack of empathy and duplicity. Her only response to deceiving me was her "principled motherly decision" that she merited time with me. Sobbing, I shouted within my heart, *Why does she deserve time with me? She abandoned me!*

After eventually finding me in the airport, she relented. She must have assumed from my splotched face and vexation that I would not go with her for Christmas unless I could say goodbye to Roger. But it never registered to her how much my psychology was being affected by her frequent let downs.

Lilith and I greeted Ray who came out of the house to feed his horse Rosie. As we watched Ray affectionately interact with his sable mare, it occurred to me, unlike my mother, Lilith didn't have to make false promises for me to come see her—I just wanted to be here.

Lilith turned to me and said, "Elizabeth, are you here?" I must have had a blank stare. I told her, "Sorry, I was just thinking about how my mom has lied to me." Lilith responded, "That's what insecure people do. Those of us who have transcended our insecurities have no need for lies." I was in awe to be with someone so spiritually evolved. My thoughts returned to what Lilith had said, that I could be her "handmaiden." I was eager to please her, like I'd always wanted to please my mother. My eyes went blank again as I remembered how upsetting it was when I tried.

BIRTHDAY TANTRUM

It took more than ten hours to sketch one of my mom's favorite photos of me as a little girl with a graded pencil. On the three-hour drive to celebrate her 50th birthday with Maggie, I was excited to gift her with my framed and matted drawing. My mother had been good at encouraging and praising my art talent, even paying for me to attend a summer program at Berkeley College of Arts and Crafts. When I was a child, she knew I preferred art supplies as gifts, and I loved showing her my new creations.

Cecille Anne had specific plans for her milestone day, and she gifted us trinkets from Cost Plus. When she opened my drawing, I was shocked by her cavalier criticism of my labor of love. Holding it up and briefly beholding it, with a flat affect she simply uttered, "Oh." Knowing my mother's typical expressions when she values something, it was obvious on her face she was not pleased with anything about it. She even appeared disappointed—like she anticipated something better as a gift from me for herself. When pressed about her response she said, "Well, it doesn't look like you!" She went on to say, "When that photo was taken, you just weren't this sad looking. It's not the picture I have of you as a little girl." Heartsick over her fault-finding words, I wept. This couldn't be further from how I hoped she would respond.

Maggie and Em were seated in the room and both of their jaws dropped. To my surprise, they began to chide my mom for her hurtful response. Em called out, "Mom!" Maggie appealed, "Cecille Anne, Beth put a lot of love in this—just for you." In reaction, my mother stood unyieldingly before us, childishly asserting I-statements while I continued to cry. She exclaimed, "I feel so hurt you are all attacking me on my 50th birthday! I have come bearing gifts for all of you! You do not appreciate me! I feel so underappreciated by all of you! How dare you accuse me on my birthday! I feel so hurt! This was supposed to be a very special day for me! Now you have ruined it!"

Her tantrum was upsetting, and I was embarrassed by her ugly behavior. Anxious to return with Maggie to Modesto, we left earlier than planned. My feelings settled into more tenuous discomfort for my mother. Her response reinforced that she had an ideal not only of this portrait of me—but of who she imagined I should be—and she disapproved of the finished product.

A Dragoon breeze blew across my face, reminding me of the present moment, and that Lilith was still sitting next to me. Unlike my mother, Lilith was a woman who valued me near her. She did not have a projected ideal of me. I trusted her to safeguard and accept me as I was.

LILITH'S VISION

Especially after recounting how different, she was from my mother, my heart melted more in who Lilith was to me. And because I felt secure that she cared about me, I became zealous to please her and follow her directions.

From the time Lilith came into being, the mission became more defined. She told us, "People who come to this retreat center will spiritually advance through meditations, and through the impact of walking the grounds dedicated to the masters." She explained that the property was to become a vortex of "transcendental spiritual energy," similar to what is felt at Sedona and Mount Shasta. "Our community will grow to include people 'called' with giftings of their own to contribute. Eventually, we will acquire more land, beyond the 40 acres to accomplish all that the master's direct."

Lilith articulated to our group, "Before this retreat center can happen, you will all need to come into strong spiritual alignment. You will become spiritual helper-leaders and guide in the new energies yourselves. To get you ready for this, we will meet to get you all accelerated and healed with inner transformation." During these meditation meetings led by her, she helped "accelerate our energies" by cleansing us of old ones, weighing us down and balancing our alignment so we could be "filled with more light." After each gathering, we trusted we were growing spiritually.

Lilith made our roles plain—Zev would build the retreat center, and Ray would help fund it with specialized parts commissioned by aerospace giants located in Southern Arizona. Lilith said Zev and Ray would additionally help lay the foundation of a "spiritual grid" upon the land. For this, Ray would make "channeling tools," and Zev would lay out the architecture in a way that best promoted her "energy work." One day Lilith vision casted, "Zev, you will construct a large gazebo dedicated to the masters. And Ray, you will create a crystal tool. We will work together on this. It will be encased in the gazebo with an inscription to the masters."

When I probed with curiosity about my part, she said, "Oh yes, Elizabeth. You are called to be a teacher to all the children born here." I smiled in response. Though I was not ready to abandon my medical school plans, hearing this initially fueled my imagination and revived my sense of purpose.

Lilith and Zev lived together in one of the three bedrooms in the 6000 square foot house. In their bedroom, as a main part of the "energy gridwork," Zev constructed a grand inlaid mantle designed to be an altar for the masters. Lilith placed large crystals in front of it that had called her at the Tucson gem and mineral show. The thick frame of the arched mantle was adorned with large depictions of the "ascended masters." It was an impressive altar to honor "the council" and the spiritual charge was palpable as you approached the three-foot-high amethyst geode in the center and other surrounding crystal giants.

While Lilith and Zev were together, Ray appeared content to be an essential part of what was about to take place, including financially aiding and protecting Lilith. The main home and acreage were owned by Ray, and once Lorelei gave him a vision for its use, he happily handed it all over to the "divine mother." At age 42, his decision to buy this land and his life was now full of purpose, culminating in this exciting new undertaking.

During the first three weeks, sometimes Ray and I found ourselves alone together, and we would talk and walk upon the land, or I would help him in his shop. Messy with bright lights and loud machinery, his shop smelled like metal filings and burning oil and we frequently left with teeny metal curls in our hair.

WE WILL SEE

This was an electrifying time of vision-casting and building. We all trusted the universe was speaking to us, through an accelerated being who was living among us, and who would help us become more spiritually advanced. Our mission began with serving her and accomplishing whatever she asked of us. We trusted in her character, her gentle smile, her appearance of complete confidence and the charming ways she asked us to do things. She was our influential leader, and she surrounded herself with other strong characters who appreciated and even adored her. I thought to myself, *She wouldn't have invited me here if she didn't believe I could help further the mission.*

Even though I planned to be there only for the summer, whenever I brought up this expiration date, Lilith would say—"We will see." Several times she spoke this, and I took notice every time she did. She was yet another figure I transferred my naïve trust to—she was my next wise life pilot. From my upbringing I learned it is normal to be controlled or "guided" by another. It was Lilith's turn to be the one that I trusted absolutely.

My devotion to Sai Baba waned and I felt slightly guilty about it. Lilith told me with a heartening tone, "Oh, he understands Elizabeth and there are no hard feelings. Sai Baba and I are like 'spiritual brother and sister' on the same path for planetary acceleration. You are not betraying him, he understands." When she said this, I was relieved I could more fully devote myself to the mission, at least until the summer ended. Lilith would often pause in reflection before telling us confidently what the next step was. In this way I perceived her as a calculated chess player, carefully considering her next move. With every decision she made, I also trusted she was concerned for my welfare.

I had very real wounds that needed healing, and I had found the "divine mother" in Lilith. With a searing hope to cauterize my pain, I believed the divine mother would protect me from the Em's of the world, the divine mother would be there for me when my father ignored me, and she would also protect me from a very different type of villain.

NINE

Mercury in Retrograde

I sat atop a broad rock along the property grounds. Scanning the landscape, I mused, *Living here feels safe. The people here—Lilith, Zev, Ray and Charlotte—they are genuine, and they make me feel secure. Their hearts are in the right place. This is all a good thing. We are on a divine mission from the divine mother.* I looked down on the sunbaked terrain and remembered being a part of water polo teams and backpacking groups. I always enjoyed the exhilaration of accomplishing something great with others, and how it required trust in my teammates. My head was spinning thinking about already belonging to this spiritual "ascension" group—*I mean, what is going on here?* This is a long-term project, far beyond this summer. Like Lilith said, there was such gravity to this mission, and I believed she could be counted on to lead us with our best interests at heart.

As I reflected on the rare safety I felt here, my thoughts drifted to a figure from my past. I felt a particular sting from the experience of a group leader I knew in the seventh grade.

MR. MERCURY

When I entered junior high, I wanted to do well in Mr. Hagen-Grave's class. A young educator in his twenties, he was passionate, humorous and intellectual about biology. He piqued my curiosity about science and recruited me to join the Science Olympiad of which he was the head advisor. After school, we spent hours as a team studying the properties of natural substances, rocks and fossils, the physics of protecting an egg as it fell, and answering science trivia. I felt free to laugh with my nerdy and fun new friends, and the year was full of fond memories for me.

My 8th grade friend Kallie, who I met in Mr. Hagen-Grave's class was also a part of Olympiad and we rapidly became close. Kallie's confident, fun-loving personality brightened me up. Competitive in many sports, voted class president and most popular, she made friends wherever she went. We bonded over practicing for both basketball and Olympiad teams, hung out on the weekends, and she invited me to family vacations that summer at a lake house and to Yosemite.

Kallie and I were Mr. Hagen-Grave's favorites, and we playfully called Mr. Hagen-Grave "H-G" which for science nerds is the symbol for Mercury (Hg) on the periodic table of elements. As the year progressed, we three shared more time together during after-school competition preparation. My mom was seldom present until late at night, and I was daily enlivened to engage with my amusing Olympiad family. Even though Mr. Hg was awkward, he was fun, he recognized some of my strengths and seemed to take a genuine interest in my well-being.

Later that year, we took first place at the city-wide Science Olympiad. A couple of months later, we earned first place at the California state championship, and you would think we had just won the Super Bowl. The elation we felt was overwhelming and the accomplishment bonded me more to the team—especially to Kallie, and to Mr. Hg. After much parental and district support, we were able to raise the funds needed to attend the National Science Olympiad in Dover, Delaware in 1987. It was the biggest thing in our little lives that had ever transpired. Being at Nationals was incredibly exhilarating, even though we did not rank high. As the alternate in my subject, Mr. Hg let me represent our team in my "Mystery Substances" event, and it bolstered my esteem.

During and following the Olympiad season, Kallie, Mr. Hg and I spent time together at various times outside of school. And that first year started innocently enough. However, now and then following our trip to Delaware, I detected something different than merely a protective watch from Mr. Mercury.

C'MON BETH, IT'S JUST ME

The sense I initially experienced about him brewed into a mild itch within my consciousness. It got to the point that I asked Kallie, "Do you ever feel like Hg looks at you or me kind of strangely?" She had no idea what I was talking about and reassured me I was looking too much at something that wasn't there. Valuing her opinion and perception, I shrugged it off.

In Delaware, we took a photo of our entire Science Olympiad team celebrating in the hotel room. For that photo and for that celebration, I naïvely, and completely unaware of inappropriateness, was sitting in Mr. Hg's lap. After Delaware, Kallie's mother, who had chaperoned the trip, told Kallie that she must stay far away from Mr. Hagen-Grave. What she saw caused her to succinctly put an end to any outside school contact between Kallie and Mr. Hg. Without understanding these kinds of boundaries growing up, it shook me to hear this from Kallie, and I was sad we would no longer be the three musketeers.

Mr. Hagen-Grave continued to find ways to connect with us following the Olympiad season. He decided to coach the girls' softball team, and because Kallie and I loved sports, we didn't need much persuasion to join. For myself, beyond softball, I kept talking with Mr. Hg, sometimes coming to visit him after school just to check in. I had bonded with him.

Beyond that year, he became a permanent fixture in my 8th grade and high school—someone I could call if needed. Even though he was primarily a nerdy intellectual and enduringly odd, he was a good listener, and he seemed to care about me.

On New Year's Eve in 1991, when I was sixteen, Mr. Hg convinced me to hang out with him and his wife because my friends who were driving had forgotten to get me, and they let me down. My mother had already moved away, and I was lonesome. Mr. Hg picked me up and once at his house, he persuasively pressed me with a series of questions like, "So, have you made out with any boys?" He asked details I was uncomfortable answering until he reassured me with, "C'mon Beth, it's just me." I finally relented and shared some particulars when his wife had left the room. Though I was nervous about the discussion, I also knew he was an awkward individual, so I chalked it up to that.

Then he casually suggested, "You know being physical with guys is supposed to be pleasurable, but I know boys are pretty dumb. They don't know what to do at your age. If you ever have any questions about it—about what it's supposed to feel like, because it's supposed to feel good—I will always be here to talk you through it." Though the topic was making me increasingly uneasy, I didn't want to believe he was being inappropriate. But at a certain point, I was anxious enough to ask him to take me home, even while he tried to persuade me to stay and talk.

On the way home, his comments became overtly creepy. "You know Angel, right?" "Yah," I answered. Angel was one of the girls in our Science Olympiad group. He continued, "Well, I've helped her explore and deal with some sexual things." Though he was vague about how he helped her—*Blech!* I did not want to know! It took this mention of his to strike at me deeper—*Ok, this is not right.* Feeling relieved we were in front of Maggie's home, I said goodbye, shut the door and didn't recontact him for many months.

In my innocence, I ignored his salacious suggestions because I had a striving plan for success, and I would not go that far with anyone until it was right. I questioned why he pressed me about this, but I knew he had been there for me on so many other issues. I convinced myself that he was not so singularly focused. Geez, but why did he stay on this subject the whole time? *What is wrong with him?*

NOT THIS AGAIN!

Later in my junior year, Mr. Hg invited me to see a Taiko Dojo performance in San Francisco. I assumed he just wanted to spend the day hanging out, and I said as much to Maggie. Innocently, I believed he was still a father figure to me, a friend I could confide in—someone who knew me and saw me.

We took the two-and-a-half-hour drive from Modesto to San Francisco, and once again, the conversation got to the sexual intimacy thing. I shouted within—*Not this again!* After asking about my recent update with boys, he said, "Beth, I care about you, and I want you to be able to experience physical love in the way you deserve." The attention was embarrassingly invigorating because, who had ever given me this much consideration?

As my mind glazed over into a kind of dissociative awareness, the boundaries of what was appropriate began to bleed all around me like a cloud of soft smoke. I remember wanting to leave my own body as he spoke to me because while it seemed right, *it wasn't right at all*. Having never gained the proper reference since I first met him in seventh grade, I absorbed what Mr. Hg said in utter ignorance. It started to seem "natural" to me, as he explained, that he could be the one to show me what I deserved, what love was—"I can show you feelings you have never known and things a younger inexperienced boy would not know how to give you."

Without knowing it, I was being charmed and groomed by him during this car ride, vulnerable to its enchantment from the deepest core of my psyche. And he knew it. My father was, for the most part, absent and not there to say, "What is going on with this man? No, you may not go to San Francisco with him!" My mother lived far away and was too disinterested to notice cues of impropriety from this "father figure" she had idealized.

So, as the day unfurled and we enjoyed Golden Gate Park, nice food and a powerful Taiko Dojo drum performance, he held my hand,

and I held it back. Needy for affection, I craved touch, and I knew he cared. I thought to myself, *I like the hand holding, this is nice*, while the rest of me rejected it—*But I am so not attracted to you! Eww! Where is this going? I don't want to lead you on!* My insides trembled with anxiety as I wrestled with an anxious thought, *What if I refuse what he really wants?* I liked the simple affection that I sorely lacked—but that was all! I had questions about his motives and at the same time, I really did not want the answer to my questions. While walking, he stopped, gently touched my face and kissed my forehead. *Blech!* I felt strange that people would be looking. Even though we were 90 miles away from anyone who knew us, he was almost fifteen years older than me. Everything apart from his concern for me felt wrong—just wrong—all of it!

The drive home was beyond strange. My mind was bursting with conflicting thoughts. *Will he still want to be my friend if I don't want to talk about this anymore?* While seated next to him in the car, I inspected his gestures and older facial features—the same way you do when you only see imperfections in a person. Inwardly, I grimaced, *Yuck!* Even though I didn't want to have to view him this way, he had forced me to think of him like this. He again tried to hold my hand, and I gently refused. I was honest to tell him I was not interested in him. We had a history enough and he had made this kind gesture to take me to San Francisco that we didn't have an unpleasant drive home, but I left the car sickened by the whole thing.

FRESHMAN FUNDS

In my freshman year of college, he continued to be a friendly person to talk with over the phone. However, while staying at my mom's for the summer, he brought up the topic of sex again. Though I tried to change the subject, I was feeling more mature now as a young adult, and I appreciated having a deep conversation. My mom heard the intrigue in my voice as she quizzically called from the next room, "Beth, who are you talking to so late?" I told her, "Oh just a friend."

Soon after, Mr. Hagen-Graves began sending me one hundred

dollars each month. He told me he would be doing so as long as he could afford it. Anyone who has struggled financially through college can attest—this was hard to refuse. The money he gave helped with everyday living, especially since I was entirely dependent upon student loans and scholarships. My mother was particularly pleased with his support. She blamed my father for not contributing to my college even though she had made it abundantly clear to me she would not help me in the slightest bit herself.

In anticipation of his check, I would run to the post office. Opening his letter, I saw his distinct writing I had known since the seventh grade when he scribed it on the chalkboard. He always included a brief note of encouraging humor which made me feel valued. He was filling a role that made his presence even more confusing. I never questioned his motives nor the money. Instead, I welcomed it because he was engaging with me and providing for me in a way that I did not receive from my own parents.

THE KNOLL

In early summer of my freshman year, however, his sudden presence on campus was an unwelcome surprise, especially due to my current mood and attire. The day had been an unusually breathtaking one, with perfect winds pushing up into the redwoods from beaches miles below. The trees were swaying so kindly, and I wore my new blue sundress I felt particularly feminine and summery in. I walked to have a picnic on the Stevenson Knoll—a broad hill set yards beyond redwoods overlooking Santa Cruz and Monterey Bay in the distance. But as I strolled back from the Knoll's spectacular view, I saw him walking towards me.

All at once, I was paralyzed. I felt icky and bare-naked in the dress I was wearing. An irritating nudge vibrated along my spine. *Did I owe him something or did he come to collect?* When he sent funds from a three-hour distance, I could infer it was freely given, but now that he was here—*What did he want?*

He approached me with a cheesy swagger and acted too familiar with me. He said, "Hi," with a smile that begged to be flirty and mysterious. Startled by his presence, I let slip, "What are you doing here?" "I came to see you," he replied. His grin fell. He seemed thwarted I did not respond to his strut. Though I didn't feel unsafe with him, I wished I was like other girls whose *real father* showed up for a visit, and not this perverted, strange one. I felt uncovered. Our relationship had forever changed because of the topic he pursued with me since I was in high school.

Still unsure if he had come to "collect," I went with him for a drive. He took me out for a meal, and it became obvious he wasn't leaving without spoiling me in some way. Though I tried to hide from him the name of my favorite store, he got it out of me and bought me 150 dollars of new oil paints, brushes and canvases. I fought to allow positive feelings to wash over all my unease. I told myself—

Maybe he does just want to give to me and that is all? Maybe I can still think of this as a pure relationship—a kind of father that enjoys spoiling me?

Who was I kidding? Anxiety about his motives rushed back as quickly as I tried to cover them up.

AIKIDO

In our high school years, Mr. Hg invited me and Kallie to his black belt Japanese Aikido martial arts ceremony. We watched him calmly glide across the dojo floor while whipping his body into different directions, deflecting stand-in opponents. Ever a lover of dance, I became fascinated with this flowy martial art, which was robust with graceful movements. Watching his ceremony was enough to capture my interest in Aikido.

As a college freshman, I signed up for Aikido and took classes every semester for three years. I showed up eager to learn from my lighthearted sensei Martha. There was something about the feel of a thick gi wrapped across my chest, fastened with a wide belt at my waist that made me feel self-assured as I twirled with poise across the floor. Obtaining my blue belt in Aikido just prior to my sophomore summer, my sensei Martha was impressed with my commitment. She awarded me a scholarship to attend the Santa Cruz Aikido conference during the summer of 1995, when I was twenty.

Hagen-Graves called to tell me he would also be attending this conference. Though I responded favorably to the news, I was ambivalent about him attending. Trying to imagine being Aikido partners with him did not sit well with me. I had built a relationship with both the UCSC and downtown dojos, and I felt generally safe with my Santa Cruz affiliates, while I had an unsettling story with Mr. Hg. Even though he was not aggressive, I didn't believe his intentions with me were pure, and he gave me reason to lose confidence in him. By now, he had been sending me money for two years, surprised me with an unwanted visit, and made licentious proposals to me. Why did he want to attend this with me? Did he desire an excuse to touch me as his Aikido partner? Did he exult he was a black belt over my blue belt and think he could assert dominance over me or be some kind of Aikido tutor for me? *Yuck!* I was even repulsed by my own speculations!

Having been hurt by faulty intentions from those close to me, I asked him frankly over the phone, "So...Why are you coming?" His response was elusive. He simply stated, "I have my reasons."

HERE IT IS–HE HAS COME TO COLLECT

One week later, he called and said, "Beth, you asked why I am coming. Well, I have a proposal for you. Can I stay with you in the yurt?" During summers when my student loans ran out, my housemates graciously let me stay in the backyard yurt for free. Hearing his appeal, I absorbed only a partial reality of how wrong it was. In my fragmented psychology, any awareness of personal boundaries or advocating for myself was dreamy-naïve—as if my psyche's moral compass was suspended without gravity in an Alice in Wonderland rabbit hole. With a common dissociative response, I spaced out realizing his true motive here.

Oh . . . Here it is. He has come to collect.

Rapidly, I deduced I had an out. "Yes, you can stay with me," I answered. I knew my housemates would let me sleep in the large front room of the house while Mr. Hg stayed in the yurt, giving me a safe zone away from his potential advances. Of course, Hagen-Graves had something entirely different in mind.

He continued over the phone saying, "When I come, I want to spend special time with you." With a creepy calm he once again messaged what he started when I was sixteen, "Young men don't know how to treat you as a young woman. But I am experienced and patient. I want to give you a very pleasing experience, something you deserve—something you haven't had and something you won't ever get from guys your age." He persisted, "I love you and I can guide you in intimacy because I care for you. So, I am making you a proposal. Before I come to the conference, I want you to think about if you will allow me to show you intimacy. I know you will be satisfied with the experience. I will help you relax, and I won't do anything you're not comfortable with. You don't have to answer me yet, but I want you to think about it before I come." After listening to his "offer," I said I needed to go and ended the call.

Everything within me cried out—*No! Gross! This is not right at all! This is creepy, this is hideous!* I was disgusted by it. But I was even more grossed out that his coercive words and evocative pitch caused me to consider his suggestion *at all*. He was a trusted teacher—someone I looked up to once before. He was so convincing. What if he was right? What if I was just being stubborn? Though I was not attracted to him in the slightest, I knew he cared. Just thinking about it, it felt so awful that I went inside to take a shower. Thus far in my young life, I had not had a long-term boyfriend, but plenty of short-lived dating chances to be intimate. I personally stopped these heated encounters to not go beyond a certain point. Why was it always about this for him?

Knowing Mr. Hg usually incited my honest, direct thoughts, I got off the phone quickly because he had a way of drawing out my concerns to the point of quelling doubts about him. But I didn't want him to talk me through this or talk me into this. *Gross! I don't owe him my private thoughts!* All this dialogue just got inside my head, and I hope it didn't turn him on. *Disgusting! Why can't it go back to the way it was before—when it wasn't all about this!*

YOUR WAY IS UNFAMILIAR

As I walked up to the registration table at the conference, I was taken by assembled Aikido masters skillfully sashaying with one another. The whipping echo of their traditional hakama split skirt pants reminded me of what I imagine is the sound of many eagles flapping their wings. I knew most people at the conference, and they respected me because I practiced with them downtown. My gaze was nervously fixed, however, on Mr. Hg while he sparred with my sensei and others. I observed closely how they responded to him.

Usually, partnering with a black belt was exhilarating. With smooth and effortless movements, I loved responding to their velvety rotations which simulated soaring on currents of air. But when I entered one of the practice groups with Hagen-Graves, he was abnormally stroppy with careless gestures. With an insecure smile and smug demeanor, his movements were both weak and heavy-handed. He unnaturally pulled his partners with a forceful lead, as if he was seeking to control the person. His poor technique was probably even more apparent to others. *Ugh!* I thought. *This is only the beginning of a weekend with him.* I was embarrassed I had introduced him to my sensei earlier because his was not the style of Aikido we practiced in Santa Cruz. I smiled at him but took a mental note, *I don't want to learn anything about your Aikido method, and I am not in awe of your skill. Your movements are strange—your way is unfamiliar. There is nothing I want to learn from you.*

This was another major red flag to refuse his "offer" in full regard. I started to move into survival mode from that first night. Feeble to assert meaningful boundaries, I looked around my martial arts community wondering, *Is there anyone here who would protect me from him?* Ironic that I was surrounded by a powerful assembly of self-defense masters, but no—*There is no one I can talk to about this*. I was alone in this strange story, and I didn't feel comfortable telling another soul.

BLAZING INTO THE WHITE MOON

That first night of the conference, after Mr. Hg had time to settle in the yurt, I came to visit him. There was a redwood hot tub in my backyard—a treasured oasis of my college home surrounded by baby redwood trees. On many nights, I would tiptoe alone along its paved path, turn on the bubbles and take a dip.

Quietly opening the backyard door, I paused with disquiet thinking about his expectations of tonight. Without distinct self-agency, I was not yet clear what I should do. Now that it would be just him and me, my defenses were down, and we were about to meet in a secluded place. Even though it was all mental for me, we had talked about it so much that I began to succumb to surrendering thoughts, *Well, maybe this is inevitable. Maybe there is this opportunity now and we should just get physical. This is the culmination of all the things he has been saying.*

Standing there, a battle raged within and all around me. I heard war cries on behalf of good and evil—good that I couldn't clearly decipher and evil that was distorted into deceptive lies of false love and lust of sexual prowess. I couldn't see what was right and my reality was blurred. Knowing this was a decision I could not return from unscathed, the two sides shrieked into the night, piercing my ears each with their resounding strength. Spacey from deafening lures to proceed one way or another, I was utterly overwhelmed with indecision. Looking up at the moon outside, I asked the universe for help. I walked on the solar-lit path which diverged to the yurt to my left and the hot tub to my right and thought about how he has been my surrogate parental morality for almost a decade. Mr. Hg's convincing tone had fueled my curiosity, and my futile defenses were beginning to crumble. I also feared his rejection if I rejected his "offer." Everything in my mind spoke of caving to it all, and his intensity about it demanded an answer from me.

When I met him at the yurt, he wanted to go right into the hot tub. He walked there in the buff, and I averted my eyes while he got in the water. Fully clothed, I sat on the deck. Keeping my toes tipped into the hot pool, I played a few scenarios in my head. *If I quickly get in so he can't see any semblance of my form . . . No, that won't work. I could sit completely opposite to him . . . No, that won't work either! If he comes close, it will be hard to suddenly get out!* All the scenarios were not playing out right. So, when he asked me to get into the hot tub, I said, "No, I am ok here."

With tight shoulders and my body curled in on itself, I looked blazingly into the white moon set against the black sky. I stared at it as if it was my lifeline of hope—certainly it represented the spiritual realm to me, and I was desperate for guidance. I considered my life, aware that if I proceeded with this, my prospects for finding true love would go into the toilet. Somehow, I knew this one act with him would ruin me. Once I saw myself as he saw me, everything would change for me. I started to get very uncomfortable. I wanted to climb out of my own skin. He seemed unphased by my apparent discomfort and continued in an overconfident manner, believing that I would come around. He said, "It's ok Beth. Come into the yurt with me. Let's just relax and talk." Once again, I averted my eyes from his body as he got out of the hot tub.

He lay down on the homemade bed of the yurt in a towel and signaled for me, "C'mon Beth, let's just talk. Lay down next to me. I won't touch you unless you want me to." Fully clothed, I lay down against his bare chest in the yurt, my legs angled away from his legs. There was a clear plastic view at the top of the yurt where I could once again see my lifeline—the moon. Looking up to it with a spacey disposition, I screamed within my mind and heart, *Is this what you have planned for me universe?* I was praying hard, but my mind was hardly there—like a surreal vision. Holding onto an amorphous thread of reality, I started to believe, *I should just surrender to the moment because—maybe the problem is me not surrendering enough. After all—everything happens for a reason, right?*

From the moment my face touched his chest, the battle raged harder. Both my options—either to stay in this yurt with him or flee to the house were being strained across my mind like a taffy machine pulls gooey confection across circulating belts. While leaning against him, I felt disgusted. His skin felt leathery like a reptile. His smell was repulsive. My mind's curiosity had not caused me to impulsively kiss him—even though there were warring voices encouraging me to just let go, be impetuous and surrender to what was in front of me.

With a sudden urgency, I felt compelled to go inside the house. I needed a minute of space, unsure of this extremely pivotal decision. This was very hard for me—especially with all his giving and suggestions—did I even have a choice in the matter? After laying in his arms silently for one seemingly unending minute of total awkwardness, I sat up and said, "I will be right back. I need to go the bathroom." Quickly, I leaped to the house.

I opened the back door and to my surprise, Martin was sitting on the kitchen couch, which was unusual. I was so grateful he was there. He was the most level-headed one of my housemates, and he asked me if I was Ok. With a glazed head fog, I spoke with a hurried survival tone about my dilemma, posing it as a hypothetical situation. He figured out this was not hypothetical and became the wise moral compass I needed at that crucial moment. He asked the right questions and reflected to me that this was not a good situation. He pointed out that Mr. Hg just wanted to have sex with me. Martin said, "It doesn't matter what he has given to you. You don't owe him anything. Certainly not that. If you don't want what he asked for—it's ok to say no. And if he doesn't understand, then he is not worth the friendship anyway." Having Martin articulate that Mr. Hg's intentions were purely selfish, I finally saw it clearly and sobered up. I was no longer confused by nebulous guilt or arguments in my head.

Now I didn't know how to deal with Mr. Hg still lingering for me in the yurt—waiting for the culmination of all these years with me. Afraid to be pulled again into his coercion, Martin kept me company and talked me through it.

Debating whether to go face him alone and reject his indecent proposal, suddenly we heard the commotion of someone trying to unlatch the side gate. Martin and I went to the front of the house. Mr. Hg appeared there, struggling to scrape his suitcase across the rocky side yard. With frustrated gestures and petulant grunts, he was having a childish hissy fit. I called out from the tall front porch, "What are you doing?" By this time of the night, I had the right perspective of self-advocacy. The kind of spell I was under regarding what was right and wrong had lost its grip and he no longer had power over me.

With a whiny juvenile tone, he said, "I'm leaving!" "You're leaving the conference?" I asked. "Yeah, I'm done! I'm going!," he snapped. I watched him open his car trunk, throw his suitcase in, and without looking back, he got into his car and drove away. I had never seen him like that before—in fact, after that night, I would never see him again. His frenzied tantrum cemented to me that my decision to not go through with his years of handling me was absolutely right. My parting view of him was from the top of the stairs, safe amongst friends, out of reach of his entrancing manipulative words and our historical relationship. Once I watched his car disappear from the road, I took deep breaths of renewed safety, as if I had escaped a menacing prowler. Martin continued to be there for me that night to talk it all out.

Weeks after it happened, Maggie noticed my demeanor was off, and I explained my shame and confusion over having been preyed upon by Mr. Hg. She knew me during the vulnerable years when Mr. Hg pursued me the most and was upset she hadn't been aware of it nor was she able to protect me from him.

She took me out to lunch so I could vent, and I am forever grateful she was there to listen with compassion. I told her I felt degraded for even flirting with the idea he suggested to me and trapped by how he made it the overwhelming part of our relationship. Asking the right questions, she helped me map out how he had been grooming me for eight years. Starting when I was just twelve, he propositioned me at age sixteen when I had no parents present, and with a powerful pull of monetary support, his intentions with me became overt at age twenty. Maggie gave me the wisdom, clarity and courage I needed to help me write a letter to Hagen-Graves, telling him to never contact me again.

Maggie's counsel and love were exactly what I needed to not only set a final boundary with Hg, but also to set a parental boundary in my brain—reinforcing the fact that the whole thing was very wrong. Maggie reacted like the parent I needed to validate my pain, and to heal.

As bad as the years of grooming by Mr. Hg was, the worst part of dealing with it was when I told my mom the full story. Her only response to Hagen-Grave's predation was, "Well . . . Are you still going to receive money from him?"

How can my mother be so wrong? When I heard her cold-hearted reaction, I could not help myself. In a voluble fury, I blasted at her, "Are you kidding me? Is that all that matters to you?" Still, my response to her indifference did not change her position regarding him—she kept asking if I would still receive his money. Apparently, prostituting myself was worth $100 per month in her eyes, and the heartbreak of her response made her injury worse than Hagen-Graves's. Though a licensed child and family counselor, she had no empathy or acknowledgement of his corrupting pedophilic perversion towards me. This was yet another narrative she gaslit regarding me. It was not the first time she refused to protect me from another's injury, and it struck a central chord inside me.

A strong desert breeze whipped across my face, bringing me back to Dragoon mountains. I felt a knot in my stomach thinking about all this. Though the encounter with Mr. Hg had ended, its imprint lingered. *I wish it never happened! But now, here in Arizona with Lilith, things are different. I found the divine mother who is a good leader, and she cares about what is best for me.*

Longing to finally feel safe and taken care of, I started to let down my guard. I reasoned, *There is no one trying to take advantage of me here. I can trust these people. I need refuge from dishonest situations.* I had old injuries to splint, and fresh wounds to lick. To shield my own desperate need for a protective environment, I willed myself to believe I had finally found a sanctuary. *I don't have to worry about predators anymore—do I?*

TEN

The Set Up

It had only been a few weeks since I arrived in Dragoon when Lilith instructed Ray and me to drive the large RV to Roper Lake. She told us Zev and she would meet us later that day, and then we would all drive up Mount Graham to camp overnight. So, Ray and I bought food, organized meals and thoughtfully packed all that was needed.

Ray and I were friendly but also tentative towards one another. While we prepared for the trip, I felt a glimmer of affection towards him which I immediately squashed. Our nineteen-year age difference flashed through my brain, and I succinctly renounced the spark between us—I did not want to entertain anything about it! The age difference was revolting to me as he was even older than Hagen-Graves.

The bumpy, hour-long ride in Ray's monstrous RV was like being on a hillbilly amusement park ride and the hilarity was greatly diverting. Ray had confident command of the beastly vessel, and we laughed at its precarious sounds and poor shocks as our bodies shook with every passing bulge in the road.

Once we arrived just outside of Safford, we had a delightful time floating in Roper Lake, enjoying the sun and cool waters. Ray also loved being in nature and together we were playful and interacted with ease. Each time a flicker of attraction surfaced, I quickly built mental walls to shut it down, holding fast to the belief that I needed to leave by the end of the summer.

On that first day at the lake, the sun began to set, and Lilith and Zev had not yet appeared. Ray gave Lilith a call to inquire when they would be coming. She told Ray, "Something came up, and we will not be able to join you. But keep enjoying yourselves and go camping tomorrow just as you planned." "Ok," Ray replied.

That night, in the RV, we slept in separate beds with awkward moments of silence. Raging thoughts plagued me within, *What is going on? Not this again. He is so much older than me! Yuck! But I feel a connection. He is so sweet, and we like the same things. Are we meant to be together?*

There was a lot to Ray that reminded me of my father. The sometimes gregarious but also gentle, protective charm coupled with a probable propensity for angry outbursts. Into the night, I wrestled with their resemblance—even down to Ray's broad shoulders and build. They always say girls tend to be attracted to someone like their fathers. Though I stopped wanting to think about it, thoughts of Ray lingered like boulders in my brain. I finally fell asleep, resolved that our age difference made it too upsetting to consider him beyond friendship.

We drove up the mountain the next day, about another hour's distance. On the way, I watched as the RV's bulky silhouette crept sluggishly along the sloped rock. The sounds of our struggling vehicle made for a noisy climb, which drowned out the mental distress of my conflicting fondness for Ray. He remained concentrated on getting us there safely, and I was grateful for a break from plaguing thoughts.

Once we arrived at the pinnacle campground, the crisp air of cooler elevation with surrounding green pacified all my hassled thinking. To this day, I cannot help but frolic and let go on a mountaintop. You would think I was Julie Andrews singing "the Hills are Alive" whenever I am near the crest of a crag. Skipping around evergreen timber in the euphoria of cloud altitude, I found a nice clearing for us to lay down camp. Together we hung out on the mountain and unloaded our camping gear.

Our day was laden with smells of forest pines, gazing at swaying branches and hearing whizzing birds and insects, bright with the sun reflected on their wings. The whole time I wondered if we were "supposed" to be together all while deciding if I was even attracted to him. At sunset, we built a fire together. Sharing genuine glances and conversation, I knew where things were headed. The connection between us had ignited to the point that by night's end, we lay down closely in adjacent, separate sleeping bags.

Examining the stars above, my mind spun relentlessly. It was like standing at the base of a Ferris wheel, its massive frame churning past, each rotation shoving a gust of wind that stole my breath. That crushing pressure mirrored the weight of my thoughts. I was freaking out! How was I supposed to view my feelings with regard to this all-important calling with Lilith? *What does this even mean for the mission, for my own goals—for my life? He's really a lot older. And it's not like this could be just a fling. We already agreed to help Lilith with this huge new undertaking. Ray was part of the triad itself. Was I even welcome to become part of the inner elite group?*

Suddenly, some sort of large animal made a ruckus in vegetation above us. Tree branches snapped from the weight of a creature. Heavy thuds were heard from its presence walking on the mountain floor, and the noises grew in proximity. Ray shot up with a flashlight, aimed it right at the sound and let out his arms with a great shout, attempting to threaten the animal. He saw the reflection of eyes surrounded by a greater form that was not discernable. After a moment of human versus animal stare-down, it crawled unhurriedly out of sight, away from us. Phew, it worked! And sorry to be the stereotypical swooning female, but that event put Ray in hero status for me. After all, he had protected us from some kind of hairy formidable beast. Maybe it was just a bobcat, but still, he saved the day! And just like young men take women to scary movies, it produced the right natural effect—we tucked our separate sleeping bags even closer together.

The event of our visitor caused me to simplify my wondering about Ray. Certainly, adrenaline was coursing through my blood which cried for a salve of assurance. But when it all came down to it, what did this mean for us? How did I feel about Ray? The tension and curiosity became overwhelming for both of us, and we kissed on the mountain that night.

The next day, we drove all the way home, my thoughts racing. We spent nearly three days and two nights together, and while we made an undeniable connection on the mountain, we both suspected Lilith had conveniently skipped out just to encourage this spark between us.

KNOWING SMILE

There's no question, in normal circumstances our mutual affection wouldn't have kindled this quickly, or if even at all. And the age gap made me very uncomfortable! I was a young and impressionable 23-year-old and he an older more seasoned 42. Years of grooming by Mr. Hagen-Graves certainly prepared me for the idea of being with a much older man. Then again—*Maybe this is what the universe has been telling me all along. Perhaps it's fated to be this way.*

So, when we drove home from Mt Graham with the seemingly personal connection we made with each other, like the tender bud of a plant you want to protect and not yet display, it felt strange to suddenly confess our feelings to Lilith and Zev. But with no time to process, Lilith and Zev wanted to meet us for lunch on our way home.

At a Benson favorite "Horseshoe Café," we all sat together in a booth. Leaning against deep-recessed seats, I scanned leather saddles and rancher décor lining the walls. At the thought of making something so new so public, my heart galloped like the hooves of a racehorse upon the track. This was too fresh, and I had many doubts to work through—including our true compatibility. It was literally hours old and raw in the relationship to form any conclusions.

Lilith sat across from the table with Zev and stared with close observation at both of us. She said, "So, how are you two doing?" with a knowing smile and a twinkle in her eye. Ray and I looked at each other—*Dang, she did know about us!* She then boldly spoke aloud about our fresh and mutual kindled interest. It was then we fully realized she had set us up for the getaway. It was quite a shock to Zev who was in his mid-30s. With raised brows and eyes bulging with surprise, he stopped swallowing his drink mid-sentence to let loose a laughing gasp—"What?? You two?!"

At that café, Lilith spoke about how our bond was important to the mission, how it would ultimately strengthen it. We laughed with her about the creature visitation we had, and she led us on to believe she was aware of it, that she had the power to "send" such an event to get us to see how we felt about each other. This was part of the allure in following her—we were fascinated by some of her apparent divine awareness.

Exposed for years to New Age fairs and books, I had learned about "soul mates," a rare spiritual connection between two souls. Leaning forward she said, "Look beyond your ages. You two are extremely rare 'twin flames.' It's no coincidence at all you have met here and found each other. Your bond is very special. If you deny your feelings now, you won't get this chance again to be together." she said. This was something I had been searching for because who doesn't want to meet "the one?" It all made sense to me—that I was here now to meet Ray. The way she explained it—our linked lives seemed to flow into a perfectly orchestrated plan from the universe. Hearing her assurance that we were divinely meant to join helped dissolve my objections regarding his age.

I knew my life was about to radically change. I had been an independent part of this group—a young college kid here for a stopover with clear intentions to leave at summer's end. But just by admitting to the start of something with Ray, this amalgamated me to the mission and split me from my autonomous purposes. Conclusions of the matter reached my consciousness like electric jolts trying to shock me into awareness—*Wake up!*

Hidden under the table, I gently pulled my hand away from the warmth of Ray's new grasp. My hard-earned goals of going to medical school were about to completely vanish into the horizon. Realizing this, my legs dangled with numbness beneath my seat. I became spacey and disembodied, just as I did as a little girl whenever things became distressing.

HOW CAN I GO AGAINST THE UNIVERSE?

As Ray and I traveled back to Dragoon that day, I thought about a new grounding thrill in all of this. I realized, having a relationship with Ray meant I would belong more fully to the triad, and I was baited to fill in holes which had riddled my psyche like Swiss cheese. It reminded me of being the baby in the family and wanting to be a part of what my older siblings were doing. But now that Ray and my connection was made public, I could be a fully participating member of the group. It was certainly an enchanting thought. I wasn't just trying to thrive from the outer banks anymore—I was invited to the prime inner pond, the center of all elite activity.

And then she dropped the bombshell on us. Just days after our lunch at the Horseshoe Café, Lilith triumphantly insisted that Ray and I should get married. "You know, the universe fully supports your union, and it will strengthen the mission for you to do this sooner than later."

I felt my stomach tightening. This was all happening too fast. My mind whirled anxiously trying to acquiesce to her insane pace! In that moment of shock, I realized we would never be two people growing together at a natural rhythm. There was no room for the heart's hesitations, for walls to melt, or for a decision born from mutual choice. From the moment we kissed on Mount Graham, marriage was no longer a question, it was a directive under Lilith's watchful eye. As she impressed upon us, the magnitude of the mission outweighed our feelings and reservations.

In the same breath, Lilith "encouraged" that our marriage take place by the end of the summer—even proposing a wedding date in early September. My eyes stared unblinking at her. Entranced by her alluring leadership, I felt compelled to comply. *How can I go against what the universe wants?* Though shaken, I yielded, naively slipping into a familiar follow mode, trusting her timing was divinely perfect.

While she urged haste for the mission's sake, she also emphasized to me the importance of securing marriage as a way to take a stand of independence from my family. Lilith recognized the inner war I faced when it came to communicating major decisions to them and how deeply this plagued my mind. She also saw I lacked a clear identity apart from their opinions—especially those of my mother and sister, whose judgments had long shaped my fractured sense of self.

BLINDSIDED

Within hours of deciding Ray and I would get married, Lilith said to me, "You know, you're going to have to confront your family about this, and I will help you." When she said this, the pressing weight of reality returned. This was the part I most enjoyed escaping from—family approval. The way she boldly addressed this fear in me deepened my trust in her.

Absent of sound wisdom, I leaned on a "divinely inspired" adult who claimed she could lead me through my family's reactions. In our conversations, she prepared me, "Elizabeth, they are not going to understand what we are doing here on the land, but you get it. You understand. Your family will not get your decision to marry Ray." I thought to myself, *Why would they? The last thing they knew was I was taking a summer hiatus to become refreshed to enter medical school. This will blindside them entirely! It will be a painful shock—a sudden turn and full throttle retreat from the bright future I had.*

She persisted, "You know your development—sovereign from your family—is a major part of your growth." Like other things she had persuaded me of, her words began to ring true. She continued, "Wrestling with your family's esteem is most of the war inside of you.

You need to assert your own decision to marry Ray and remain on the land regardless of what they think."

Maybe she was right; I had to stress my choice no matter how they responded. All this did, however, was make me discount any remaining doubt *I had* about marrying Ray. In the place of cogent uncertainty, all the pieces of myself rallied behind one voice that cried, "Yes, this is how I claim my independence! They can accept my decision or not—it is their choice! Let them reject my decision!" This fueled an immature drive to detach from my family's opinions all together.

With her reinforcement, I was emboldened to fight and even protect my decision to marry Ray. After all, as she pointed out, my family did not know what was best for my highest growth *like she did.*

THE CALLS

For me to set boundaries with my family, Lilith told me to call a few family members stating my decision to get married at the end of the summer and not to enter medical school. I remember clarifying, "Just a few?" to which she responded, "Yes, just pick a few to call . . . at first."

Initially, I called my mother and my brother Patrick. When I called my mother, I had rehearsed an opening statement which I was sure was bulletproof. It was bloated with spiritual language I knew she could not easily deflate—the very language that propelled her into her own major life decisions. My mother responded with a soft, muffled voice as if she were on a drug of avoidance herself, "Oh. Well, Beth, I am not happy that you have chosen to throw away your goals that you have worked so hard for, but if this is what you want." I did not stay on the phone long with her after conveying I would send her a wedding invitation.

What I love most about my brother Patrick is his honesty and lack of a filter. When I phoned him, he came right out with it and said, "I heard you were in a cult!" *Presumably from my mother and sister,* I thought. After I told him about the wedding he said, "I'm not happy you are leaving everything behind! You're being 'controlled' by the head woman!" I snapped, "I am not under Lilith's control. This is my own independent decision! I want to marry Ray!" Within myself I shouted protectively, *No! Lilith is pointing to what can heal me and my higher calling. She is influential yes, but I trust in her!*

Patrick became increasingly frustrated, "Elizabeth, I can't believe you are leaving behind medical school. You calling me is another ploy of the cult and the head woman wants to disconnect you from your family and control your life!" As he always did, Patrick passionately voiced exactly what he felt. The conversation ended unpleasantly and abruptly. Though his words made me defensive, my determination was greater than when I had traveled all the way to India convinced that Sai Baba was god. Here, I was chosen for an elite spiritual purpose, addicted by its promise to heal my brokenness.

Once I felt defeated following that first tough confrontation, Lilith became more emphatic—"Look at how hard this is! It will not go any better for you to call your remaining family members. It's clear that they will not be supportive! It's no longer good for you to start your life with Ray at a marriage ceremony with your family here. It's best for you to just write them letters and get married to Ray *without them.* Do you really want them here with their unwanted opinions and feelings while you have this ceremony? At your wedding, you want those here who will be supportive in your new life. If that means just the four of us, then so be it. All the universe is supporting you. This is your chance to decide for yourself, Elizabeth."

LETTERS OF CONSEQUENCE

Repulsed by more potential confrontations with my family, I realized they would never validate my "decision" to marry Ray and leave my goals behind anyway. I started to agree with what Lilith was saying. It ignited a flare of adamant resolve within me—"*Yah, they just don't understand. This is my life!*"

Within days of first mentioning our marriage, Lilith talked to all of us about the great value of the mission, "We may need to make sacrifices and cut ties with those who hold us back spiritually—ultimately leaving behind those who don't understand it." She looked directly at me and said, "Elizabeth, your own family is holding you back from all the universe wants for you. Your family does not understand the bond you have with Ray. This is a spiritual connection that they don't get to have a say in."

I did not resist when she instructed me to write letters to my family, asserting my conviction to marry Ray and my disappointment that they disapproved of my decision. To my older brothers and sister, my mother, my father, and most of my aunts and uncles I wrote that my wedding would be at the end of that summer of 1998, but that it would be on the land without a ceremony. Ultimately, I was to inform them they were not invited. I struggled through the process, knowing they would not understand, and that this would effectively hurt them. I really hated it, but she had flipped my awareness towards self-preservation. As I wrote, she guided the tone—soothing my doubts and validating my need to protect myself. She proclaimed, "This is the first time you have made such a bold decision for your future without their input. This is a giant step in your self-determination, and your growth. You are your own soul, Elizabeth."

Lured by her influence, I fully trusted Lilith. And these letters felt like a necessary step to stand by my decision and silence voices pulling me back to the path I'd left behind. She said, "Once sent, these letters will advance and accelerate your spiritual position. They will set a boundary to not allow your family to pull you back into an old life."

MAILED

Though it took me a while, I mailed the announcements. Thinking my artwork might soften the blow, I spent time crafting each one with watercolor pencil drawings. Lilith put pressure on me to make haste in completing them, stressing the importance of focusing on my new life. If it were only that simple.

The day my sister received her letter, she left a message on the landline recorder, and we all listened to it together—Lilith, Ray and Zev and I. In typical Em fashion, she chastened me saying she was "very disappointed" in my decision to marry Ray. But I was pleasantly surprised to hear Lilith, Ray and Zev mock and ridicule her tone! Their perspective of how ridiculous Em sounded trying to browbeat and control a decision I was making as an adult was incredibly reassuring to have.

Em had visited the land the first week when I arrived for the summer. At that time, she considered becoming part of the mission, but while she was here, she created a fiasco fighting incessantly with her husband and demanded many things of Lilith. When my new land clan made fun of her phone message, it was the first time another adult verified to me Em's inappropriate control over me, and the first time someone seemed to be protecting me from her! It solidified safety I felt with the triad.

From all the letters I sent, I heard back from only a couple of family members. My brother Finn was kind enough to send us a heart-shaped infinity sculpture for our wedding, and my Aunt Katy sent us a colorful Afghan. Their support provided a thread of familial warmth and acceptance.

CONTINUED GROOMING

Weeks prior to our wedding day, Lilith nudged me to stay in Ray's room. Persuading me to sleep with him before getting married, she pressed it was necessary for us to bond as soon as possible in this way. This intimacy she pressured between us would have progressed more naturally in a normal relationship, but it was somehow vital to the mission.

As I came to find out, Ray and my relationship would never be a private endeavor. We all lived in the same large house connected by one kitchen. Lilith held private meetings with Zev and Ray regarding the triad, and she would invariably "find out" information from him regarding me. I don't know exactly how, but she knew details of our intimate life. As a twenty-three-year-old innocent about the subject, I was oblivious, and, to a great degree—humiliated.

THE OUTSIDER

In late July, my friend Heather who roomed with me at the ashram in India, came to visit me on the land. First, we drove north for five hours to Flagstaff to attend a Sai Baba conference. After a couple of days, we returned to Dragoon. Heather stayed in the RV, and I wanted to sleep over with her so we could catch up. While she waited in another room, Lilith had a talk with me about staying in Ray's room instead of staying with my friend. I was very conflicted about this. Desiring to talk with Heather, Lilith insisted, "You need to remain with your fiancé in his room." She asserted, "Because you are engaged, it is not appropriate for you to stay with her. You need to stay with him. This is part of your growing up Elizabeth—part of marriage. You are not a child having sleep overs anymore."

Heather was weirded out by Lilith, and this situation only made it worse. She had many alarms about her, and I spent time convincing Heather how spiritual and "awesome" the situation was on the land. She figured out my looming expedited marriage to Ray without family was suspiciously very wrong, and she admitted she was worried about me.

Lilith gave Heather funny looks, like a twitching pain was contorting her face. My friend could not leave quickly enough! After telling me her concerns once more, she drove away. Watching the dust from her departing vehicle settle, I thought to myself, *I know she cares about me, but Heather just doesn't see the spiritual significance of all of this. That's ok, Lilith said not everyone will understand.*

MATRIMONY

Our wedding was moved up an entire month to early August. At an altitude of 4,600 feet, we were married in front of a sizeable divine mother statue located near the north end of the acreage. When the ceremony's appointed time came, we all took a saunter on the path leading to its position. Walking at a leisurely stride, I looked up from the earth that had accepted my intense stare. With my eyes glazed forward to the horizon, a nervous rush of energy surged through my face and arms. *This is all really happening!*

Assailed by the searing desert sun, the soles of my suede moccasins pressed upon pebbles strewn along the footpath. Promenading toward a new destiny, my body was caressed by the flowy texture of ivory linen attire purchased from a boutique in Tucson. My wedding ring was an opal stone surrounded by two smaller amethyst stones that I chose from a New Age bookstore.

It was a brief but simple ceremony with the six of us, including the dogs "Honey" and "Cosmo" who were of course invited. While hot breezes pummeled us in the wide-open Dragoon desert, I moved flying hair away which kept sticking to the lipstick on my mouth. Lilith spoke a few words and commemorated our union in the light of the mission. As an on-line ordained minister, she led us into basic wedding elements, and we verbalized our "I do's." By the time of our short-lived matrimonial kiss, we became bothered by the elements. With quick footing, we flitted back to the house to sign the marriage license.

On that day, I sealed my fate. Now I would stay on the land, be married to Ray and never return to earlier endeavors. Before this day, there was a great deal of drama surrounding whether my family would attend and accept my marriage, but in the end, the whole thing lasted maybe ten minutes, and it was back to the business of the mission.

Soon after our ceremony, Zev and Lilith were also married. There was no officiant other than Lilith, and she signed "Lorelei" as the official upon the state document of her own wedding. After more than a year of knowing each other, they were genuinely locked into one another—the main merging couple of the mission.

During the first few months we were married, Lilith recurrently teased us about having children. She suggested we would have a "star child"—born with a kind of spiritual enlightenment—specially chosen just to be raised upon the land. Although I never spoke it, the thought of having a child so early in this rushed marriage was not something I wanted to entertain. Then again, everything was viewed through the lens of this mission. So, because I was already bowed to all her influences, I tossed my own preferences aside.

This was no typical marriage. We were all living in the same house. Although the home was spread apart, and we all genuinely liked each other, this was a messed-up living arrangement. We ate meals together, spent time together, and retired for the night to our respective parts of the same house. Lilith continued to have meetings with just the two men, while I performed other tasks or relaxed in Ray's part of the house. On a few nights, I attempted to cook ambitious meals for the four of us, but merciful to them, that role ended. It became obvious I never learned to cook, but I sure tried to please! They made fun of my fancy recipe concoctions and wanted simple meat, potato, vegetable meals anyway.

A HOUSE OF CARDS TOPPLES.

Not long after we were married, I could no longer contain the escalating conflicts raging inside me regarding my family's disapproval of my abrupt marriage. Competing arguments amplified in my heart and all of it became too much for me. Ray and Lilith reproached me, saying I was immature. Go figure! As a young woman in my early twenties compared to a forty-two-year-old man, I could not live up to their expectations. Their words echoed, "You are not getting it." I was a college kid living with people twice my age. Beyond the folly of immaturity, my poor life coping skills were hampered with severely repressed memories.

Having had a sudden marriage imposed upon us, Ray and I fought incessantly because our personalities and brokenness clashed. My tendencies were too great for Ray who six months after our wedding had to process his mother's sudden diagnosis of pancreatic cancer.

And within months of her bleak prognosis, he also had to process her death. Sad to admit that in my own dysfunction, I was not able to be there for him in the way he needed. Though I tried to hold it all together for him, I had amassed childish echoes which clamored for my attention. I was not in a stable mental state enough to be present for anybody.

After only six months of our supposed marriage, Lilith decreed I was no longer equipped to help make the triad stronger by being Ray's wife. At her direction, we separated. They sent me to a week-end retreat center in the Saguaro mountains for a final chance to "get it." As was communicated to me—I was given that time to "consider the gravity of the mission and possibly prevent a separation." At the retreat, the quiet and stillness was also a reminder of confusing mental chatter which had evolved inside my mind. Try as I might, I did not "get it" during this sanctuary.

When Ray picked me up, it seemed we initially were creating better patterns of relating, but I fell deeper into a mirage of presenting what I thought the triad wanted from me, without any real change in my spirit. I was asked to sleep separately in the middle room of the large house. Quietly, I kept to myself while the three of them spent time together without me. Essentially, I fell out of favor with the "triad."

By this time, I had already started a job as a phlebotomist in Benson, AZ. Two months after I was married to Ray, Lilith had brought us all together, encouraging us to find work to contribute money to the mission. It was a passive way of telling me to get a job since I was the only one not working at the time. With my biology background, I was hired on the spot at Benson Hospital working as a lab tech making minimum wage. I drove the mission's yellow chevy truck 90 minutes round trip to work. Commuting without air conditioning was insane in the blistering Arizona heat. Gusts of hot air blowing through open windows on the freeway was my only reprise. The car guzzled gas like a thirsty camel slurps water and its tires constantly required leak repairs or full replacements.

When Ray and I separated and I moved into the middle room of the house, Lilith asked for rent money from me—$250/month. I really did not mind. I wasn't concerned with money because there was nothing I desired to spend it on. My only longing was to stay part of the mission here, and if that meant I could serve financially, then I was willing. But I knew who called the shots. It wasn't Ray in his own home or Zev. It was Lilith in every detail of every decision, great or small.

Once I moved back to the middle room, I was convinced the land was still where I needed to be. I decided I just needed to "get it," and one day return to Ray when I had finally "gotten it." Plus, I was gripped with fear of leaving, and there was nowhere else for me to go. Never would I consider returning to California near the clutches of my sister and mother—it was crucial I secure this clean break from them. Emotionally, I was in no position to finish my medical school dreams. I already felt substantially worse than when I had first traveled to Arizona "just for the summer." My prospects had melted like ice in the sweltering heat, and my countenance was like those deflated tires I constantly had to fix on the Chevy.

I lived without clear boundaries or a firm sense of self. Easily shaped by others, I drifted in a fog of uncertainty. Even in this scattered state, I continued to feel sheltered residing on the land with this group of people. They hadn't given up on me and appeared to have continued affection for me. Genuinely, I felt the same fondness for them.

And though I feared I was becoming hopeless to her, I believed Lilith could eventually remedy my messy instability. Blind or not, I had faith she had the answers for how to repair me. Simply being myself and residing comfortably in my own skin was a riddle I could not solve—surely the "divine mother" could still help me discover wholeness. For all its manifold hooks and alluring assurances, I was attached to this place, determined to remain bound to it.

PART TWO

The Chrysalis

You think that I am impoverishing myself withdrawing from men, but in my solitude, I have woven for myself a silken web or chrysalis, and nymph-like, shall ere long burst forth a more perfect creature, fitted for a higher society.
—Henry David Thoreau

ELEVEN

Isolated

The caterpillar, once ravenous and restless, now surrenders to still-ness. What was once instinct becomes mystery. She spins herself into a silken tomb, not knowing what awaits. Inside the chrysalis, her body liquefies—every cell undone, every structure dissolved into something unrecognizable. It is not death, but a sacred unraveling. Veiled in suspended solitude, she is neither what she was nor what she will be.

THE TABLE

After a few months of living in the middle room, Lilith called me to the round oak table for a meeting with my housemates. It had been a long time since we all sat here. From the time Ray and I separated, they avoided me, and beyond work, I kept to myself.

When we were still together, Ray was comfortable going toe to toe with me. Without reservation, he directly called me out on what he didn't like. I hated how defensive I was.

One day Lilith and Ray brought home an animated cat toy, saying its hissing animatronics mimicked my behavior. But I couldn't laugh at this painful prop. It was a living hell to be me without understanding why I was the way I was—I had no memories of independently surviving years of abuse as a child. They did not stop teasing me about this dumb cat, and I stuffed my grief about their reference.

The match between Ray and I was never the right one not only for him, but also for me. Lilith, who clearly orchestrated our marriage, magnified my faults before them all. I walked around paranoid to express anything they did not like. Constantly on edge, I never relaxed again around them, a stark contrast to the light-hearted way I was at the start of the summer.

Now I was surrounded by the three of them at the table. Before Lilith spoke a word, I felt the burden of bad news pending from her lips. Bracing for the worst, my chest flushed beet red, and my breath shallowed.

Lilith sighed, then locked eyes with me—her gaze heavy with unspoken weight. My abdomen quaked, dreading what she was about to say. *Can they see me trembling?* She began, "Ok. Since you and Ray have separated, this has not been easy—for any of us. You have not been able to move forward and shake the opinions of your family. You are having difficulty becoming an independent woman and supporting the mission in the way that is needed." *Oh god, what is coming next? Where is she going with this?*

"We have to move forward with the mission, but your process will need to be separate from what we had planned. I wanted this to be different, but I have come up with a way you can still be a part of us and not leave the land," she said. Inside I panicked, *Leave the land? This is real! My worst fears are unfolding. Oh no! I failed at what I was supposed to get! I've disappointed her!*

I flashed back to Lilith's instruction and tried to assess where I had screwed up—because her techniques to help me should be infallible, right? Was I really that hopeless? She was the divine mother—who else but her could help me? In one of her methods weeks ago, she told me to sit still all day and listen to my inner self. In a room for hours, I tried to meditate deeply on who I was at my core, but only chaos surfaced, and this exercise left me weary and more discouraged that I would ever heal.

She went on, "Look, this is just not working with you in the house. Ray is uncomfortable, we all are. I think what you need is time to yourself, time to find out who you are, separate from your family." Tears slid down the curves of my face. She continued, "We want you to still be a part of us. You will move out of this house, and you can move into the single trailer. It's really up to you."

The trailer was only 500 ft from the big house, but the thought of being separated from them was terrible. How could I not be seized with failure and rejection—all the worst of fears—all the most unpleasant of feelings?

Zev and Ray watched me hear her decree. My face was full of hot tears that would not cease. Looking at me intently, Zev struggled. Leaning forward he said, "Please, please stop crying." I had clung to hope of reconciling with Ray. Instead, I was banished from the "triad" house. To soften the blow, Lilith began to smile with her usual charm and tried to spin it that this was a way for me to become truly independent. "Just think of how you can buy your own set of dishes and decorate the trailer just the way you want to," she said. For some reason, the simplicity of her idea offered me a bit of comfort.

I sat frozen at the table, her words hazy. I nodded, but I couldn't feel my limbs. Later, I found myself in the trailer, unsure how I'd gotten there.

CUTTING TIES

Days after our round table meeting, Lilith approached me. "Elizabeth, you need to send letters to your family again setting a firmer boundary. The hardship you have now stems from your inability to do so before." My eyes were glazed over, dazed yet compliant. She was aware of my scattered self-margins, and I was grateful she still had a plan to help me even though I missed the boat with Ray and the triad.

I had no strength to write them again, but she convinced me it was necessary. "Your family let you down, creating your struggles with Ray and ruining your destiny on the land." she said. Her intense gaze bore into me—"Don't you see what they did Elizabeth? You need to assert who you are to them, not the other way around, or you will never become who you really are!"

Once set up in my trailer, I tucked myself into my new draft table to write my family. Lilith outlined what I needed to express. There was no mention that Ray and I were separated, nor that I was living alone in a trailer. Instead, I wrote it was my own decision to marry him despite their disapproval and because their response was distressing to me, I needed distance from communicating with any of them.

Though the wedding announcements were shocking but "gentle," this second set of letters was assertive, even cutting—written to detach from my family's "condemnation." With doubts about the generalized theme of these letters, I appealed to her, "But *not all* of my family disapproved! Some probably didn't reach out because I told them they weren't invited to the wedding. And my brother sent me a sculpture!" She persisted, "It doesn't matter, every member of your family expressed disappointment whether they were silent about your marriage or if they told you directly. They all condemned your decision to marry Ray!" Even though I received different responses from everyone, she framed them all as one lump response. And because of the conclusions she fed me, I started feeling victimized *by all of my family members*. She pressed, "You will never heal unless you do this Elizabeth!"

Broken-hearted, I eagerly lashed out in the way she said would give me catharsis. But once mailed, I became sorrowful that I created a rift with everyone in my family. The letters were a final blow designed to separate me from them. And this separation with words broke down any resistance, leaving me dependent on Lilith. I was now estranged from everyone who loved me. Tears fell down my cheeks because no one I wrote would know that I was alone and already separated from Ray. My only option was to hope for Lilith's benevolence.

With numbing alienation, I believed living in the trailer was a temporary exercise, or maybe it would bring healing as Lilith said. Having separated already from Ray, after abandoning my dreams and botched attempts to mend myself, I was one lost puppy. I longed to be back in the triad's favor—to satisfy a deep, stunted need for community, refuge and love. My sole focus was to someday become worthy again to rejoin the inner circle and finally "get" whatever Zev and Ray were "getting."

But weeks rolled into months rolled into years, and I became embarrassed and ashamed that it wasn't working out—or rather that *I wasn't working right*. Solitary on every level, I drove to work several days a week dulled with dissociation.

VOICES

It was in solitude that I became desperately lonely. In the trailer's crushing silence, voices grew loud, hundreds of them—a jarring chorus that proliferated like a virus in my mind. I didn't know if they had always been there and were now louder, or if they had multiplied in severity here on the land. I didn't recognize they were separate expressions; I thought their confusing mess was just my mind. Their haunting cries each bore a separate opinion, yet no distinct identity—fractured laments spun to shield me from abuse I could neither name nor remember. Overcome by their chaos, and growing intensity, my tears became a cascade of despair.

Lilith started calling me "the weeping willow," but this wasn't comforting to hear. Rather I was confused, she knew I was so sad and offered no balm of relief. As some sort of exercise, I once painted a weeping willow, but painting did not bring me solace. Brush in hand, I sat frozen staring at a blank canvas which reflected a void inside me. Meditation also made everything worse! I thought I could organize and look at each thought at a time, but the process frustrated and pained me so much that I would begin weeping again. These quiet tears flowed from an emptiness in my soul, so starved that I would have clung to any drop of affection from anyone.

With no consolation, my suffering could never be soothed by kindness or the relief of a good laugh. My soul felt trapped, caged by invisible walls. And though there was no bruising, nor hand raised against me, I felt bound as if every part of me was quietly imprisoned.

Perpetually, I was tormented by negative energies and strongholds which fell right in line with my own harmful thought patterns—so much that I believed they were all my own thoughts. Dark images burst into my mind without warning—thoughts so gory and perverse, I couldn't believe they came from within me. Because I felt guilty about them, they were like needles trapped inside my brain. In many moments, the struggle was very real as one voice among many would praise some part of me while another voice tore me down just as that thought was forming.

Other than when I was at my job, in order to perform my duties, I had no concrete thoughts. Sometimes the only temporary relief I found was while taking a warm shower. I forced myself to listen to the gentle sound of the water stream instead of the torrent of my own voices. This was also a fight. Incessantly, I wrestled to hear something other than emotive echoes. Whatever I tried became hopeless. I suffered alone. The crying ensued. *What does it matter? No one can hear me. No one sees me.*

BAD MEDICINE

Isolation wove my broken psychology into the land's spiritual darkness, keeping me rooted in fear. I couldn't leave—drops of respect from the community convinced me that I was still wanted, despite the triad's rejection. Lilith's remedy, meant to forge independence, was bad medicine. Voices surged whispering words of shame and doubt. Loneliness slammed me like the hot Arizona winds, chapping my skin, making each breath heavy.

Lilith often told me, "Elizabeth, just surrender to the divinity within," but her words were like a heat lamp in the middle of the scorching desert, they offered no relief and were grating to hear. My psyche split further, and the voices intensified every emotion. They had taken the driver's seat—and I had lost control. There was no way

I could just "grow up" and become a mature adult. No, this separation had proven to be an abject failure. I was a cracked vessel barely holding together, unsure if I could ever be whole again.

In spite of the fact that she was the "divine mother," and for all of her channeling of the "ascended masters"—she had no special insight or wisdom. She simply did not have the answers for me. The added quarantine of miserable loneliness only magnified the volume of suffering I experienced. Apparently, *Lilith was not divine enough* to know that I was dealing with an identity disorder with severely suppressed memories from years of childhood distress.

She wanted me as a gift for Ray, a devotee to mold. But I was too broken for her vision. Monthly meetings about living "vibrationally higher lives" left me trailing, unable to grasp what the triad "got." The independence she promised served to amplify chaos for me—not the transformation she promised. Still, a faint hope flickered. Maybe this trailer, my chrysalis, could one day give way to wings.

CATALYST

Getting banished to my bunker was the eventual means for my metamorphosis. And at the culmination of my time here I did spin my chrysalis—as if I knew I needed to sojourn in a covered cocoon to heal. But while this trailer may have been the place, it was not the right time. First, there was a long time of wading in the mire. I didn't have the tools to be remade yet. Entering a chrysalis now— before I was ready—would have been like forcing a caterpillar into wings it hadn't earned.

While still consuming spiritual concepts from Lilith, I sat motionless, halted by life, in a kind of paralysis. And instead of contemplating the right spot to attach and spin a silk web forming my own chrysalis, I was tired with indigestion and weary of trying. Somehow, I knew I was never going to find the answers I was seeking. Instead, I just needed shelter. For the moment, I existed in a trailer, sequestered without companionship in the middle of a desert.

Because I was fully dissociated, those years are a blur to me. With a split awareness, divided among hundreds of auditory echoes inside my mind, I suffered an excruciating, disconnected existence and it's why I chose to forget it. It was another traumatic time in my life where I escaped profound sadness by blocking out most days entirely.

MY COMFORTS

With my mind blurred, I leaned upon the beauty of the land, and its scenes would soften the blow of my harsh inner world. Watching dusk from my plastic chaise lounge, brilliant pastel colors that swirled in creative cloud formations lit up my sullen eyes. I took solace in the uniqueness of the desert—with its sudden temperature dips in the evenings, precipitous heights midday. I loved to inhale the musky, earthy aroma of Arizona rain, with the powerful sound of rushing monsoon waters bringing me comfort. The hum of the cicadas was also calming—much like the white noise of crickets acoustically magnified near a lake. The dry, arid desert heat with its breezy evening was like a welcome pause to the oppressive melancholy which had consumed me.

My creature comforts weren't much, but they would engage me for a moment, albeit as briefly as a snowflake stays intact in your hand. My TV/VCR combo provided me with diversion, and I was comforted by the weight of my quilt wrapped around me as I looked at the moon and stars above my bed window. On my meditation altar, I placed a sculpture of an angel figure that Lilith had painted for me, together with a few crystals and candles. Grateful that Zev bought me my first guitar at a pawn shop, I practiced chords he taught me which tuned the more pleasurable parts of my brain to the stirring of music. The simplicity of my shelter felt safe to me. Content with salt-of-the-earth living, I was not looking for extravagance. But for all its beauty, the land still bore an unnatural weight, an oppressive heaviness, that reminded me I was somehow its captive.

UH OH–I NEED HER AGAIN!

Every three or four months, despite trying to prove my successful independence to the triad, I would panic and lose heart, needing a one-on-one talk with Lilith. Despair drove me to ask Zev to arrange a meeting. Living so close, Lilith was like an approachable guru, and I still believed she could help me fix myself.

Just knowing that a meeting with her had been arranged caused my mood to brighten. Though I came for guidance, what I really craved was "the mother's touch"—her love. She relieved the hot-tempered rocks of my mind and still had a soothing influence on me. Really, I needed to be reminded she still cared for me and to make sure she would not abandon me like my mother had.

Sometimes, our conversation would give me assurance that it was the right time to speak with her. But as months and years passed, this became the exception. More often than not, I left ruminating over what she had said, realizing asking to talk with her proved I still couldn't "get it" on my own.

Even in her comforting voice, she reminded me, "Nothing is new that I am saying to you, Elizabeth." She viewed me as stuck and not moving forward. I was ostracized from the group for not getting whatever they were getting—seemingly proving to Lilith that her methods don't work for everyone. I truly never understood what I was supposed to do. As it was, what she asked me to inwardly do was impossible with my peculiar psychology.

Then I got more news.

FINALITY OF PAPERS

Two years after we were married, likely spurred by my latest desperate talk with Lilith, Ray walked to my single wide trailer where I had been living alone for the past eighteen months. A firm knock, "Elizabeth, are you there?" I opened the creaky door, and he stood in the doorway, eyes intense. He cracked a slight smile, that quickly faded to a somber, furrowed brow. Devoid of tenderness that once warmed me, he handed me divorce papers, "Um . . . here. We thought it would work out, and I wanted it to, but it hasn't. You can still stay on the land. You're still a part of us."

We lived together only six months, a year and a half ago. I'd clung to the hope we'd reunite. His words shattered that dream. With nothing more to say, I knew Lilith's hand had guided this. "Ok. Goodbye," he said. Softly closing the door, I heard his fading steps. It was a sad evening, unlike any other. Tears fell for hours.

This was the loss of all hope for me. Having no other soul to express to, I didn't think I could take it anymore. His promise—"You're still part of us"—and early memories of the land hung threadbare in my heart. I had stayed loyal, never looking at another man. Safety was my soul's deepest need, and Ray, with his broad shoulders and kind heart, could have shielded me from Em, my childhood's lingering threat. I stood alone, clutching the papers, tears blurring the desert sky where a single star flickered faintly. I didn't know what it meant, but it seemed to be a silent witness to my tears.

TWELVE

Frenzied Emptiness

THANK YOU, HORSE

After the divorce, the calendar turned quietly. Birthdays, holidays—each one slipped by without fanfare, just another day in the desert.

For three years, I remained in isolation. On my 26th birthday, I decided to attend horseback riding lessons at a local Dragoon stable. While enjoyable, my companion teacher asked questions that I didn't want asked, "So where do you live? And with who? Are you married or do you have a boyfriend? How long have you lived here? Why are you here alone today?" Her constant probing was overwhelming. I had come to forget my situation, not explain it. And with mounting paranoia, I retreated from her intrusive curiosity.

By then, I had adopted the unspoken Arizona motto, "Trust is earned." Even from myself, I had hidden away the key to unraveling the last few years. My experience on the land was its own trauma shoved in its own Pandora's box. I hadn't spoken to my family because I felt remorse over letters I had written cutting them off.

Trying to take delight in my paid horse ride the best I could, my guide's constant questions left me depressed. Feeling agoraphobic, I wanted to return to the introversion of my trailer. She took pictures of me—some of the few photos I have of myself during those years. Mounted high upon a mare, my smile was flat, my eyes troubled and glazed. Still, I was proud I had made an attempt to enjoy myself. And I was happy to have the horse's quiet company. *Thank you, horse!*

CRACKLING PAINT

Because of my spacey existence, I can recall only flickers of how these years passed me by. Though I became proficient at sudden alertness and selective listening when necessary, all other times, the pain was too much for me to remain aware. Sadness overwhelmed me until I could no longer hold back the tears. Even when I received a letter from my friend Zahira who wrote that she was greatly concerned for me, I just cried, because I didn't know the girl she had written to anymore.

My greatest regret during this time was a thoughtless decision made at the height of my mental unraveling—when nothing could numb the pain. My mom had just sent me a large batch of my old paintings. I looked at them one by one, and with each image, a wave of emotion welled up within me. But instead of comfort, they brought anguish. These pieces, once vibrant expressions of who I was, now felt meaningless, like lies from a person I no longer knew—a life I no longer recognized. My identity, already fractured, felt more distorted than ever.

What did any of it matter now? What good had expressing myself ever done? *I'm still filled with confusion.* I sat outside alone, depressed, surrounded by ghosts of who I once was. One by one, I placed them into a large metal garbage can. Studies of birds, flowers, self-portraits, faces—colorful sweeps of paint and detailed images from high school through college. And the one of my father—that one stopped me.

I had poured so much into this piece. My father in a brown business suit, his tie of paper mâché money and me as a child in the background. It was more than a portrait, it was a question I never dared to ask aloud. Was I feeling so disconnected because I lacked nearness to him? Does he think about me? I glared at it, my breath catching. I didn't want to feel what stirred in me. Not now. Not here.

I struck a match.

My art ignited quickly. I stared as the edges curled, the colors blistered, and the paint began to crackle. The smell of burning canvas and acrylic exhaust filled the air. I sobbed as flames consumed them—my memories, my questions, my voice. I couldn't reconcile the destruction of something that once brought me joy and confidence. Some of these pieces had hung in college galleries or received awards. But in my distorted thinking, if they stirred emotion, they had to go. I believed I had to detach from them completely. Everything was still filtered through the lens of the mission, and these paintings had no place in my world here. No one here would want to see them, let alone remember who I had been.

The fire hissed and popped, and I stood there, watching the smoke rise into the desert sky. There was no person to witness or stop me, just the ashes and the silence that followed.

STILL INFLUENCING

After the divorce, though I rarely spoke to Lilith, Zev and Ray, they remained the hollow source I went to looking for love. I convinced myself that their distance wasn't rejection, but rather Lilith's way of fostering my independence. My drive for acceptance was relentless. The isolation from them was unbearable, and I believed that if I could just make them happy again, I might earn back their approval. With nowhere else to go, my instinct was to bridge the gap the only way I knew how—by finding my way back into their good graces. Then, maybe I could reclaim the sense of community I once felt. To belong with them again, that meant love to me. That was all I wanted.

By this time, I was too tied up in voices and identity fragments to reflect anything authentic. I probably expressed a disingenuous smile or projection of what I thought they wanted me to be just so I would feel accepted. I had nothing sincere to offer because I was far from myself.

Especially in light of the divorce, Lilith likely saw me as an obstacle to the mission's momentum. The dream of Ray and me raising "star children" together on the land had unraveled, and with it, her vision for my role. So, she shifted her stance and eventually redefined my purpose altogether.

In a rare meeting with her, I expressed great sorrow about the failed marriage and how I missed Ray. She told me, "Elizabeth, all this time you have been so focused on getting back with Ray that you haven't spent time getting better within yourself. But now the relationship is over, and you can change your focus." She continued, "Remember how you used to want to become a nun in Mother Theresa's convent in India to help the suffering?" "Yes," I replied, recalling how I thought being compassionate towards the poor might help me escape my own agony.

But her related offer to me was a little odd. After mentioning this former dream of mine, she again lured me that I could be her *handmaiden*—by similarly taking a vow of chastity and abstinence to her, saying it would make me better able to serve her. After our talk, she had me sign a contract of commitment making this vow, and this did have the effect of taking my heart off of losing Ray or focusing on any kind of romantic loss. As she explained, "Now you can center your attention on growing spiritually and being there for me." She told me the vow was our secret, which made me feel special to her. I didn't fully understand what I was agreeing to, only that it made me feel chosen, and that was enough.

Following our secret agreement, land meetings and interactions remained sporadic. Sometimes I saw Ray walking from his shop, and he would wave at me which helped me trust he still wanted me here— now as his friend. When we did officially gather, maybe every three months, we met inside new areas Zev had built. There, Lilith would continue to channel and guide us into "energy shifts."

Though I rarely spoke with Lilith alone after our agreement, she still managed to assert her influence upon me, even with a mere suggestion. One day when I dropped off my rent check, she commented about my "gaunt-like" weight which had dropped below when I was a swimmer in high school. After her mere hint, I rapidly began consuming more of what I wanted to eat. Her approval alone was enough to make me want to shift my behavior.

RUGGED AND ROUGH

Life on the land was not gentle—it was coarse in texture and relentless in spirit. Even though aspects of crunchy dry brush and temperate breezes were comforting, the desert's harshness amplified the ache in my heart.

One day, a massive, aggressive rattlesnake slithered towards Zev. It was standing a meter tall from the ground in fury and seemed to be exerting dominance that he had been king of this land. Zev pulled out his shotgun and put an end to that. Too curious, I had to touch it after it was dead. Both my hands barely wrapped around its circumference. Even headless, it tried to strike me the following hours. When it did, I screeched aloud and dropped it! Zev was nearby when I did; he cracked a smile and walked over to also examine its carcass.

On occasion, I went on ascending walks into the mountains behind the land. One day, I drifted from the trail, high onto a ledge overlooking Dragoon. Though it's never smart to stray from a desert path, I felt myself rebelling against Ray's advice to stay on the trail. After a few minutes of resting where I had trekked, I heard a loud rattle. Swiftly, I darted back down the mountain in a bit of a panic and scurried home. Slamming the trailer door behind me, I was relieved that my abode rested high above the ground where menacing creatures were unable to enter.

Another time, jogging on a trail, I nearly stepped on a coiled rattlesnake in my path just feet from me. I rapidly braked my body, turned around, and sprinted the opposite way, my heart pounding. Both situations were too close for my comfort.

The land and all of its "negative spiritual energy" began to take its toll on all of us, including the animals. One day I asked to take Honey, Lilith's little Schnauzer on a walk along with Cosmo, Ray's dog who was suspected to be part wolf. Cosmo usually played nicely with Honey, and they were companions. But when we were far off on our trot together, Cosmo suddenly began viciously tearing and ravaging into Honey—down to sinew and bone.

Screaming as loudly as I could, I called out to the others! Honey was shrieking in terror and pain, but Cosmo could not be stopped. It was a dangerous venture to break up the attack, but I strove to pull them apart as much as I could. The others dashed out as quickly as possible. In the gruesome aftermath, Honey was barely alive. She was rushed to receive lifesaving care and after a long recovery, she survived Cosmo's violence.

That next day, Ray took Cosmo deep into the Dragoon mountains. In *Old Yeller* fashion, because of his rabid and murderous behavior, Ray shot Cosmo for his crimes. I took this as more evidence of the bad medicine growing on the land.

PREPAREDNESS

Around this time, a recent high school graduate named Michael moved onto the land. Lilith knew his mother who had temporarily stayed with us. Zev took Michael under his wing with construction projects and even built him a temporary two-story home at the edge of the property.

Zev, Ray and Michael began making emergency preparedness plans to ensure the land was self-sustaining. Zev installed a sizable white propane gas container, so we had ample power source if anything knocked us off the grid. He also fixed handpumps on the four corners of the property so we could have access to water in the event that we had no electricity.

Michael showed Zev a website called, "The Cutting Edge" which Zev and Lilith began to read and digest. The text spoke about how "the Illuminati" were working to control the outcome of a "New World Order." This included a plan to control people by removing their ability to protect and feed themselves and eventually place Americans into forced labor camps. This especially struck Zev whose orthodox Jewish family had survived the Holocaust. Provisions were made not only to protect Lilith and the mission, ensuring we could all flee and survive a government takeover, but also to fortify the land from outsiders with bad intentions.

As part of this preparedness, the men began to buy guns and learn to shoot to protect against potential governmental stripping of rights. From his research, Zev handed us a list of supplies that we should have ready in a "go bag" for sudden escapes, whether from disasters or threats. Our role to seek protection was always in the light of the mission and to shield Lilith. We would defend her first as she was "the vulnerable one" that required guarding.

Charlotte and I followed Lilith and Zev's directions, buying the survival items and preparing for quick escapes, just as we followed everything else they told us. The men prepared mountain bugouts where they stashed supplies and bought two motorcycles for quick escapes. Of our own volition, Charlotte and I even cut our hair short for practicality. But my pixie cut pricked at my already low self-esteem, especially when I couldn't feel the soft truss of hair along my neck.

At the bottom of our list was to purchase a gun. Thankfully, we drove as a group to the Tucson gun show one day and Zev helped me buy my first firearm—a Beretta .25 ACP. We ventured to outdoor ranges to practice. The men taught me gun safety and how to clean it. Though it took several minutes of emerging courage to fire the first shot, the power of the blast was exhilarating. I was proud of myself for becoming proficient at my aim.

Spending time on the range with the land clan was invigorating after months of solitude. I reveled in the thought that we were preparing for something—that *something* was happening! And beyond anything, I enjoyed that we were doing it together.

In front of the main house, we attempted to cultivate a large garden. Hardened caliche, or rock-hard clay, resides beneath the Arizona topsoil and Michael and Zev used a jackhammer to try and break it up. Turns out desert earth does not yield great results. Squash and pumpkin thrived in our soil, but not much else took a liking to the scorching weather and solidified sand.

I attended a horticulture conference and a medical emergency preparedness class for the mission, but the concepts taught proved to be way over my head. I only remembered what I was able to tell Lilith about planting fruit trees below the porch of the main house.

The wilderness medical emergency conference was set in Dragoon led by a fire captain who fed us delicious food. In a class of fifty medics, nurses and firefighters, they looked at me curiously as I explained where I lived and that I had no medical experience other than being a phlebotomist. But I believed I needed to be prepared to take care of my land clan.

I'm not sure how I took on the whole "preparedness" effort with sudden conviction. It seemed to give me a renewed sense of purpose. But just as quickly as it began, it faded. The triad may have continued the conversations, but after those first few times we shot guns together, I was no longer part of it.

EARNING MY PLACE

Since Lilith's words and meditations had been taped all these years, I asked if I could scribe them. Wanting to serve, I was compelled to prove my worth. I hoped that by transcribing them, I might absorb their meaning more deeply. This project took me several months, and I was satisfied handing it over to Lilith and Zev when I was done.

For educational pursuits, I received a $500 scholarship from Benson hospital. I had applied for the award intending to hand it over to the mission, desiring to give something more than my rent check. One day I passed the money proudly to Zev and he responded with a kind smile and thank you. Fragmented and lost within myself, I clung to the belief that my land clan was the key to the safety, dignity, love, and community I had always lacked. Eager to win back their approval, I was willing to give them anything—whatever it took to be accepted again.

I felt increasingly desperate. Like a battered woman, I stayed for the sake of receiving even the smallest drops of their affection. Entranced by the charisma of Lilith's coercive allure, I was stripped of all support, and this was the only "family" I now knew. I tried to put on a good face because they were watching, and I longed to be seen as worthy—if not for who I was, then at least for still trying. So, I kept striving—stretching out for a mirage of water on a searing endless desert. My main coping mechanism of ruthless determination propelled me into a forced hope, because I refused to give up. This spiritual ship that we were on, even though I was cast to the lower decks, I was still a part of the crew. But my position now felt entirely dispensable.

DESPERATE EMPTINESS

During these years, I couldn't remember the last time I laughed. Even my reflection looked like a stranger—eyes dull, shoulders hunched, as if bracing for a blow that never came. In the deepest reaches of an inescapable cavern, I sat within myself, immovable with sorrow. My life was a quiet wasteland, barren, and littered with the remains of dreams I no longer dared to name. And I was only 26. How could a garden grow in the rock-hard caliche that my life, my very existence had become?

Was there really any hope for me? If she couldn't heal me, *Maybe this is my fault just like Em taught me as a child*. I certainly felt too defeated to fight off echoes of her voice which flooded my mind, exacerbated by dark spiritual strongholds surrounding me. My memories' recordings rose up to confirm that *I had done this all to myself*. I was in this place—companionless, without family or true community because of me.

Even with the bright future I once had, I was merely surviving. Drained of sustaining nutrients, I was laden with noisy weeds that choked my reality—and the reality of who I really was. Without an extension of love, I would not prosper. No one knew the starkness of my reality or the nearness to a complete breakdown of my psyche.

New Age platitudes like "think positive," "have gratitude" or "find love within yourself" would have been as cruel as telling a new widow, "Time heals all wounds"—useless against my deep childhood injuries. The only ability I had was to lean upon the soothing colors of an evening sunset, the songs of birds or the wind on my face. These were my companions when I could not talk with a single soul on the earth.

Lilith would tell me that I put her "through things," emphasizing repeatedly that if one of us was weak, it weakened her. This phrasing of subtle but overt blame placed upon me made my own mental self-beating even stronger. "You don't realize how much your energy drains me," she once sighed, shaking her head, "It's like I'm carrying your process for you." And when she retold stories of my incessant crying with a chuckle, "You should've seen yourself last week—tears, tears, tears. I thought we were going to have to buy a boat," it only added to the embarrassment I already felt. Still, I made excuses for her. I told myself, *Maybe she is just trying to lighten the mood. Maybe this is her version of tough love—pushing me to heal in the only way she knows.*

This supposed mission of promises to elevate the spiritual and psychological landscape of the soul resulted in a deeper, more frenzied emptiness. It didn't help heal me, it only intensified my childhood issues whose memories were locked and unknown. Most of what I was feeling, I didn't have the capacity or recollection to understand. My heart was a tightly wound ball of twine without knowing why it was so intricately coiled that way. My nervous system was paralyzed, grief stricken and chained by emotions for which I had no tools to detangle.

But I was petrified with fear of leaving the land. She was my only hope. She was the link to the spiritual world which had promised to be the answer—the end game. With a mix of naïveté and a desperate longing for wholeness, I handed over my control, my submission, and my trust to her willingly. What had started with Sai Baba, from one "master" to the next, I exchanged my trust from one to the other. In doing so, I descended into greater darkness than I had ever known.

I perceived the land as a place I could hide in, and hide I did—trussed by aloneness, wrapped tightly in the illusion of safety. In my trailer, no one could see my glaring faults, failings which consistently engulfed my senses. Caught in a relentless wheel of survival, I moved through each day burdened by fear, guilt, and shame; chained to deceptive voices that reinforced a reality I could no longer trust. It was maddening—not the kind that makes you scream, but the kind that makes you disappear. The kind that prefers silence and solitude, because the shame, the disappointment, and the aching loneliness are too heavy to carry in front of anyone else.

Without some sort of intervention, I feared I'd never emerge. Stilled as a caterpillar, unable to transform into a chrysalis. Years of caterpillar indigestion had led me to the truth—that I was critically sick from seeking love in all the wrong places. Was there no light which could deliver me from its clutches? Without speaking it aloud to another living soul, never before had I become so desperate for love.

THIRTEEN

Stunned!

In late November of 2000, Lilith called us into the main house. Zev, Charlotte, Ray and I all sat on the living room couches—an area I had not been invited to for nearly three years. Within me a giddiness surfaced because I was finally in the house again, hanging out with the crew. *I am not alone today.*

Then I noticed Lilith. I could tell by her unwavering gaze she intended our meeting to be brief. Just as I had perceived, she got right to the point, "Well, I gathered you all here today to give you something—an early Christmas gift. Here. I bought one for each of you."

I was absolutely stunned when she handed us large leather-bound Bibles—enormous three-inch-thick texts. I could not believe it! *What!? What is going on here?* I was given my gargantuan volume enveloped in forest-green binding. Even with its small lettering appropriate for my young eyes, it sat with a major weight on my lap. I glanced quickly to see if she had signed the front of it—*Yes, there is a short scribble.* I would look at her inscription later, but now I was riveted to hear her explanation. I had many aversions to this book, and to Christianity in general. Trying hard to not make an audible gasp or widen my eyes, I was thrown. My mind swam with questions. Perhaps she wanted to reference "like truths" she had been feeding us these past several years? Was she caving to Christianity as the truth or desiring that we find reference to her inside the Bible? *How is this possible?*

Lilith's eyes drifted to the floor, like she had nothing more to give us. This surprised me all the more! I was thunderstruck—*uh . . . I just spent months transcribing every taped thing you have ever said to us about love, integrity, peace, joy, and kindness. And what about the mission? What about plans for the retreat center and how we are to be a hub of spiritual transformation?* And what of the power of crystals, portals, energy vortices, elevating the planet's consciousness, and transcendental psychology? After absorbing teachings drawn from Tibetan Buddhism, Taoism and Middle Eastern philosophies—why this sudden shift into traditional religion? Now she's leading us to the *Christian Bible??* Devoid of her usual confidence, Lilith offered only a few cryptic words.

"This is the next step for us."

That was it. No elaboration, no context. After years of spiritual teaching and channeling the masters, this abrupt pivot left me reeling.

Handing us massive texts with meager explanation, she gave us our first reading assignment. Though I resisted this book, which seemingly opposed all we had learned, I decided maybe she had a different purpose I hadn't considered.

I headed for my trailer to read the entire book of John, our first task. On the way, I thought, *Did Zev influence this?* He had been studying emergency preparedness framed by Christian end times prophecies connected to world events, found in the "Cutting Edge" series. He had shared these with Lilith and she in turn shared with us. We have been readying ourselves for some kind of world emergency, framed in relation to the mission. *Maybe this all led them to want us to read the Bible?*

When I arrived home, I sat down to look at Lilith's written words on the first page. My eyebrows lifted as I read her inscription, "My prayer is that you would find the answers you seek. With love, Lilith." *The answers? Why would she say this?* Frustrated, I closed the book. Immediately all my aversions to this Bible flooded my mind, even though it was dressed in genuine leather and smelled nice.

A high school scene came to mind when I attended a Baptist church with my friend. The pastor ranted in a fire-and-brimstone manner against gay people, accusing the congregation of secret sins. My college friendships with the LGB community deepened my revulsion.

Christianity felt judgmental—unaccepting of those I cared for. My life cried out against its harshness.

I stood up from the desk and nervously tidied up the room for several minutes, bothered by more reasons I avoided Christianity. The Bible's talk of wrath, sin, and heaven-or-hell boundaries clashed with my New Age freedom, where multiple lifetimes let me evolve my own path. One "Christian" life meant I was really stuck with myself. And I was nowhere near transcending into some blissful state of nirvana or becoming one with the universe. Christianity seemed close-minded and old, its followers joyless compared to the mystery I craved. I liked defining my own path—wherever my heart led me. *I don't want to yield my discovered way to one deity!*

Still moving about in the trailer, I experienced a major philosophical crisis. This would be a departure from years I had invested in my spiritual growth. *And where is Lilith in all of this?* Feminism from my upbringing churned too. *Why point us to a male-centered religion? Just why are we reading this?*

Was I judging it unfairly? Perhaps. But I knew right and wrong were defined in these pages and my childhood belittlement made me sensitive to anything unkind. Why is there talk of mercy when it's all about sin and judgment? How is that loving? Certainly, God is limitless and the way to find God limitless, but the Bible touts only one way.

I sat back down, arms folded, staring at this Bible. I was stubborn to even open it up! It opposed every spiritual vantage point I had reached and seemed a radical step backwards, negating all my earlier efforts. I thought, *We on the land know better, right? We are on a more enlightened path than others. Maybe the Christians have it wrong, and Lilith wants us to see that?* The volleying in my head was dizzying.

Yet, she had gifted us this book which stirred a faint curiosity. *Could it hold answers beyond my fears?* A few moments passed when I unfolded my arms and shifted in my seat.

Placing my hands on this book, I opened it slightly, pausing to feel the delicate gold-edged sheets between my fingers. It evoked a memory years ago when I touched pages from a Bible my father had given me for my first communion. After a deep sigh, I began to incline to her inscribed words. *We were only told to read one chapter.*

I decided there might be possibilities in these pages. *There are so many words. Maybe something here might help me?* Really, I was desperate for an inner change. Billions of people rely on this book. Apart from Old Testament excerpts during college, I had never read any of it. *What will I find here?* I really had no idea. The mystery of its pages intrigued me.

As much as I didn't want to admit it, the fact that I was given an actual book I could follow made me feel secure. My New Age leader had just told us, "This Bible is the next step in our evolution." If I accepted that completely, I now had tangible spiritual instructions. This huge study Bible seemed concrete and not abstract like Lilith's instruction was for me. Maybe I could "get this" and once for all be transformed. Finally resigned within myself, I opened it up.

BLURRED BRILLIANCE

Tucking myself into my chair beneath the desk, I found the book of John. "In the beginning" were the first words I saw. Initially, I tuned out from this statement, deciding I would not just accept everything willy-nilly. I glossed over a personification of "the Word" that made no sense to me, "And the Word was made flesh." Who was the Word? Moving along in the passage, I read about "the children of God." My curiosity was piqued. I thought to myself, *I am probably already considered a child of God.* But then, it seemed to refer to a group who knew something which I was not entirely clear about. I read all of Jesus' words written in red, and I was riveted by how he expressed love. I recognized scripture verses Sai Baba had claimed were his own, however, clearly, they were first written here in the Bible!

As I read it for the first time, I didn't understand what I was reading. I thought, *Is there a code? Is this encoded as a riddle?* Though

I couldn't grasp it fully, there was something undeniably different about these texts.

They stirred and awakened sensations which were usually numb inside me. I didn't know what it was, but I was stimulated by how reading these words made me feel. They seemed to order the anxious unrest inside me into a hush of rare stillness. I sensed every word had meaning and was affecting me.

Though I couldn't articulate it, reading this book made me feel good—it made me feel hope. Truly hope was new to me. Hope was a feeling I had never known before.

There was something about these words which were pure and kind. Reading them had an alleviating effect upon *all of me*. For some reason, unlike anything else before, reading the Bible stilled every one of my voices. Contrary to their nature and purpose, they agreed to harmoniously shut up—as if their usual cacophony was lulled by a resounding, consoling bell produced by merely considering these words.

I began to sense an intoxicating warmth, like a soothing oil pouring over my chaffed, harsh interior. I could not get enough of how this was affecting me. Inside I cried, *I want more!* It didn't seem to matter that perhaps my soul alone comprehended what I couldn't consciously follow. It was like I heard a muted clip of heavenly sound I had to urgently tune myself to. As if through a veil I saw a blurred vision of brilliance that I had to keep pursuing.

Before I knew it, three hours had passed, and I fell asleep. For the next six days, when I wasn't traveling for work, I came home anticipating returning to the pages of John. Absorbing this new language imparted to me positive feelings, shrouding me with an emerging courage. Filled with wonder, the relaxation and clarity that covered me was like drawing near to an endless expanse of sky. I didn't want this awareness to end. I wanted to keep coming back to that feeling—so I kept reading.

Some of Jesus' words kept echoing in my mind, especially when

He said that God seeks those who worship Him in spirit and in truth. Since God is spirit, that's the only way to truly worship Him. My ears were open. More than anything, I had always longed to know the truth—the real nature of God.

Jesus also talked about being the light of the world, and that anyone who follows him won't walk in darkness because those who believe him have light and life. Contrasts were also made about light and darkness which attracted me. I had learned so much about being a person "filled with light" in the New Age, but I never experienced what this should feel like. The darkness mentioned in the Bible was talking about a spiritual darkness—the darkness of deception. Immediately I wondered whether I knew the light or in fact if I was one living in spiritual darkness? *No! I can't think that!* I hushed the thought which crept into my mind.

John also contrasted the unveiling of reality—the way things really are, versus the darkness in the world. Again, I wondered, which camp am I living in? I was not happy, and I was honest enough to admit this to myself. Though afraid to name it, depression had crept into my innards like a tightly bound reinforced grip. I longed to be a child of God, and I started wondering if I knew what that meant. I certainly intended to find out. As soon as I desired to know the answer, I heard a whisper of hope calm my incredible impatience, witnessing to me, "Yes, in time you will have your answer."

WHAT DID SHE KNOW?

One week after we received Bibles, we were called into the main house again. This time I was not interested to linger with the gang as I had been so keen to do before, instead I was enjoying my reading time alone. Once dismissed, I walked with quick-footed pace back to my single wide trailer, eager to begin reading our new assignment—the book of Romans.

As Dragoon winds beat upon the metal exterior of my abode, they shook interior walls with a faint rattling vibrato. While this background noise soothed me, I located where this little book was within the Bible. Straightaway, I digested more of these words which had begun to uplift me. The first four chapters of Romans seemed to lay a foundation. It was a wonderful mystery of God, and why Jesus came to the earth—God incarnate as man. Riveted by the story, still I had trouble following what I was reading. Again, in Romans, I read mention of "the children of God," and the phrase kept tugging at me. Then I remembered how it stirred a memory of someone I knew—Sara.

My interactions with Sara had been affecting me deeply. I was drawn to her sincere, gentle manner, swathed with a depth of kindness I could not comprehend. When I drew her blood weekly for a terminal cancer diagnosis and asked how she was doing, she would answer, "I am at peace, ready to go whenever God wills." Her words were breathy, with a weakness that only allowed three words per utterance, and soon our conversation exhausted her. Her appearance went beyond her frail frame and pale skin; there was an alluring beauty proceeding from her. She emanated a brilliant warmth which did not match her haggard presentation, and I couldn't figure it out.

It's hard to take your eyes off of someone who is terminally ill, especially when they are comfortable stripping away all pretenses. They know their time is short, and even if those surrounding them don't want to admit it, they are real about it. I remember in my pea brain thinking I could encourage her in her suffering. One day, she saw my pictures of the "divine mother," and as I talked about God with a strange application to Christianity, she looked right at me with her typical humble gaze. With calm resolve she told me, "I look to God's son. God's son Jesus is the mediator between God and us." I said back to her, "But why would I go to his son if I can just go to God?" Always appreciating efficiency, I found it ridiculous I couldn't just skip a step and go straight to God, like I thought I had already achieved or was supposed to by now. Sara turned to face me. Imparting a peace that rested warmly upon her eyes, she smiled at me with genuine concern. Without saying another word which would have tired her, she slowly turned to walk away.

She knows something. What does she know? She is dying—why do I want to know what she knows? Her peace stung my pride, exposing the emptiness of the supposed "light filled" life we were striving for with Lilith's guidance. She was content to die whenever God "called her." She spoke assuredly what she knew of God in the midst of her suffering with much greater conviction than I was able to express from lessons of my young and "spiritually elevated" path.

WIND OF HOPE

As my experience with Sara surfaced into my thoughts at home, I wanted to talk with her, especially about this. She knew she was a child of God; she was so confident she belonged to God. Now more than ever, I wanted the guarantee she had. Having been abandoned by many figures in my life, I needed this assurance I had seen in Sara and been reading about in Romans!

Then, something entirely different happened while I read Romans chapter five, six, seven and eight. The whisper of hope I had sensed while reading John now swelled into a tangible, gentle wind that stirred effortlessly through my trailer. I looked around to see if something had entered the room. I felt a palpable spiritual existence peering in as I read—as if the personification of *Hope* itself had come to visit me. In that moment, its presence felt like it was even resting upon me as an eternal weight. Instantaneously, I was aware this existence knew me, and knew what this moment must have been for me. It was then I experienced a wonderful sensation—as though scales which had previously blocked what I could comprehend fell gently from my eyes.

There is no other way to describe this moment in time for me.

A spiritual veil had been lifted from the way I saw *everything*. Whatever I could not understand before became relatable and clear.

I sat there astounded at the simplicity of it all. I thought to myself, *Can it really be that easy? This can't be all there is to this!*

I had been working so hard just to "get it" on the land, with the triad, with the masters, with Lilith's teachings, even with Sai Baba for two months in India. Every other system of belief involved some kind of work to attain enlightenment and here Jesus purported to be *the* truth, going as far as to say that no one could even get to the Father except through Him. There was no giant mystery—no great riddle to solve. I was not reading a series of rules about how to be a Christian. In fact, I had not even read the word "Christianity" or "Christian" in the Bible at all.

It was just about Jesus—his healings, miracles and his individual, loving attention towards all people. It was Jesus' words that entirely captivated my attention. He called himself a door through which we could be saved and find pasture. This was a picture with words I could grasp. He lovingly called his followers sheep who would hear the shepherd's voice and follow him. He said he would be willing to give up his life for his sheep and even promised to give them everlasting life!

Could it really be so straightforward to meet with God—to be close to God? I remembered learning about the trinity from my Catholic beginnings. The Father, Son and Holy Spirit are all God just like a body, soul and spirit is all part of a human being. I started to marvel, *Did God become a man just like us in the form of Jesus—the Son of God?* Did Jesus really restore us to the Father? Did he take on himself the consequence for all the sucky ways I ever acted and for all my imperfections, for all my selfish, judgmental thoughts—for every lie I told—for every hateful word I said while angry? Did he really promise to cleanse me and make me a new creation? It seemed too simple to be true. But it sounded like a major transformation—something I desperately desired.

When I read what Jesus wrote that man must be "born again," the verse made me flinch a bit because the term "born again Christian" had such a negative connotation for me, probably from movies which depicted them as stuck up and judgmental. Then I read about what it might actually mean with the veil that had been lifted from me—with my newfound understanding. Being born again meant a second breath from God. I was already born and created by God—why did I need a second birth from God? Falling into an old mode of needing to figure out a mystery, I wondered, *Is there something I need to perceive here? What work do I need to do to be worthy?*

I had come to the end of myself—exhausted from trying everything, only to be met with emptiness and deep sadness. But then, like tiny flashbulbs going off in my mind, the dots began to connect. I saw what was required of me. It had been one week of reading this Bible, and something pierced through. I had to face the truth—*I don't know the light. I am living in spiritual darkness!* Though I had spent years chasing what looked like spiritual growth, it had always felt dim. I wore a mask of light, pretending I was moving toward wholeness or enlightenment, but deep down, I was sinking further into a psychological pit. Even among so-called "elite" spiritual circles, I was unraveling. Now, sitting in raw honesty, I asked myself, *What do I really have to lose?*

Yes, I was deeply flawed, I had always known that. But could it really be that those flaws, those sins, were what kept me from God all along? And now, was it truly possible that the way across—the healing, the cleansing—was not something I had to earn or achieve, but something only He could give me? I just needed to acknowledge that I'm imperfect—that I can't get to God without Him? I can't reach Him on my own, not even in some unique way that I prefer. Just ask for forgiveness from God? That is all? Because Jesus already paid the price for my sin which was death. Either I die in my sins, or I receive Him and get to live with Him for eternity. *Ok, I understand this.*

But could this be real?

There was no one to explain any of these connections to me. They became clear after reading the same theme in verses from the book of John and Romans. When I looked at cross-referenced passages in my study Bible, the whole book was congruent, supported from books in the beginning of the Bible I hadn't read yet. I was not used to people or ideas which did not at some point contradict themselves, but thus far, I saw none in the Bible. Other verses instead added to a layered harmonious story. I considered what it all might mean for me.

ASSURANCE

The day I first read Romans, I couldn't stop. I also reread verses in John's gospel until nightfall when it was time for bed. I found scripture saying the results are assured—that his word is true, that I will belong to God, and I will know that I am his. Then I can be with God forever? I felt a growing excitement. There were many verses saying this transaction would be complete; once I belong to him, he will never forsake me. What comfort to my soul that he would never let me go, never desert me as others had done to me! And I took Jesus' words to heart that once I am his, no one can snatch me out of his hand. I was very relieved by this! No ill-intentioned family member or jealous person could ever take me away from closeness I had with God. The security of love and to never be abandoned had not ever before been promised to me in life.

Encouraged that the transformation was not dependent on me, but only upon God, I realized, *I can't mess this up! I can't "not get this" or undo it.* I just need to ask Him and acknowledge that the Father sent Jesus for me personally. He knew I would perpetually fall short of the glory of God. When I receive this second birth from God, I will become a child of God. I will receive a cleansing within and have a more intimate closeness with my creator. Finally, I absorbed what this all meant.

Engrossed in scripture from the book of Romans, I reread the eye-opening passages just to confirm what I thought I understood. As I did, once again that pure and loving existence began to pervade my trailer. Its presence was starkly different from heavy spiritual sensations I had felt before in my life, the kind that used to make me feel short of breath. This presence was pure, light, and seemed to blow gently around my whole body—filling me with an awareness of eternity and an arresting of love. My eyes were wide open, my jaw relaxed open in amazement. Could it really be this simple? Is this really it? The truth of the words resonated within me and the spiritual manifestation I felt in my trailer seemed to witness this, that it was the truth. This caring spirit in attendance rested on me like a mystery.

It took time to contend with these words of the Bible steeped deeply in my being. For one month following, my mind remained in wonder—my mouth figuratively gaped open in disbelief and awe. I grappled with the gravity of it all, still I felt too "dark and complicated" to receive such a sacred gift of salvation. While I digested how sobering this all was, the pride of my futile search kept me from the simplicity of what was requested, and pieces of me puffed up with resistance.

But I knew what was before me now, a concrete answer to true transformation. Yes, I had been desperate to be free from emotional-mental duress, but my heart's overall cry was to know God's love. If the positive feelings and mental calmness I experienced while simply reading the Bible was any indication of a greater burst of God's love I would find through salvation, I was willing to sell everything I had for it! My initial hesitation was because I was afraid to admit I had been wrong. But my fear of missing out on the opportunity to know God's love, to live with Him and receive His healing was immeasurably greater than my arrogant conceit.

THE ENCOUNTER

One night in January 2001, after weeks of soaking in the words of the Bible, I watched a TV program with a preacher who led viewers in prayer for their own salvation. This completely struck me.

When the preacher finished, I turned off the TV. My body and mind became intensely focused on my desire for transformation—for salvation. It has been said that truth must enter the soul, penetrate it and saturate it, or else it is of no value. Certainly, after weeks of marinating within me, this truth had become extremely valuable to me.

A passion had escalated in me to belong to God and for God to make me whole. After all my internal wrestling about Christianity and the Bible, it was the only flame of fervor which remained. There was no more opinion, preference, embarrassment, insecurity or fundamental argument which could hold a candle to my soul's desire to find God. If there were music within me, it had intensified into a crescendo of stringed instruments which played until sustained on an ardent note of tension. I knew the music strained within me would fail to resolve until I had opened the door of my heart that the Father Himself had been knocking upon.

Within a matter of minutes in my little trailer, I became acutely aware of God's holiness flooding my senses, and my own fearful respect and reverent awe in response to Him. He came to meet me. God Himself manifested to me. In an instant, He shut off the noisy heckling I heard outside and inside of me and in that sacred stillness, time stood still. It was just Him and me. I was immediately aware that He knew who I was. He knew all of my struggles, but at the same time He was unfamiliar to me. He *knew* me, but although I had an innate understanding of Him, I didn't *know* Him.

In this sliver of eternity, there was a separation between us, and I was afraid of Him—not afraid He would hurt me—but afraid I would miss this chance to be with Him. The authority of His presence was overwhelming. I pinched my own skin to shake myself—*Do not dissociate from this moment! Don't mess around, this is what you have been waiting for.* God the Father was leaning into my trailer—here, now. In the middle of the desert, in the middle of *nowhere*, the living God had come to personally meet with me. He spoke to me deeply, in a way that only God can be heard and perceived by the human soul—

"Are you serious about Me? You have been searching for Me

all your life. You've been looking everywhere. Philosophies, rituals, tarot, crystals, teachings. Where are they all now? I AM here now. This is who I AM. I AM not a riddle to be solved. I AM not a mystery to be comprehended. I AM a reality to be received, and I AM not to be taken lightly. I AM a Holy God, and My eyes are upon you. I see you. Now, what is your decision? Will you come to Me with all of your heart?"

The weight of His presence and words wholly arrested me. In response, I got down on my knees and spoke aloud a version of the prayer the television preacher helped viewers to speak. My whole body trembled as I spoke with a quivering voice, "Father, I have sinned and fallen short of your glory. Forgive me God. I receive your free gift of salvation through Jesus who died in my place on that cross. Please turn my life around, my life is in Your hands now. You are my Lord."

I hoped God could see past any uncomfortable smiling that was on my face. His presence cut to the sincerest part of me, even though pieces of me felt ridiculous as there were still hundreds of childhood voices within that bellowed for my attention. But He silenced every phantom thought and contrary voice surrounding and gripping me from within so that, devoid of distraction, I could have an honest encounter with Him. And so, the miraculous exchange of His salvation occurred.

I remembered reading that no one comes to Jesus unless the Father draws them. And I knew that was what had happened to me. The Father made Himself known to me, revealing the vast chasm between us that only Jesus could bridge. For many, salvation is tender. For me, it came with trembling, as I stood in the fear and holiness of God, painfully aware of my pride. I had spent years striving to perfect myself, chasing divinity through effort and secret knowledge. But all it produced was a false sense of superiority, not true spirituality. Then, in the quiet, I sensed God answering my heart—"It's not about you uncovering mysteries or working your way to Me. It's about Me letting Myself be found by you. This is My work—not yours."

SHUDDERING

It all began to dawn on me. If there is a creator that is infinite and all powerful and I am His creation, how dare I think that I can become divine? I had been trying to attain this, to attain divinity. But this was way more than divinity. This was *holiness*. Holiness is mind-blowing. It's not necessarily goodness. Holiness contains goodness, but holiness is being set-apart.

In those moments with God, I realized His holiness as He revealed Himself to me. I comprehended that God is set apart, perfect in truth and righteousness, entirely different from me. I am His created, given free will to choose whether to accept His true nature, to believe in the name of the one true God.

He made Himself known to me, and I understood with absolute stupefied awareness that there is no virtue I could have ever unlocked within myself—nor could I have ever attained to the heights of His holiness by my own created standard. In His presence, all my spiritual striving fell away. I saw how small my efforts were, and how great His love was. And when He made me aware of Himself, the fearful reverence I felt for Him turned into a fear that I would miss the opportunity to be with Him forever—just because He wasn't fitting my expectations or understanding.

Awestruck for the following days, I returned to that moment again and again. *Wow. He is a Holy, Awesome God! And He just restored me to Himself!* His offer of salvation is made through His Son. His free gift towards me was expensive—the life, death and resurrection of Jesus Christ. There was no other way for me to get to Him, just like I had read there is no other name under heaven by which I could be saved. And now it was clear to me that it was the only way that would ever be acceptable to God. I am not a little god who gets to decide whatever path I want to get to God—*He alone is God!* None of my arguments or justifications can stand against Him.

I never knew until that night how great the chasm was between us. Intimately, He came near to me in my trailer just so I knew how to be with Him forever. Answering the call of my soul to know the truth about Him, He also revealed the way to get to Him. This was not a long transaction, it all occurred within minutes. *How can this be?*

In the nights that followed, still with audible breaths of wonder, I would shudder at the fear I had of Him that night. But the weight of His glory also reminded me of the mercy and security I now had in Him as my Heavenly Father. I quickly learned to prize the Sovereignty of God that newly blazed in my chest. He promised to never leave me or forsake me; He would never let me go. There was great consolation in knowing who He really is, and His power to protect me, watch over me—to lead me.

With my first new breath as a believer in Christ, without yet having the words, I understood from the psalms, "Your rod and your staff, they comfort me." For someone who had never experienced safety before, nor been shown the boundaries of loving discipline, this was a great new kind of love and comfort my soul needed. The internal voices of "children" who normally created havoc within me—like a classroom of pediatric screamers, felt calmed, reassured and ordered by the margins of holiness that God commanded in that moment.

FOURTEEN

Spun in Silk, Set in Truth

In that sacred encounter, God revealed Himself in a way I had never experienced—pure, steady and deeply real. Connecting with Him was the most authentic moment of my life.

Having been consecrated by God's powerful presence, my trailer became the place I could begin my transformation. Now I was ready to form my chrysalis, firmly attached by a newfound love from Christ. Secured by this assurance, a silk web was spun all around me, and my caterpillar body slowly became undone and unrecognizable. I was a soul in suspension, waiting for God to transform me. Stillness overtook me as I contemplated this newly discovered truth.

After I received salvation in early 2001, I started to understand who God really is and it challenged everything I had once believed. My New Age spirituality was the opposite of what I was now discovering in the Bible. As truth unfolded, I had to reexamine beliefs I had been clinging to, and over the next year, I made deductions on my own. The first realization was undeniable. God is very real, He is who He is. And just as He did that night in my trailer, He transcends all space and time.

My assumptions about Him had been limited. I thought Christians had a rigid, boxed-in view of God, but it was my view that was narrow. I had imagined God as an impersonal essence or force, but He is very personal, genuine and even scary—not in a way that made me afraid. It was a reverent fear, a humbling respect, knowing I was in the presence of the Creator of all life. This wasn't the universe whispering back—it was the One who made the universe, the galaxies, and every intricate detail of creation. The universe itself is contained *within Him*.

When I used to refer to God as "the universe," it was easy to assign Him whatever traits or values suited me. But now I knew He was an actual being with a rich, multifaceted nature. He had come close and spoken to the depths of my heart. I read in the Bible that because He is so holy, no one can see God face to face and live, yet He introduced Himself to me in a way that was undeniably real. The same God I had been reading about had prepared me for that moment. Somehow, He even used our New Age leader to hand us Bibles—an incredible plot twist! From that first meeting, I learned that when the Father draws someone to the truth, nothing can stop Him—not even Lilith, who had her own plans to steer us elsewhere.

For months afterward, I was amazed how personally God engaged with me, how deeply He cared. He met me when I was brutally alone, in the middle of nowhere, with a powerful, gentle kindness that reached every part of me, body, mind, and soul. What I once hoped the universe might be doing—listening, watching, protecting me—was no longer just a hope. It was a certainty. God met me at my lowest. He became my Savior, rescuing me from a spiritual desert. This shattered everything I had believed in the New Age—that God was distant, detached, and only accessible to the worthy. The true Almighty God knew I could never make myself worthy, and He accepted me anyway.

Around this time, I read a verse that said God is not like man, He doesn't lie. That struck me. Unlike people, He isn't bound by facades or the need to please. He alone could see the truth of my heart. It was more than I had ever imagined of God. My heart felt free, and my mind filled with wonder, and this was only the beginning.

FINDING THE PEARL

While doing everyday life, surrendered in my newly woven chrysalis, I spent time thinking how He had changed everything for me. Contrary to the U2 song, "I still haven't found what I'm looking for," in receiving His salvation, I found *all I had been searching for*. I had been straining toward spirituality, trying to fill an aching emptiness. But amid all my seeking, He came for me. He sought me out! My mind was blown. That first encounter—intimate and terrifying, left no room for delay. I knew that if I hadn't repented, if I had clung to pride and continued climbing my paper ladders of self-effort, I would have missed the chance to be with Him forever. He came unmistakably near, and I knew it was now or never.

His presence and voice had overwhelmed me, yet I was captivated and surrendered to who He was. I thought, *I'll do anything just to stay near Him.* When heaven's King Himself visits you, nothing else satisfies, no matter the cost. Though I couldn't see Him, I felt his righteousness and perfection face to face. His presence, like a sublime fragrance from another realm, left me longing for more.

In the place of profound loneliness and brokenness, God met me. Right when I was tender beyond belief, He fiercely loved me, and it was absolutely amazing! He became my everything, the greatest gift I had ever received.

No one had ever cared for me like He had. In the middle of nowhere, the story of Christ's love became my own. He gave up everything—even His life—just to dwell in my heart. I read in John's gospel that the greatest love is shown when someone lays down their life for a friend, and that's exactly what He did for me. Since that moment, His peace and love have lived in me. I read a verse saying if you seek God with all your heart, you will find Him. And I did. Just when I was desperate for even a sliver of hope, He revealed His love and filled every void. He was my pearl of great price, and when I was ready, He let Himself be found.

HEALING WATERS

Throughout 2001, it was just me and God, my closest companion. In that sacred solitude, He filled my love tank and began healing the deep well of grief within me. I knew He was with me, lifting me out of the miry clay, setting my feet on solid ground, and clothing me with His righteousness. The world had left me sick with complicated confusion, but God promised to cleanse me from within and love me without end. In those early days of knowing Him, it felt like I was soaking in warm healing springs prepared just for me. God began washing away old narratives and the emotional chains I had carried for so long. Knowing I had much to be cleansed from, I kept returning to His Word, letting it renew me.

I was in awe that He wanted to dwell within me, that I was His child. Still, it took time to believe He truly wanted to stay with me. But I clung to the promise in scripture that He would complete the work He began in me. Slowly, I began to trust that His love wasn't going anywhere.

As He continued to free me from the mental wilderness I had built, I felt lighter. I began to believe the darkness would eventually fade. Scripture says that when Jesus sets someone free, that freedom is complete. Though it would take years to fully emerge from the chrysalis of healing, I was already resting in His care. Only the One who made my heart and mind could gently unravel and restore them. And in the meantime, His Spirit remained with me—quiet, steady, and faithful.

BEAUTY OF LIFE

Embraced by my new certainty, it took months from the time I was saved for my spiritual eyes to fully open. Like waking from a long slumber, I gradually became aware of the world around me. But once I did, all my senses felt enlivened by His presence and forgiveness. The life and truth I read about in the gospels was now living in me. I never felt more alive! Colors seemed brighter, birdsong sweeter, and even my breath felt infused with warmth of kindness. I began to see beauty everywhere—in the shifting light of trees and grasses, in dancing tumbleweeds, in the grandeur of distant peaks. Even simple drives at sunrise or under dusk-colored skies stirred a deep awareness of His glory.

In the evenings, I would lounge on my fold-out chaise to watch the sky transform into a living painting. Arizona sunsets never disappoint, each one a vivid display of color and imagination. In those quiet moments, I felt close to the Great Artist, struck by the thought that I was made in His image, and that He had given me a creative spirit, too. As I reflected on our growing relationship, I could sense His nearness. Breathing in His solace, I felt overwhelmed once again by the beauty of who He is. I thought about how Jesus called Himself the way, the truth, and the life, and how He came to offer us life in abundance—that's exactly what I was beginning to experience.

FERVENCY

I learned from scripture that God promises to give us a sound mind, and I started to get a glimpse what that felt like. It was a sense of order that quieted the chaos inside me. Tucked away in my trailer, in the middle of nowhere, I found sanctuary in the stillness. The only sound was the wind tapping against the walls. I would read the Bible for hours, soaking in words that cut through confusion I had lived with for so long. More than anything, I wanted to feel mentally whole—to escape the edge of madness I had narrowly survived.

I began writing my favorite verses on index cards and taping them to the wall above my bed. Before long, the entire space was covered. Each morning and evening, I would read them. Often, tears would come, not just from sorrow, but from the comfort of knowing I wasn't alone. For the first time in years, I was feeling my emotions fully; my tendency to numb myself became less frequent. Even in loneliness, I sensed His presence beside me as a compassionate witness, gently healing what had long been broken. I had read that the Holy Spirit is called the Comforter, and that's who He became to me.

I knew God had begun healing my mind and emotions, but I also sensed there was a long way to go. I read in the Bible that transformation comes through the renewing of the mind, and I clung to that idea. The more I read the Bible, the more I felt something shifting inside me. These words brought comfort and life, speaking directly to places in me that had felt unreachable. In that season, reading scripture became my refuge—the one thing that brought peace and reminded me that I was being made new.

Overnight, I felt like I couldn't get enough of the stories and wisdom in these pages. I learned that Zev had previously studied the Bible extensively and I asked him, "What else should I read?" He suggested the other gospels—Matthew, Mark, and Luke as well as 1 John and the Psalms, especially Psalms 23, 51, 91, and 139. Reading these grounded me within myself and made me feel stronger in my mental constitution. Using calligraphy and watercolors for the first time in years, I illustrated these psalms so I could absorb them more deeply. My rendering of Psalm 51 still hangs in my living room, a reminder of that early season of faith. Zev encouraged me to read the Bible like a novel from Genesis onward. "You'll love it!" he said. He was right. I delighted in the unfolding mystery I had never seen before.

EVAPORATING OPPOSITIONS

As the truth grounded me more, all of my objections seemed to evaporate in light of my divine encounter with God. So much of what I thought Christianity represented or even what I thought Christians believed, turned out to be wrong. And my faith didn't begin in a church or through someone else's guidance, it began with God Himself.

For years, I had tried to do things which I was told would please the universe or earn good karma like volunteering to help those in need. But then I read that good deeds don't play a role in salvation. They hold no weight before God. What makes a person right with Him is accepting the gift of salvation through Jesus. That realization radically shifted my understanding and confirmed what God had spoken to me that first night. It was never about unlocking divinity within myself—it was about God revealing Himself when I was ready to receive Him.

All my so-called spiritual accomplishments suddenly felt hollow. I had felt proud and enlightened when I stumbled upon "new" discoveries or personal breakthroughs. But now I saw that eternal life wasn't something to attain—it was something freely given. And if it's a gift, then bragging about it makes no sense. I hadn't earned any special status or spiritual rank. It was all a supernatural work of His. All I did was open the door to His patient, persistent knock.

Another truth became clear. Truth wasn't relative—it was absolute. There was no more room for "my truth" or "your truth." There was only God's truth. My opinions about morality, how God should operate, or how I thought I could reach Him no longer held weight. When I encountered the Creator of the universe, I had no arguments left. God didn't conform to my preferences. He simply was who He was. I remembered reading that when God revealed His name to Moses, He said, "I AM WHO I AM." That truth now lived in me.

The idea of "finding my inner truth" had never made sense to me anyway. With so many conflicting voices inside, I couldn't trust a single one to guide me. But God, unlike my voices, was eternal, sovereign, and far more loving than I had ever imagined. He wasn't just a projection of my hopes—He was so much better! And while I still respected that people have different perspectives, I came to see that when it comes to God, truth isn't subjective. He is real, and He is who He says He is.

FRAIL STRENGTH

Up until this point, I didn't know many Christians, nor did I belong to a church community. But at my workplace, I began to recognize Christian friends who showed me kindness even before I came to Jesus. Once I gave my life to Him, I felt a sincere connection with them. These were my nurse friend Dawn, my front office friend Belinda, and of course, Sara—she was still alive.

When I saw her, I was overcome with elation to share that I had asked Jesus into my heart, that I had made Him my Lord. Sara's usual frailty was invigorated as she embraced me and called us sisters in Christ. In the weeks that followed, during her regular blood draws, she would linger just to talk with me, encouraging me in my walk with Christ.

I was deeply honored to know her during her final days. That's when I learned more about her story and why her gentle, radiant presence seemed so angelic. She chose early in life not to marry, instead devoting herself entirely to God. He had been her closest companion all her days.

One day, I found out that Sara had been admitted to the hospital for chemotherapy. I visited her room and sat beside her, holding her hand as she continued to speak with trust in Jesus. When she became sick, I held back her hair and comforted her. Those tender moments planted a seed in me—a desire to become a nurse.

When Sara passed not long after, her sister called and asked me to pick up something Sara had left for me, one of her treasured Bibles. As her sister handed it to me, she said, "Sara talked about you. You were very special to her!" We both began to cry. Then she asked if I would sing at Sara's funeral. I did, I sang "Amazing Grace" at her burial, honoring the woman whose faith had helped shape my own. I watched Sara's body being lowered into the ground in a cardboard casket she had selected for herself, and I marveled at her fervent love for Christ. Sara's life, along with the kindness of a few others at the hospital, quietly showed me what it meant to follow Jesus.

OLD PARADIGMS EXPOSED

Though my perspective was shifting, I struggled to reconcile these new revelations with the life I had been living. The mission started to feel completely at odds with what I read in the Bible. Truths I now grasped changed how I saw Lilith and the entire focus of our community. Had the mission come to a halt? I wasn't sure. But I began to wonder how everything would change.

By Spring of 2001, our meetings no longer centered on hearing from Lilith, who had grown silent. For all I knew, she was secluded in the house. I never saw her. Having been on the outside for so long, and now focused on God, I was not dripping with neediness to connect with the big house family. I was enjoying my time with God alone in my trailer. And even though I still struggled, I felt a lot better. Filled with hope, I had answers about God which lifted my countenance. My spirit, now communing with His, gave me a thrill that couldn't be overcome by the unrest that still lingered. There was a newness in my soul like morning light. Joy once suppressed was bubbling up from deep within me.

Unlike my experience with Lilith, when I came to Jesus, I didn't need others to validate what I was experiencing—He revealed Himself directly. He confirmed Himself by His own presence. Every cult personality I had followed needed to convince me, "This is the truth and here's the proof." But Jesus didn't need to prove anything—He was the Truth. Both Lilith and Sai Baba had to perform or persuade, offering fleeting "feelings" or illusions of spiritual progress. In the end, all they gave me were scattered drops of so-called energy. But the God of the Bible Himself said to me, "Hello. I AM true, and the proof is, Here I AM."

In the place of mission meetings, Zev began gathering us weekly to teach us biblical concepts. Returning to his faith, his love of scripture, and being the only one who had previous experience studying the Bible, he took us through passages to help us break down what we were learning. He gave us a foundation in the story of God's love as revealed in in the Bible, teaching us about Jesus and the nature of sin, salvation, fallen angels and the origin of Satan (or "the enemy"), just to name a few subjects. Zev was adopted and raised Jewish by Hungarian Jews, and he gave us a valuable understanding of how the old and New Testament was intimately interwoven—how Jesus was the fulfillment of all that had been spoken of since the beginning. I was deeply grateful he was the first to teach us in such a rich and insightful way. I left our weekly meetings desiring that the information would marinate deeply inside me. After furiously taking notes, I would come home and scribe them into a nicer bound book with crisp penmanship. Having been muddled by a cesspool of obscuring New Age concepts, we required this renewal of our minds.

During these meetings, I wasn't sure if Ray, Charlotte or especially Lilith had truly been born again and received the same Spirit of God that I had, but I kept to myself. It wasn't important to me. To be honest, I still questioned whether something really happened to me because of inner noises that remained. Regardless, the lessons were invaluable. My mind was hungry for truth, and I soaked up every word like a sponge.

Since Lilith was not present for these meetings, we were all very curious about where she fit into everything. Zev didn't have an answer. She was always too "busy" or in an emotional slump, and when she did finally lead a meeting or two—which notably avoided any biblical content—I sensed sharp, disapproving stares from her. Zev would later reveal that Lilith did not attend because she was deeply morose and did not say much for weeks.

I became increasingly aware that the "energies" Lilith worked with were not from God. Compared to what I now experienced as a born-again believer in Christ, her so called "impartations" had only ever left me confused or inflated with pride. I read in the Bible that God is not the author of confusion, and the deceptive powers that I once pursued, tied to her influence, weren't just misleading, they were tormenting. They amplified voices already inside me, manipulating my thoughts for years. Because of my identity crisis and fragmented memories, I had been especially vulnerable. These lying impressions would pit the voices against each other, creating chaos in my mind. It was a nightmare. I remember hearing what felt like 500 voices at once, all shouting conflicting things—and that's no exaggeration.

Now that my relationship with God had been restored, I noticed a profound internal shift. The once overwhelming chorus of voices quieted. What used to be five hundred had dwindled to fifty. Though I still needed healing, I could already sense the beginnings of restoration. Remaining voices grew especially quiet when I read the Bible. The Holy Spirit and language of the Bible seemed to bathe them in love, gently soothing their needs, long before I had the tools to address them one by one.

ELEVATING MUSIC

During this time, I also discovered worship music. It stirred my heart, much like reading the Bible did. I even began composing my own simple praise songs. Zev invited me once a week to practice guitar and play worship music in the upper room above the garage. We jammed to a few of his original songs. After years of distance, he felt like a friend again, and connecting with him gave me a sense of community. Though we didn't talk much, music became our shared language, and I treasured this time with him. He had taught me guitar during my first months on the land and even bought me my first six-string from a pawn shop. I still remember his challenge, "You're either going to practice until you get calluses—until your fingers bleed—or you won't ever do it." I respected him because he was so talented and willing to teach me.

Zev needed a singer for worship songs he had written, and I was glad to learn them. One evening, we performed a small concert for Lilith, a rare opportunity to spend time with her. But her response was distant. She managed to make a faint smile, still her face was pale and her expression heavy. She looked unwell.

GODLY SORROW

Although it wasn't required, after receiving salvation, I felt compelled to write out all the ways I had acted selfishly or hurtfully. I was deeply moved by a passage I read in the Psalms about acknowledging one's transgressions and asking God to create a clean heart. It seemed that the more I became aware of my own brokenness, the more space I gave Him to cleanse and restore me. I cried aloud, "Forgive me God! You alone are God!"

After a while, I sensed God wanted me to stop. He didn't want me to keep punishing myself or dissect every failure, He had already forgiven me. He came to set me free, not to watch me spiral in guilt. I remembered reading that if we confess our sins, He is faithful to forgive and cleanse us from all unrighteousness. That meant I didn't need to name every wrong, I could trust that His forgiveness covered it all. Repentance, I realized, lifts the burden of perfection. Over time, I came to believe that His sacrifice was more than enough. I would still stumble, but now I knew I could whisper a prayer, leaving my shame at the foot of the cross and keep going. He didn't save me to make me perfect—only He is perfect. And I still had a long path of healing ahead, especially as I began to understand that many of my past behaviors were survival mechanisms shaped by pain.

Inconsequential

During my first year of reading the Bible, many of my earlier concerns faded into irrelevance. Reincarnation, once a concept I entertained, now felt exhausting and unnecessary. I no longer feared becoming a wasp or a sloth in another life, nor did I dread merging with an impersonal universe. I didn't need a thousand lifetimes to find Jesus; He had already found me. I read a passage in scripture that it is appointed for people to die once and then face judgment. That truth brought immense relief—there was no longer a burden to justify myself before God. Through Jesus, I was already accepted.

When God met me, He tethered my heart to His and gave me a glimpse of who I was always meant to be. There is nothing more freeing than being known, loved, and set free by the One who created me. To someone who struggled with dissociation, this was permission to be whole. I didn't need to transcend my body or become nothing. I wasn't the sum of my thoughts or the pain I had endured. I was who He said I was—created in His image, wonderfully made, and deeply valued.

And the most terrifying idea of hell wasn't fire, it was separation from God. After encountering His love, I couldn't imagine life without His presence. That, to me, would be the true torment. But He promised never to leave me, and that promise became my anchor.

TURNING JUNCTURE

In the summer of 2001, Lilith began to reemerge, almost as if she were embracing the Bible herself. Maybe Zev had influenced her understanding of repentance. Whatever the reason, it felt sudden when she told us, "Get rid of all your idols. Scour your homes, including relics, pictures, writings, crystals, anything tied to New Age beliefs and burn them." What shocked me most was her insistence that all the crystals be removed from the land. These weren't just decorative, they formed the "crystal grids" she once used to channel energy. I thought, *Wow, they're even getting rid of the giant geodes on the altar in the house.*

I didn't ask what this meant for the mission, but I assumed this must be its end. And honestly, I didn't mind. I had found the one true God, and I was finally growing. We were all studying the Bible now, and that was all I cared about, aside from the fact that we were still together.

I spent time searching my trailer for items tied to old spiritual practices—crystals, books on Sai Baba, astrology, occult materials, and spiritual artwork. That evening, I stoked a small bonfire outside encircled by large rocks and watched the flames consume everything I fed it. When only embers remained, I felt lighter. It was a clear, physical declaration of my break from New Age spirituality. Even without Lilith saying so, it was obvious the mission was ending. I couldn't help but wonder, *Does this mean Zev is going to lead us now?*

OUR OWN VERSION

One day in July, Lilith called me on the phone unexpectedly, her voice urgent. "Elizabeth, it's now or never," she said. "It's time to repent and come to God!"

I understood what she was getting at. Even though I believed I had already been saved, the persistent voices in my mind made me question it. So, just to be sure, I reaffirmed my devotion to Jesus that night. Still, I felt annoyed. *Why does she think the decision hasn't already been made?* For the first time, I realized that my relationship with God had nothing to do with her. She didn't have psychic insight about me, and she never did.

Later, God helped me understand that I had received His gift of salvation the first time I confessed my sin, not the forty-fifth. The voices in my mind had cast doubt, each one weighing in on whether I was truly saved. But God knew the moment when He silenced them all to speak directly to my truest self—my free will. And in that moment, I chose Him.

At that time, our community meetings shifted to focus on the Bible. Lilith never addressed the former mission directly, but she began acting as our leader again, seemingly relying on Zev's teachings.

It felt like a strange but innocent version of church as we gathered to study the Bible together. We were all still emerging from a very different worldview, and none of us fully understood what we were stepping into. Our first teaching was about baptism, and soon after, a day was set for us to be baptized at the gazebo in front of the main house.

Before the baptism date, Ray approached me with questions about Jesus. We met near the house, and I did my best to respond to his doubts. He was still uncertain about salvation, but he could see something had changed in me from the way I spoke during our Bible studies. As I shared what God meant to me and how real His presence had become, Ray seemed genuinely surprised. If anyone could recognize a difference in me, it was him. Later that week, he told me he had given his heart to Jesus. It felt incredible to know I had played a small part to lead him there.

On the day of our baptisms, Zev immersed me in a large metal tub. Everyone participated—except Lilith. I found that strange. Was she above baptism? A new discernment began to stir in me, challenging the pedestal I had once placed her on.

One evening, we held a foot washing ceremony that Zev explained beforehand, a humbling act meant to reflect how Jesus served His disciples before His crucifixion. Lilith and Zev made sure Ray and I didn't wash each other's feet, likely to avoid any discomfort. Using prepared tubs of water, we washed the feet of our assigned partner. At other meetings, we were assigned topics to prepare short "sermonettes." I took the assignment seriously, but I wasn't ready to teach, and my delivery was awkward.

It was clear we were trying to create our own version of Christianity. Lilith often claimed we had deeper spiritual discernment than other Christians because of what we had come out of. But the truth is, we hadn't truly let go of our former beliefs, and we certainly didn't have any special spiritual edge because of them. Without repentance her claims only reinforced a sense of pride and a works-based mindset. She wasn't an authority on the God of the Bible, though she tried to position herself as one to maintain influence.

FIRST LOVE

I often think back to that trailer in the middle of nowhere. What began as isolation, spiritual strongholds and emotional torment became the sacred ground of my transformation. I had no idea that in that quiet space, held in God's care, true renewal was beginning. Once He entered my heart, He formed a chrysalis around me—preparing me for the change to come.

I welcomed the solitude, soaking in His Word as if He were teaching me directly. Replacing the oppressive spirit that once surrounded me, His presence became increasingly real with a gentle stirring—like butterflies in my chest. I can still recall the sound of Dragoon winds brushing against the trailer, a backdrop to the divine romance unfolding. Jesus became my first love, the only One who fulfilled every longing of my heart. I had no close relationships, no possessions of value—but I delighted in Him completely.

I began to see myself through the eyes of someone who loved me deeply. And the change was visible, even in my old driver's license photo from a gothic gaze to a face lit with joy. God answered the deepest cry of my heart, and His truth set me free. In one divine exchange—His life for mine—He became everything I had searched for.

FIFTEEN

Leaving the Land

EXPOSING SHADOWS

Zev had a backstory that would prove to be pivotal. Though raised orthodox Jewish, in his youth he was deeply moved by a television program about Jesus and later described feeling the presence of the Holy Spirit while working on a construction site. This experience led him to seek the truth and study the Bible intensely. After years as a Christian, Zev became disillusioned with his church as it collapsed, and then following his divorce and the dissolving of his company, he began to doubt his faith. Disenchanted, he turned to New Age spirituality, which is when he met Lilith. Eventually they married, and he became central to the mission's plans.

When Zev began teaching us scripture with the depth we needed, I had never seen him more alive. He described it as a film lifting from his eyes, restoring his understanding as a both a Jew and a follower of Jesus. His love for scripture returned quickly, and he helped us see how the Bible contrasted with our previous beliefs. At a certain point, even he questioned where the mission, or especially how Lilith fit into the context of the Bible.

In August 2001, when Lilith began joining our foundational Bible discussions, she added her own "biblical insights" blending them with lessons she had taught us before. Because I had not read the entire Bible, I didn't recognize how her interpretations conflicted with the words of Christ, only that they didn't quite fit. I questioned what her true role was, and why we had been convinced of her authority for so long.

It's clear she shaped Christianity to fit her previous teachings, referencing the Bible the way many in the New Age do by using selected passages, distorting the message and denying the fullness of what Christ accomplished. If she hadn't tried to reshape the Bible to fit her teachings, she likely wouldn't have introduced it to us at all. As I tried to reconcile biblical teachings with what Lilith had taught and the new ideas she was now adding—nothing fit together. Reading scripture began to clarify my thinking, and I found myself resisting her opinions more and more.

Even though it was Lilith who gave me the Bible, I doubt she ever imagined what would come of it. Perhaps she thought it would reinforce her influence, but instead, the pedestal she stood on began to crumble. We all received our Bibles in December of 2000. I was saved in January 2001, and after nearly a year of learning the Bible from Zev, he suddenly left the land in November 2001. His abrupt departure shook us all.

The day before he left, I asked Zev if he could help with some questions about scripture. He agreed to meet, and I looked forward to the conversation, not just for answers, but because he was the only person I talked to on the land. I felt a brotherly affection for him, and I valued his guidance as my first Christian leader. But when he sat down in my trailer, I never saw him so uncomfortable. He seemed restless, almost as if he was trying to jump out of his own skin. His eyes, usually honest and confident, now looked deeply troubled.

After I finished asking my questions, he said, "I'm sorry Elizabeth, I know you have questions, but this isn't my role. I am not your . . . your pastor. I . . . I just need to go. I'm sorry." He was burdened by something I couldn't name, and I wondered what was really going on. It felt like he was saying goodbye to his role as our teacher. The next day he was gone. He had left in the night.

Zev told me later why he left so abruptly. Hours before we met in the trailer, he became increasingly aware of dark entities operating through Lilith. He had asked her, "Who are you really?" In response,

Lilith's eyes turned black, her face contorted, and she answered with a sinister voice, that was not her own—"Who do you think I am?" With that chilling response, Zev knew—he was not just dealing with deception, but with multiple demons. He said to himself, "I'm out!" and made the decision to flee.

From the time he returned to reading the Bible, it took less than a year for Zev to discern, through the Holy Spirit, that the woman he married was not just spiritually misled but demonized. What we had once believed were "ascended masters" were, in truth, unclean spirits masquerading as light. Though he cared for Lilith as a person, he understood that there could be no fellowship between a follower of Christ and one who is under the influence of fallen angels. Once he saw clearly who she was serving, he was not only disturbed—he was genuinely spooked!

THE UNRAVELING

During the days following Zev's unexpected parting, Ray and I become Lilith's closest confidants, supporting her through this devastating time. Her husband had left her, and we rallied behind her, listening to her process through it all. As a result, we became very protective of Lilith, and to our fault picked up her reasoning that Zev should rightly return to the land as her husband. She also highlighted to Ray that Zev had abandoned him not only as his friend but as a joint business partner in their LLC company, which, as she would press, had outstanding debt. We were left to make sense of Zev's absence and the strange heaviness which lingered.

Within a month of this tender time, another layer of grief settled over us as denial lifted and Lilith tried to make sense of Zev's absence. It seemed to break her. She became contrite—almost needy for our company—which, after years of her distance, felt oddly comforting. I saw a vulnerability in her I'd never witnessed before, as if she'd been unmasked and left delicate. The loss left her reaching for connection, and for the first time, her power over us seemed to waver.

All this time I had longed for a connection with her, but now I found myself needing to be there for her. Having just experienced years of my own private hell, compassion for Lilith came easily. She seemed so fragile, she wasn't eating well, and I was concerned. I took her to town, bought her the expensive cigarettes she said she needed, and tried to help with whatever she asked. I was determined to be there for her.

REACHING

In a typical New Age fashion, I found myself impatiently searching for meaning. Reconnecting with my "land family" meant I didn't have to swallow the loneliness pill anymore. Even in the sad after-math of Zev's exit, freely conversing with Lilith and Ray was like water to my parched spirit. Was this coming full circle? Could we become a community again? I let myself believe I belonged once again. And I rushed toward the hope of restoring my place and washing away the failures of the past several years.

So, when I came across a passage that says God hates divorce, in my immaturity, I took it to mean that God never acknowledged my divorce from Ray. Acting on impulse, I went to Ray the next evening and asked him if we could talk alone. By then, the three of us had been meeting and talking together about Jesus, and both seemed to have given their hearts to Christ, at least that's how it looked to me. For the first time, though, I realized my relationship with Ray was separate from Lilith and I needed to talk with him apart from her.

Under a clear Dragoon night sky, we sat on a big log as the wind fanned our faces. Even though lights emanated from Ray's shop, the Milky Way galaxy remained clearly visible above us. What I had to tell Ray I had inferred from scripture all by myself—applying one verse to conclude what God must feel about us. But I hadn't heard clear direction from God at all. Instead, I responded hastily to what I had read so I could validate my own desires.

After taking a few breaths, I looked right at him and passionately made my case, "Ray, God never acknowledged that we were divorced. We were never divorced. We were made to be one flesh and not break apart." He looked surprised at the assured way I spoke; with confident intensity, I was thoroughly convinced of my discovery. In the light of all that did not work between us before, we talked about how we were now Christians with softer hearts. With new eyes, we looked at each other, and we were attracted like old friends with a new kindling.

After hearing me, he took full breaths of his own. He looked up at the pathway of stars, and I watched his eyes taking time to deliberate it all. He seemed to be deeply considering what I was saying until he said, "Well . . . maybe this was God's plan all along." He also expressed hesitancy, but he was warming up to being with me again. We said aloud that it felt nearly rebellious to make this choice without consulting Lilith, but we concluded that this had to be decided by us alone. He hugged me close, and we kissed, sealing the understanding that we were still married in God's eyes. Not long after that, I moved into his room.

I was overjoyed that there was not only a purpose to all of this suffering, but that I hadn't failed in the marriage—it could just continue. This was a bit of sunshine and rainbows for me. Yearning for full deliverance from loneliness and isolation, I wanted the blessings of a new life. And impetuously, I strove to make it all come together. Ray was agreeable to it because it seemed right, it seemed from God. We were so new in our faith that we were a little innocent in our understanding about how God would be working in our lives. But in the end, He would make things right anyway.

Lilith's reaction to Ray and me rekindling our relationship was tense. She seemed unsettled, increasingly vulnerable and afraid she was losing control.

THE CONVERSATION

One month after he left, Zev returned for several nights to seek closure and retrieve some of his belongings. During his brief stay,

Lilith asked me to be the chosen spokesperson to convey all of her feelings—ultimately to try and convince him to remain with us. In the room which he built above the garage, I met with him privately. Beyond all of Lilith's agendas, I had genuinely missed him.

Zev confided that he no longer recognized Lilith and felt compelled by the Holy Spirit to leave. I tried to convince him that Lilith had changed, but he challenged me to consider whether things were truly different. I wasn't ready to accept his perspective, still hoping our community could be restored. Zev gave me a piercing stare and said, "Don't you ever just want to get out Elizabeth, and start somewhere new?" But I couldn't see beyond these forty acres of land, still clinging to the hope of restoring this community we had invested in for nearly four years. Not many days following, for the last time, he rode away on his motorcycle. When Zev's departure was final, Lilith seemed even more fragile.

LEAVE THIS BED NOW

After I moved back into Ray's room, we believed our marriage was not lost, but that it would just continue from this point. Several weeks after Ray and I were living together again, Lilith asked Ray to drive her to see Zev who was living on the East coast. She wanted to have more closure with Zev and the business, and to bring him items she wanted him to have. While they traveled, I waited at home, still hoping Ray and I could rebuild our life together on the land. When they returned, Ray seemed distant, and I sensed a shift between us.

As I lay in our bed one night during the following couple of weeks, I felt a literal push from the Holy Spirit to remove myself, and sleep somewhere else. This shove from God was spiritual, physical and even audible to me. His unwavering voice resounded within my spirit—"Leave this bed, now!" So, I left to sleep in the middle room. The next day, I told Ray that I wasn't sure what this meant from God, but that I needed to pray about what was the next right step. So, I returned to the familiar middle room, back to where I had first started, more than three and a half years ago.

One night there, I dreamed that God had never honored Ray and my original marriage because we were never married before Him. Our original marriage was from Lilith channeling dark entities, and so, He never honored the union. In the vision, God also told me Ray was not right for me—He had someone waiting for me and I would have a family of my own.

The next day, I told Ray what God showed me. The two of us shed tears as we conveyed love we have had for one another over the years. Together, we marveled about how crazy this whole ride has been. But we also expressed that we trusted God knew better all along.

At just 26, I was already divorced, feeling like a failure and wishing I could tell my family I'd succeeded despite my years in the cult. Yet, I would eventually leave the land with the greatest reward—the gift of Jesus. As my relationship with Ray ended, I struggled to believe I could ever marry again or be loved, not realizing how much healing I still needed. I clung to the safety of the land, unable to imagine leaving or losing the makeshift family we'd become.

We began attending a small Nazarene church, where I was baptized and found my first true pastor, Pastor Lyle. He truly loved the Lord, and he loved people. One day soon enough, his counsel and guidance would become vital.

UNBEARABLE HOUR

A few weeks after I told Ray of my dream, I witnessed something that took my breath away. Standing in the shared kitchen between Lilith's room, my room, and Ray's, I looked out through the large windows into the front yard. There, I saw Ray and Lilith feeding Rosie, his horse, laughing together. Then, they held hands—and kissed. My heart sank. I didn't want to believe what I saw. After years of holding out hope for a life with Ray—a hope Lilith had once encouraged—I was blindsided. From the moment I arrived in Dragoon, I had done everything she asked—moving into the trailer, working to pay rent, driving her to town. I had been her champion and her "handmaiden," doing whatever she needed, believing she was helping me, believing we were close. She knew how deeply I longed for Ray, how much I had confided in her in my struggle and my hope of reuniting with him. That kiss wasn't just a betrayal—it was a collapse of everything I thought was true.

So, when I was alone with her in the kitchen, still reeling, I asked, "You and Ray are together now?" Instead of acknowledging it, she deflected and turned the moment against me. "What? No! No, don't do this. Stop this! Don't come at me with this!" she said, gesturing with her arms like she was angrily pushing me away. "Elizabeth, don't do this to me. I am done here. I am done!" She thoroughly twisted the confrontation, casting herself as the victim, and walked away, refusing to talk about it. It was a strange, yet familiar pattern—classic narcissistic gaslighting. And at that moment, I was left alone with the truth she wouldn't admit.

Anger and betrayal overwhelmed me as I realized Lilith and Ray's relationship probably began after I moved in with him again, while they went on their trip to see Zev. It felt as if everything I'd done for her was meaningless, and she'd simply taken what she wanted, regardless of the cost to me. Her evasive response worsened the sting, leaving me isolated with my pain. I stared at the ceiling for hours, unable to form a single prayer. My mouth stayed shut as if even reaching out would betray the bitterness I couldn't let go of. My fists clenched under the blanket. I bit my lip until it stung, trying to keep a scream from rising.

One night, Ray and Lilith came to my room claiming they sensed a "demonic force" I needed to confront. It was not a loving conversation—it felt punitive, like a parent scolding a child, which only made things worse. At the time, the enemy still had me believing that evil thoughts I heard came from within me. That lie kept me from seeking comfort in Jesus—I felt too unworthy to come to Him. I didn't yet understand that His sacrifice had already made me worthy.

A few days later, it came to an unbearable head for me. The middle room that I was staying in was adjacent to Lilith's bed. Through the thin walls, I heard the two of them giggling—playful lovers laughing during intimacy. It was all too much for me. Because of their recent confrontation, I did not feel at liberty to leave my room. The pain of their betrayal exploded within me! Breathless and heavy-hearted, I fell to my knees. I quietly pleaded, "God, I can't take this anymore!" I wanted Him to take me right then. The hurt was too much for me to bear alone.

Overwhelmed by intense pain in my chest, I broke down completely. My body shook with torrents of stinging grief. As if God was waiting for me to ask for His help, within seconds His comfort flooded over me, my uncontrollable sobs stilled by His love. He showed me that I was to forgive Lilith and Ray, freeing me from my tortured thoughts. I prayed for His strength and was able to forgive them. That was when I felt the anger lift. In its place there was tremendous peace. Profoundly relieved, I breathed deeply and thought, *This is Your peace that surpasses all understanding, written in Your Word.* God met me with a love that held me together, assuring me with His voice, "Daughter, I know your sorrows. I will never leave you or forsake you. I will carry you through this."

Within minutes, God spoke deeply into my spirit about the new life and new love He planned for me. He said He promised to give me a family who would love me, and that I would never again be alone or cut to the heart like this ever—*ever again*. He made that promise to me on that night and He has fulfilled every word of it.

I felt Christ beside me, sharing my heartache. He reminded me that He, too, was betrayed by those closest to Him. He also knew this profound pain. In my grief, I sensed not only comfort, but deep empathy from a God who walked this path before me and truly understood. In my darkest hour, God met me, transforming my torment into awe and peace. That night, He became El Roi—the God who sees me.

THE UPPER ROOM

After that night, I sought solace at church. Once Pastor Lyle delivered his sermons, I would return to the altar at the front of the church in tears, desperately praying for God to heal me—to heal all of my life!

When Ray and Lilith announced their engagement, I was moved to the upper room above the garage. I no longer had their friendship as a refreshing solace, and my heartbreak was driven deeper. Except for Sundays, I rarely saw them. Several times I drove myself to church when they did not join me. Humbled by life and aware of my brokenness, at the end of many church services, I returned to that Nazarene altar to cry out in surrender to the Lord. Once again, I was isolated, now with no hope of remaining on the land. It was a sorrowful time, and I cried daily.

Because I was spiritually bound to this land, clenching relentlessly to an injurious false hope, the forceful rip of a Band-Aid was so very necessary. With nowhere to go and fearful to leave my "safe haven," I was now pressed to leave it by mid-summer. I could not bear to be there for their wedding, and they did not want me around as a hindrance. Lilith was forthright to tell me so one day, "It's time you find a new place to live. We want to start our lives together just us, and you have your life ahead of you." The land was now a directionless place—a reminder of loss, failure and rejection.

How much can the human heart take? Only God knew I was near that limit in my soul when loneliness gripped my heart like a vice. Only He could delicately remove its clutch without causing more damage. He alone could heal me. Though I clung to my faith, I struggled to see a hopeful future. Pastor Lyle sat with me in that upper room, reminding me that God had good plans for me, and his compassion during this time meant so much.

As I prepared to leave, small incidents, like being sharply reprimanded for almost damaging Ray's motorcycle, made it clear I was no longer welcome, deepening my sense of rejection and confirming it was time to go. Even small misunderstandings with Lilith reinforced that my time there was over.

During these remaining days, Lilith also became unhappy with me when I asked her what she was going to do with Zev's twelve-string guitar. Zev had taught me to play, and I knew she would have no use for it. Several months back, I had noticed it sitting in her closet when I had more access to the house. Even though all that time had passed, she saw me walking into her closet as an egregious invasion of her privacy and made me feel particularly bad about it. She considered it a breaking of trust with her, overriding anything she had done towards me or cancelling any good thing I had done for her. Several months back when I confronted her about being in love with my ex-husband, she exhibited no remorse but rather victimization from my response. And she never expressed sorrow over leading us into a deceptive cult situation for the past four years. But apparently after years of devoting my life to her, I had permanently stepped over a line by entering her closet.

LAST DAYS

As I prepared to leave, I trusted God to guide me, even without a clear path forward. I felt called to a helping profession, maybe teaching or nursing. A church connection led me to substitute teach in Pearce, AZ, just twenty minutes from Dragoon. I covered first, fifth, and seventh grades on separate days, and wow—those experiences made it painfully clear that teaching wasn't for me. At the time, I wasn't aware how overwhelmed I already felt by the voices of children in my own head. No wonder I couldn't handle a classroom full of real ones, I hadn't yet learned to manage my own inner chaos. I decided to pursue nursing, enrolling in classes in Sierra Vista to complete my prerequisites.

My search for a new home was going nowhere until, just before Lilith and Ray's wedding, divine providence stepped in. My friend Belinda from work happened to have a place available in St. David. It was the perfect location, halfway between Benson, where I worked, and Sierra Vista where I took classes. Belinda and I had been friends since our first day at Benson Hospital four years earlier when she helped me fill out my W-4. Her prayers, fellowship and generosity had been a steady blessing.

Of course, there were tears when I left the land. Echoes of past traumas convinced me I would not feel safe or loved anywhere else, but I still had to go. God spoke to my heart reminding me that He would keep me safe.

As I finally drove away, four and a half years after first arriving, I said a prayer in my heart—*Oh Lord, how amazing You are. You lifted me out of the pit, and You've begun to set my feet on solid ground. This has been painful, but You showed me that even if I had nothing else left, all I needed was You. You gave me what I had been searching for all along— love, worth, and healing—blessings I was seeking in all the wrong places.*

SIXTEEN

The Promise of More

It was time to place my hopes in the second act of my story—one God was rewriting just for me. He promised me a new husband and family. Though He didn't reveal all the details, knowing my tendency to overthink, He guided me gently like a loving Father, step by step. For now, He brought comforting friendships into my life. These early Christian relationships meant a lot, especially since I felt so alone with little contact with others.

Belinda's offer was gracious. She let me stay on her parent's land in a triple wide trailer while her family temporarily moved to another state. With plenty of room to stretch, her friendly parents resided close by. For four months, from September 2002–January 2003, I commuted between my home in St. David, the hospital in Benson and school in Sierra Vista.

One of my work friends, Dawn, a nurse leader and single mom with three young children, was consistently kind to me. Knowing she was a Christian, I asked her to lunch and shared what happened to me on the land. Because I had kept my home life private, she was shocked to hear I had been in a cult, and how I came to know Jesus. Her eyes widened in amazement at what God had done in me. "Wow. Now that I realize all of this about you, I can see a real difference in you," she said. Her compassionate ear encouraged me. She invited me to meals with her sweet family and supported me throughout nursing school.

As I prepared for nursing, I quickly gathered everything I needed, completing my biology degree at UCSC, securing financing, and finishing prerequisites. When I discovered a new accelerated nursing program at the University of Arizona in Tucson, which offered a bachelor's in nursing in just fourteen months, God gently assured me He would get me in. The program was highly competitive, with many steps to complete in just a few months, but I felt God's encouragement throughout. In my continued solitude, He was continuing to heal me from a dark season. He became my Kinsman Redeemer, my loving Savior, my Good Shepherd. I could sense His voice leading me, reminding me that those who belong to Him recognize His voice, follow Him, and are held securely in His care, never to be lost.

TRIP TO MONTEREY BAY

To complete my biology degree for nursing school, I returned to UC Santa Cruz to take my final boards. I had prepared thoroughly. This was the same daunting 200 question exam that had driven me to leave school and move to Arizona to begin with. Thankfully the university had since revised the format, offering a preview of the exam to help students succeed. With guidance from Sierra Vista college faculty, I studied hard and memorized key answers.

In the fall of 2002, I arrived in Monterey and visited my mother who lived about an hour from Santa Cruz. Though our time together was pleasant on the surface, I kept my guard up. I avoided her subtle attempts to draw me into her Sai Baba beliefs, which I now recognized as spiritually deceptive. After years of torment, I had developed a keen sensitivity to spiritual darkness. I knew that staying in her home, steeped in New Age influence, would have been unsafe for me emotionally and spiritually. She didn't understand my refusal, and I didn't expect her to. I knew she couldn't grasp the spiritual boundary I was drawing.

Thankfully, I had arranged to stay with the Young Life Christian group at UC Santa Cruz. From the start, I was welcomed into a warm, joyful community I wished I had known during my college years. We went to the beach, attended a campus gathering, and worshiped in the same classroom where I once studied theatre. It was a powerful contrast—now filled with joy, truth, and comradery I hadn't known before. After taking my boards, I wandered the campus, walking through the sequoias and resting at my favorite ocean view on Stevenson knoll. With new eyes, I marveled at the beauty and felt the presence of the One who had always been with me. I grieved for years lost to deception and loneliness, realizing how close I had been to the truth all along. But as the coastal wind stirred around me, I turned my heart toward God's hopeful promises to me.

TRIPLE WIDE TRAILER

Back in my triple-wide trailer in St. David, AZ, I prepared for the future God was gently steering me towards. I spent time walking, leaning against trees, and watching water bugs skim across ponds. Twice a week, I drove to Sierra Vista Community College to complete my Anatomy and Physiology prerequisites. There, I met classmates whose sarcastic humor made me laugh again, something I hadn't done in years. It felt like a release, a reminder of joy. I also began a high-protein diet and lost fifteen pounds, weight I had once gained from a single offhand comment from Lilith. This time, the choice was mine, and I felt empowered. I continued to pray and seek God through Scripture, even trying a three-day fast. Though I had to end it early due to dizziness, I broke a tortilla in bed telling God I loved Him but needed to eat. I sensed His pleasure in my effort, a reminder that when we draw near to Him, He draws near to us.

Two months in, Ray and Lilith visited. The awkwardness was palpable; we all felt it. Though we still cared for each other, their marriage had shifted the dynamic, and I no longer fit. I sensed Lilith still wanted influence over me, and I remained vulnerable to it. During their visit, I followed her suggestion to get Dish Network and watch *Shepherd's Chapel*, which she called the "truest source" of biblical teaching. Despite her continued attempts to steer me, I found value in the program's line-by-line teaching and used it to deepen my study of Scripture. Still, loneliness lingered, especially after seeing Ray and

Lilith move on. But I knew God was healing me and setting me on a new path. I felt His nearness in my brokenness. He surrounded me with songs of solace and filled that trailer with His presence. His love poured over me like warm oil, assuring me I was not alone.

COMFORT AND PROMISES

During my time in the triple-wide trailer in St. David, God was profoundly real to me. With no close family, no reconciled relation-ships, and only a few acquaintances, I leaned entirely on Jesus—my one true friend. He strengthened me from within, healed my heart, and wrapped me in His love. I often return to those moments when He was all I had, and yet, He was more than enough. In my suffering, He never left me. No one understands pain like He does, and still, He lifted my spirit with His enduring comfort. On some days, I felt Him invite me to dance again—something I hadn't enjoyed in years. So, in my kitchen, I danced to worship music, sometimes through tears. Though I didn't fully understand my pain, God did. He knew I would one day need to release it all, and He was painting my life with brushstrokes of His compassion, in His perfect timing.

In prayer, I often cried out, "Redeem my life, Father! Let my life bring you glory! It has been so hard, make it all new!" Sometimes, His response was quiet assurance. Other times, He filled me with strength and courage to keep moving forward. He even began to give me glimpses of my future husband. One day, He prompted me to write a list of qualities I desired in a spouse—thirty-eight in total, most centered on a man who would put God first. Writing it down felt like a release, a prayer He already knew but wanted me to express. Later, He asked if I'd be willing to be with a man who had a child from a previous marriage. I said yes, first in my heart, then aloud. He assured me this man would be a true man of God. That promise stirred hope in me, aligning perfectly with the deepest desire of my heart.

PERSECUTION AND BLESSING

While working at Benson Hospital, I experienced my first taste of persecution for my faith. A lab coworker with an agnostic or atheistic background began targeting me, trying to enforce non-existent rules against reading my Bible during downtime. His attitude toward me had noticeably worsened after I came to Christ. Though I wasn't confrontational, I felt his disdain and was relieved to spend more time drawing blood in the hospital than working near him. I wore a shirt that Lilith had made for us which read "Foot Soldier of the King of Kings and Lord of Lords," a bold statement, perhaps, but one that reflected my deep convictions after being delivered from a cult. Despite the pushback, I wasn't ashamed of the gospel. I shared it with patients whenever I could, learning along the way to temper my zeal with sensitivity.

My lab director, Garret, laughed when I told him I was applying to nursing school in Tucson, doubting I'd follow through. But I trusted God's promise. Around that time, Belinda told me she'd be returning to her trailer soon, and I sensed God prompting me to prepare for a move to Tucson. Though I was afraid, I followed His lead, applying for a job at the Red Cross—which I got. It paid more and fit my experience. On the same trip for my interview, I searched for a place to live, which was a daunting undertaking in such a big city. Stopping at a Waffle House, I overheard two men discussing violent crimes in their neighborhood. I asked them where not to live in Tucson, and they kindly advised me to look for housing in the northern part of the city, near the foothills. Their help, though unexpected, was a blessing.

I found an apartment in north Tucson, close to the university, and moved there in January 2003 with the generous help of Belinda's family. I began working at the Red Cross and quickly bonded with my new coworkers. Though the nursing school application process was stressful—gathering transcripts, finalizing my degree, and meeting all requirements—I held tightly to God's assurance that I would be accepted. I knew my work at the Red Cross was temporary, a provision until the nursing program began in June. Despite the challenges, I moved forward with peace, knowing He was leading me.

THE ONE FOR ME

God had promised me a husband, one hand-picked by Him for me. I trusted that this person would come, but would I spot the right one? My heart was in its early stages of healing, and I didn't know if I would be ready for such a person. After all these years of severe solitude, I was intensely longing for companionship. Not only that, but I felt very alone in the "huge" city of Tucson.

During this time, I attended a couple churches that had been recommended to me and even appeared at their "single's meeting" following service. The very definition of the group made for awkward encounters with shelled out superficial glances, and I left knowing, *The one God has for me is not here.*

Out of haste in my loneliness, I placed my profile on a Christian Café dating site and went on several dates. Matched three times with different pastor ministry leaders, one of them ended up slightly more compatible than the others. But this individual didn't tell me until later that he was working it out with a former girlfriend, and it was a bit of a heartbreak—well, only a bit of one. Ultimately, he was not the one that God had given me a vision of. Mostly, it just reminded me of disappointment and that I had to wait on God's timing for the right one.

In the midst of all my dating, my friend Dawn from Benson recommended I attend Grace Chapel. She told me, "Oh, you will like this one Elizabeth. I go there myself when I can." One Sunday, she was going to meet me, however she was unable to make it. Of the few churches I had attended in Tucson, I felt the most at home here, and I knew God wanted me there. The week after I first attended, I received a phone call from one of the ministry leaders named Ed, who was checking in to ask if I had any prayer needs. For some reason, I felt safe to tell him part of my story, and how much I loved Jesus. At the end of a long conversation, Ed told me that because of my age, he wanted to connect me to Grace's College and Career Pastor.

PROMISES STILL TO COME

In February 2003, after Sunday service, while talking with Ed, a man with a confident stride approached. Ed introduced us, "Elizabeth, this is Henry, our college and career pastor. Henry, meet Elizabeth." Like most single people, we quickly sized each other up. I thought, *He's too proud.* At the same time, he didn't seem interested, and I wondered if he could sense that I had a lot of baggage. Henry invited me to attend the college and career meetings and gave me a way to contact him.

Not long after, I received my acceptance letter into the accelerated nursing program. I was thrilled, I knew this was God's favor. In under a year, He had helped me move to Tucson, complete my degree and prerequisites, secure funding, and submit a strong application. His promise had come to pass—I would become a nurse in just fourteen months. I felt carried on wings like eagles, filled with courage and hope for the many promises still to come.

HIS VOICE

When I attended a college and career gathering in May, everything changed. Earlier that evening, I had felt out of place among the younger crowd. Most were really just getting started in life, while I had already endured a cult, a divorce and deep emotional wounds. By age twenty-seven, I had lived too hard of a life, and sitting in the meeting, I decided not to return to the group. Just then, Henry arrived—late. As he began to speak, something in his voice immediately calmed my anxious thoughts like a salve. Every unhealed voice attuned clearly to his words, at full trusting attention. I was stunned at how just hearing him talk brought me peace.

After the meeting, we sat on the tailgate of his truck and had a long conversation. Henry's voice remained soothing, and I found myself effortlessly opening up. Normally guarded and cautious, I felt completely at ease with him. Sharing parts of my life I never thought I'd reveal so easily, I noticed his remarkable spiritual discernment. He knew things about me that I had never shared. I left that night knowing I wanted to keep talking with him, and be near him.

As He walked me to my car, I noticed his tall, full frame and shadow upon the concrete under the streetlights. There were pockets of silence as my mind raced—*I really like him. But for me? Is he the one God gave for me? He is not what I expected.* I was in a little bit of shock. We exchanged numbers, and he was very respectful as the pastor of Grace Chapel's college and career group.

Henry invited me to coffee, and we began meeting regularly. He listened to my story with compassion, often with insight he couldn't have known on his own. His discernment wasn't mystical or manipulative like psychics I had known in the occult—it was godly, healing, and deeply personal. He seemed to know that understanding brought me peace, and God used him to help restore parts of me I didn't know were broken. I started realizing Henry was not only someone I could trust, but someone God lovingly placed in my life for a purpose. Little did I know then, but God would not only use him to help minister to my heart, but he would also fulfill every one of the qualities on my list of what I desired in a husband.

One Sunday, I was excited to see Henry again. Scanning the congregation to see if I could spot him, I saw him with a small girl perched upon his shoulder. I quickly discerned that she must be his daughter. They sat alone and she snuggled him lovingly. The sight was so heart-warming and then I remembered, what God had asked me about being OK if my future husband had a daughter. After service I walked over to where Henry was, and he introduced me to his daughter Amanda. Amanda was a smart and precocious four-year-old who loved Pokémon, and we became fast friends.

Over the next two months, Henry and I quickly bonded and felt that God brought us together. Our compatibility continued to surprise us, given our personalities, our shared love for God, music, art, and smart nerdy things. Overall, we felt an undeniable companionship which God had blessed. The fact that Henry and I had both been handed divorce papers in our previous marriages created an immediate trust between us. We both knew the heartache of betrayal and rejection, and it's something we never wanted to replicate.

Just nine months after we started dating, while I was still in nursing school, Henry and I were married. Two years later, we welcomed our son Elisha into our family. From the time I met him, Henry has been Jesus' loving arms around me.

THE REAL DEAL

During our engagement, I was still in the throes of spiritual torment. Alone in my apartment, I often felt overwhelmed by the enemy's taunts. Though I had been rescued from demonic oppression, I longed for the spiritual covering that only marriage would bring. Henry, a lifelong believer who had given his life to Christ at age five, carried a peace that seemed to radiate from him. Whenever he was near, the tormenting jeers would vanish, and I felt safe. It was as if his relationship with God created a spiritual shield around me—one that offered real protection, not illusion.

For years before knowing Jesus, I had been drawn to false spiritual leaders, people who claimed to channel divine insight but were really offering counterfeits. I had been desperate for truth and healing, but what I found in those places only deepened my confusion. With Henry I saw something different. God had given him a gift—to hear and speak truth from the Lord. What he shared about me were things only God could have known, and they helped me see that God had been watching over every detail of my life with compassion.

From childhood, I had buried everything, but now I gained a tender witness to certainties of my past and was released from a tangled mess of confusion, lies and deceit. Even when truths were painful, God was gentle and healing. It took many years of unraveling, the tender touch of the Father and the patience of my husband to inquire from God on my behalf. God graciously meant for me to meet Henry to help me heal, and for Henry to sharpen his gift—because I surely stretched him with it. In the beginning of our marriage, on most days I would ask him, "What does God say about this? Why am I feeling this way? Can I have a word from God?" Hearing loving encouragement and insight from God immediately stilled my nervous resolve to heal from an identity crisis that neither I nor Henry knew existed.

Henry's soothing voice that first captivated me had become so much more than the resonance and pace of his speech. Now the words he spoke became a refuge—a source of comfort and perceptiveness. Henry made me feel loved even while everything inside me unraveled. He cared for me during my discomforting liquification as a caterpillar.

Because I still had multiple voices of my own, I didn't always have a clear ability to hear from God for myself. But my husband could cut through all that chatter I projected and lovingly lead me to what God wanted me to see.

Many years later, however, I found myself with terrific heaviness. The familiar, comforting shelter of Henry's voice abruptly fell silent. *Would I ever hear his soothing words again?*

SEVENTEEN

Room Nineteen

A bright light never shines so brightly as it does on the darkest night.

There's a common misconception that when you become a Christian all of your worries, pain and trials disappear. Nothing could be further from the truth. In fact, because you have aligned yourself to be subject to the sovereign rule of God, it is likely you will find yourself thrust into situations where God is your only hope, your only comfort and your only friend. That can be scary.

It was the evening of August 21, 2019. Henry had lovingly cooked us chimichangas when, without warning, he grabbed his chest, sat on a kitchen chair, and pressed, "Call 911!" Henry had previously been a medic, and I had been an ER nurse, so I asked him more about his symptoms. But instead of answering, he looked straight into my eyes and repeated with a stronger tone than the first, "Call 911, *now.*" This time I jumped at the insistence in his voice and called the emergency line.

While waiting for paramedics to arrive, I assessed him both as an ER nurse and as his wife. Previously, I had taken him to the hospital for chest pain which turned out to be an anxiety reaction to medication. Any experienced front-line nurse will tell you that it's hard to gauge medical urgency when it comes to our very own family members. Our minds teeter between the worst possible scenario to being nonchalant when assessing symptoms because—we've seen everything. Still, my head was spinning with a possible diagnosis for Henry's chest pain. I tried to convince myself that this wasn't a serious cardiac event, but my concern was rising.

The ambulance arrived three minutes later. As the crew rushed in, I apologized for our unkempt home, and then instantly felt guilty for caring about appearances. I was worried about Henry—alarmed by the way he looked at me with penetrating urgency. Recognizing a couple of the medics from ER's where I recently worked, I said hello. One told me, "You look tired." I thought to myself, *Why would you say that in my own home? Of course, I'm worried out of my mind for my husband!* The comment jerked me out of thinking about anything related to my history as an ER nurse or regarding all the emergency colleagues we were about to see at the hospital. I hovered over the EKG to see any indication of heart attack, but there was none. My mind was spinning. *But why is he pale, sweaty and in pain?* The medics decided to take him to the hospital in a lower alert basic life support vehicle instead of advanced life support. When they tried to get him onto the transport gurney, however, Henry became dizzy and nearly passed out. *Why is he suddenly droopy? What is going on?* It all happened very fast, and he was on his way to the hospital.

Running around the house, I grabbed what was needed before driving my son Elisha and myself to the ER. I was panicked and Henry was usually the one who drove us everywhere. Our guardian angels must have been on double duty just to get us there safely. Driving half aware of the road, I tried to call Henry's mom, but she didn't answer. I got ahold of Henry's dad, and he told me they would come right away. I replied, "You're going to come *now*?" He said, "Of course." My response to him was colored with both shock and avoidance that this could be serious.

I walked into the ER of the hospital where I worked shifts less than three years ago. I wanted to wake up from this nightmare. Knowing things were beyond my control, I raced quickly toward his room, nineteen. I forced myself to be calm by desperately, repeating in my mind, *This is not serious. This will not be life-threatening for Henry*.

As soon as I got to the room, I was met with the day charge nurse, a former co-worker who said, "Your husband—he is not acting right.

They took him for a head CT scan right away. He was seizing when he arrived." Apparently, Henry became unconscious on the way to the hospital, and they urgently shifted to drive code three—with lights and sirens.

I took an anxious breath and abandoned any thoughts for a benign outcome. *No, we won't be going home tonight to have a nice chimichanga meal and just be together all safe and sound.* My breaths stifled by anxiety, I whispered, "He's not acting right?" Nurses and techs who I knew filled the room. Everyone looked puzzled. They explained that Henry arrived at the ER in and out of consciousness, and we all tried to figure out what was going on with him. Was this a stroke, a pulmonary embolus or some kind of heart event?

Just then, Henry was wheeled back to his room from the head scan. With a glossy-eyed post-seizure gaze, he recognized me. "Hi Behb," he said. I responded, "Hi Behb" with a troubled smile. Racking my brain for his diagnosis, I couldn't stop staring at him or the monitors we hooked him to. It was during shift change around 7:00 p.m., and I was reassured to hear that Henry's nurse would be my kind friend, Sarah.

Even more reassuring was Henry's doctor, Dr. Seifert, in whom I had the most trust. Over the eleven years I had worked with him, I'd grown accustomed to asking him questions. After our greeting, I got right to it—"So, the head CT is negative for a stroke and there is no heart attack. Are you thinking PE (blood clot in the lung)?" He said, "Yes, I ordered a chest CT." During my years working with Seifert, I knew he had a good poker face, but tonight his expression really worried me. With a gentle, empathetic smile, he gave brief replies, appearing quietly resigned as if he already suspected a grim diagnosis.

HEIGHTENED HOURS

Our time in room nineteen was traumatic. While waiting for Henry to be transferred to the chest cat scan, he went in and out of consciousness with repetitive head jolting seizure-like movements—a very frightening thing for any loved one to witness! Overwhelmed with emotion, I tried to hold it together like any ER nurse has to, but I was barely hanging on. Across the room, I saw Elisha sitting in a chair nervously watching his phone and repetitively moving his crossed leg. At thirteen, he was no longer the small boy who clung to my side. I walked over to check on him just as one of my nurse friends, April, began to sweetly talk with him. She knew of his Autism diagnosis and kindly took him outside the room to shield him from the scene and so I could be there for Henry.

Even though I hadn't worked there in three years, God had especially staffed our family with eight trusted colleagues that came just to hug me or to help take care of Henry. This included the night-charge nurse whose family Henry had photographed, and another staff member Tara, whom Henry had counseled and prayed for in our own home. They knew me as their ER team member and let me fidget and put monitor leads on my husband. I said to them with tears, "I'm sorry, I just need to do . . . *something!*" They were all concerned for us.

Amanda, now age twenty, arrived in the room together with Henry's parents. We hugged, and I cried while trying to give them an update. No one knew for sure why Henry was all over the map with symptoms or what was going on medically. Henry's mom took Elisha to another quiet room while we waited for the results. Henry continued to exhibit periods of alertness with moments of groggy lucidity.

When Sarah briefly stepped out of the room, Henry—sitting upright in bed—became unconscious, seizing and vomiting, his head bobbing forward into his chest. It was the scariest scene emblazoned on my mind. Immediately, I reached for suction and shouted from the room, "We're losing his airway! We're losing his airway!" Staff rushed in as I struggled to lift his head, trying to open his airway and suction it. Thankfully, within a minute Henry became lucid again, and I was deeply relieved we didn't have to intubate him. That could have cost precious time and altered the trajectory of the entire night.

The urgent suctioning I performed likely saved him from an airway obstruction or severe pneumonia. I really disliked having to play a role in my husband's survival.

From that moment on, the atmosphere in the room shifted. A heavy, spiritual weight seemed to descend, clouding my awareness. I watched Sarah quietly roll a CODE cart next to Henry's gurney. Feeling disembodied, I asked softly, "Why is the CODE cart in here?" Then I saw the monitor change. Henry's heart rate dropped into the 40s, and his blood pressure plummeted. My body was completely tense as tears streamed down my face. My worst fear was unfolding before me. I watched as my husband was about to crash.

Doctor Seifert walked into the room. His face and body appeared heavy with news. Presently, Henry was alert, and I squeezed his hand. Fighting back tears, Dr. Seifert said, "It's not good. Henry is fully dissected with a tear from his carotid artery through the aorta from his heart, all the way down into his lower abdomen." Henry and I looked at each other intensely, knowing what his diagnosis meant. In Henry and my medical careers, we had both seen people with dissections deteriorate rapidly—they usually do not last through the night, and some not even thirty minutes. Henry had transported suspected dissection cases straight to the operating department. He also knew the story of my first year ER nursing at University Hospital when, as the main triage nurse, I gave my last available bed to a patient who died within the hour of a dissection.

Faced with the imminent possibility of Henry's passing, we had only that moment to take it all in. I gripped his hand tightly, holding on with everything I had. We looked to Dr. Seifert, whose eyes were soft with compassion, more than I had ever seen from him before. Through tears, I asked, "What can be done?" Dr. Seifert replied, "Henry needs cardiothoracic surgery for his aorta. The dissection is also affecting one of his kidneys and a major artery to his colon." The way he spoke made it clear he wasn't confident that there was much hope. He said he would call the resident cardiothoracic surgeon. Knowing time was slipping away, panic surged through me, and I cried out, "Well, let's get on it!"

God was taking my husband.

I had no time to comprehend it and spend these last moments loving him, hearing his voice, seeing him look at me and being a family. I could not take this! Especially as Henry began to look at me and say, "Lizzie, look at me." I cried, "No, I can't! This is too much, you can't leave us!" He answered, "Just trust God. No matter what, trust Him. We have a good God. Our God is amazing. You have got to trust Him."

Upon hearing he was about to leave this earth, Henry immediately told me to trust God—"Always trust in God, no matter what. He is good Lizzie." God had given him otherworldly peace to deal with news that these could be his last moments on earth.

Nurses and techs kept glancing up, visibly moved by what Henry was saying. As the weight of the situation hit me harder, I broke down, drenched in panicked tears, pleading, "No! Stop saying that—I can't lose you! I can't do life without you! I can't do life without you!" In that moment, nothing else existed—only my husband and our family. Realizing my mother-in-law wasn't in the room, I ran to find her and tell her the news. I begged her to pray hard. She pulled me into a prayer for peace and faith, but I gently pulled away, saying, "No, you don't understand—this is very serious. We need a miracle. Don't worry about my peace or my faith!" Then I rushed back to Henry, desperate not to miss what could be our final moments together. She soon returned, bringing Elisha and Amanda into the room where Henry lay on the gurney.

Henry spoke with his daughter Amanda as she cried, "Oh Daddy!" He spoke lovingly to her, "Baby, keep trusting God no matter what . . . and take care of Elisha and Lizzie." With tears she said, "Ok Daddy!" He was giving his last wishes, and it tore me apart. He called Elisha to his side and told him, "Elisha, trust God and take care of Mom and Amanda." "Ok Dad. Ok Dad!" I was concerned how Elisha was comprehending everything. When Elisha turned to walk away, I told

Henry, "Kiss him!" So, he kissed him. Rightfully so, both Amanda and Elisha had difficulty staying in the room. Later that night, I learned that they sat outside the room crying profusely with family members.

From that moment, I was glued to Henry's side. Henry lacked strength, but he kept tenderly responding to me as I said through tears repeatedly—"I can't lose you Behb, you're the love of my life, I can't do life without you!" "No Lizzie, you need to trust God no matter what," Henry answered. He didn't want me to become angry at God for taking him, but honestly, I was afraid I would. This all felt senseless. My loving Father had given me Henry who was the first and only one I ever truly trusted and loved, and now He would be taking him away? No, I felt that this was the end of me too. The end of my joy, peace and love—the end of my loving Behb, the love of my life. *This is not ok!* My whole body tensed, my soul was in agony. My heart had never felt heavier.

Henry's mom began to pray for a miracle, loudly and fervently, and we lost awareness of anyone around us. The nurses and staff appreciated the enormity of what we were facing. They had seen Henry's CT scan. Some peered in, seeming to marvel at the love and faith that was being expressed. I wasn't having any of this however— our family crisis viewed by others at the potential end of Henry's life. No, I was overcome with not being willing to let go of Henry.

The cardiothoracic surgeon at this hospital was not available to perform Henry's emergency surgery, so he would need to be airlifted to University Hospital, where I started my ER nursing career fifteen years prior. This actually relieved me because I had heard stories about the CT surgeon on call here, at this hospital—stories that would have haunted me all of the upcoming night.

While we waited for the helicopter, Dr. Seifert called me outside the room to talk privately, "Lizzie, Henry's prognosis is very grave. You should prepare to lose him. Henry's is the worst dissection I have ever seen." Dr. Seifert was not convinced that surgery would do any good. I stared past him, everything went blank. I couldn't hear anymore. I pulled away from Seifert's side and walked quickly back to my husband. The dagger to my heart almost felt tangible.

When the flight crew arrived, I was comforted to recognize Joy, a medic I had once worked with at another hospital. I made her promise she would take good care of Henry on the flight. She was extremely compassionate and reassuring to me. Joy asked for my phone number because she knew I was driving alone to meet Henry at University Hospital. In my current state, I did not want to risk having my son in the car with me. She could see I was an emotional wreck, and her desire to make sure I arrived safely was the kindest gesture she could have made.

Several nurses and techs came into the room to console me while they packed Henry up for the flight. Our nurse, Sarah, hugged me and prayed aloud for us. The kindness of my former ER colleagues was overwhelming, their concern and subsequent texts to check on me felt like the very tender hand of God.

As Henry was wheeled down the hallway to the helipad, staff members lined the hall. As we walked by the charge nurse, she called out, "Henry you need to get better because I'm going to need family portraits for Christmas!" He nodded back at her with a smile. Her comment was not a comforting goal for me, but I appreciated every degree of consideration for him. I was not even sure he would survive the flight.

Before they moved him into the tiny craft, the crew allowed me a moment to hold his hand and kiss his face—in case it was the last time. I stood outside the gate of the helipad watching for what seemed like eons for them to get him loaded and settled.

The helicopter's rotor finally began to spin, building into a loud, vociferous wind, and I found myself shouting out to God. With everything in me, as the helicopter lifted, I cried out for mercy—"Oh my God! Heal him, God! You can do anything! This is all in Your hands!" My prayers rose with the wind, pleading for a miracle. "God, I can't lose him! Please don't take him away from me!"

Trembling with tears, I shook with torrents of emotion, crying out—"My God, You have always been there for me, now God, turn this around! Tonight is bleak! This is scary! Please God! My God! My loving Lord, please come as a light and take away this dark end which only leads to a lifetime of grief! Heal Him God! Things look so bad! Please take the threat of death away!"

My body quivered in agony as I screamed as loud as my body could muster—"Fix the leak in Henry's heart! Heal and hold him together! Please God! Don't take him! I am afraid I will be angry with You if you take him! He is all I have! The love of my life! I can't handle this if you take Him! Please don't take Him! I would crumble God! Heal Henry! Heal him! Heal him!"

I stood there watching the helicopter ascend, worried that his vital signs would tank or that he would code arrest during transport. Then I ran to my car. My drive was twenty minutes, and his flight was only seven. If he survived the flight, then I was determined to see him before surgery. I needed to get there fast!

As I drove, I meditated on Henry's words earlier. Just as I had always done when something didn't make sense, I asked Henry, "Behb, what does God say about this?" He simply answered, "I just feel His peace." "Nothing else?" I asked. "But will you survive this?" He answered, "God's not telling me. He's just giving me so much peace."

I wish I could say I was comforted by that, or that I felt secure, trusting in His perfect will. But I didn't. Not even Henry's words, spoken so gently from the ER gurney, "Trust God no matter what," could calm the storm inside me. I was gripped with dread because I didn't know what God's will was. If He intended to take Henry, I was fighting it with everything in me.

I had always relied on Henry's ability to hear God's voice to steady me. But now, with his voice fading, I was left to rely on what God was saying—and I wasn't sure I could hear Him through the fear.

EIGHTEEN

The Longest Night

Watching the road through my tears, the tenderness of God slowed my heavy foot. He placed me between my in-law's vehicles so that I could be guided safely to the hospital. I felt as though angels were driving my vehicle, and not me. In our entourage of cars traveling to University Hospital were my mother-in law "Bellis," Henry's father "Papa," Vanessa, our "adopted sister" and angel, my son Elisha, my stepdaughter Amanda, and Amanda's mom.

Once we arrived and hugged each other, my steps were quick-footed and strong, leading our group to the ER to ask where Henry was. I was hoping they would take him right to surgery and that he would not have to stop in the ER first. Time was ticking.

THE DREAM

As I hurried toward the hospital doors, I recalled a dream God had given me just three weeks earlier—the last time I clearly heard from the Lord. In the dream, Henry was driving along the California coast with me in the front seat and Elisha in the back. Suddenly, Jesus appeared behind me, serene and radiant. His presence was arresting—gentle, humble, and completely content just to be with us. I turned to Him, amazed, and said, "Jesus! You've never been to California before. Is there somewhere we can drive you?" With a soft smile, He replied that He was simply there for the ride, with us.

Then He looked at me, and the seat beneath me vanished. He cupped my jaw in His hand and said with tender affection, "My girl." His incredible warmth poured into me like liquid peace. I tried to focus on His face, but it became pixelated—each feature made up of thousands of tiny scenes from my life, moments He had witnessed with compassion, including every trauma. I couldn't make out the full picture, but I understood—I was fully seen and known by God. He had been present for every part of my soul's formation. Then He took my hand, and for several minutes, I was swept into waves of His glory. The borders between His hand, His power, and my being dissolved. Eyes closed, I saw brilliant light and felt His sovereignty, love, and strength. It was as if I had been transported to heaven and given courage for what was to come. I held His hand until I sensed He wanted us to stop the car. When I asked if He wanted to get out, He pointed and said, "Over there is fine." Henry pulled over, and we were giddy that Jesus had been with us. But when we looked again, He had disappeared into the crowd.

I awoke from my dream with a sense of euphoric freedom and resilience, believing it was simply a beautiful gift. But now, racing through the hospital, I cried out inside—*What about the dream, God? You were content with Henry driving! He was driving the car! Please let him still drive our car, Father. Let him live to lead our family. Please—he still needs to lead us!*

I'LL DO MY BEST

The ER directed us to pre-op, and they took me right back to where Henry was. I was zealous to see what kind of state he was in. It was 10:30 p.m., and the pre-op area was dark except for his room lit at the end of a long hallway. I briskly ran-walked to find him lying on a gurney surrounded by his surgery team of about seven individuals.

Thank God he appears alert and oriented! Cardiothoracic surgeon Dr. Kazui introduced himself—his hands would be delicately sewing my husband's body together. As I signed all needed forms, Henry's team explained they would do as much as they could, but that there was a risk of death. They quickly figured out with my medical background that I knew doing nothing would certainly amount to death.

Miraculously, Henry's vitals looked good, and he was alert

enough to ask, "How long is the surgery, and what time is it?" The reply came—about eight hours, and close to 11:00 p.m. With his usual wit, Henry quipped, "Hey doc, are you sure you don't want to get some coffee first?" Dr. Kazui gave a relaxed half-moon smile and replied, "I will be okay." I marveled that after a night of seizures and looming tragedy—Henry still had his sense of humor. Dr. Seifert had explained that the dissection affected multiple arteries, so I asked Dr. Kazui if he would be working on all of them—the carotid, the aorta, the kidney, the artery to the colon. With calm resolve, he answered, "Your husband's aorta is leaking and will require the most emergent work to repair." His steady manner was comforting—clearly, he had seen this before.

Henry had not been sent with scans from the other hospital, so they needed to do another set before the surgery. I thought to myself, *Geez, how was that missed?* In the next breath, however, I reassured myself that God had all these delays in mind when He already decided what would come of this night.

Just before Henry drifted off under the anesthesia, I leaned in and said, "Behb—I love you." Tears welled in my eyes as I turned to Dr. Kazui and pleaded, "Please take good care of him—he's the love of my life." At first, he glanced uncomfortably to the side, but then his expression softened. Looking directly at me he said, "I will do my best."

I watched as the surgical convoy whisked Henry away. For several seconds, I stood there dumbfounded. This was completely out of my hands. Henry was now utterly vulnerable—in the care of strangers. At least they seemed exceptionally calm, confident and mild mannered. I didn't have the mental capacity to think past "risk of death" and the ticking sound of a second-hand clock resounded inside my ears. The charge nurse told me she would be updating me throughout the surgery.

In the waiting room, my level ten stress relaxed a half notch. Henry's family was assembled which now included two of Henry's aunts, their spouses and Amanda's boyfriend. Pausing for a moment,

I knew they would look to me to relay medical information. Knowing I had to be strong for them, I was not strong. Absolutely and completely, I was freaking out. But like a nurse giving a report to a family member, I told them what his surgical team told me with as much injected encouragement as I could muster, which wasn't much.

WAITING ROOM

We hunkered in for the longest night, gathered together as a vigil for Henry's life. Papa took Elisha home while Bellis stayed at the hospital with us. Pillows were brought in by family. I leaned my head against the wall and let the tears fall as I prayed—attuning my ears to the quiet, gentle talking around me. Henry's loving Mexican family was in for the long haul. Henry had always jokingly said of them—"When one bean hurts, the whole burrito suffers." I was comforted knowing they were praying solely in faith without the burden of the medical understanding that I had.

I tried not to think of the operating room—that they would actually bypass his circulation and temporarily stop his heart to perform the surgery. I tried to suppress images in my mind of Henry's blood and organs separated, and the awareness that they would be pumping him with multiple liters of emergency blood just to keep his perfusion stable. It was all too overwhelming. My mind was racing.

From what Dr. Seifert had told me earlier, I already knew the odds were against him. Every complication I feared now loomed large. *If he survives the night, will he make it through the threats of ischemic bowel, aspiration pneumonia, stroke, or kidney damage?* I knew there was a risk of bowel death or severe debilitation. In the ER, he had probably inhaled some vomit into his lungs—an easy path to a dangerous pneumonia. Plus, the tearing of his carotid arteries—he had been drifting in and out of consciousness from lack of oxygen to the brain—*Will he wake up with stroke-like symptoms?* And then there was damage to his kidney—*How bad is it?* I knew too much. Above all, I was terrified he wouldn't even survive.

With trembling hands, I googled the survival rate for aortic dissection—five percent. *Five percent! Five percent survival is practically a death sentence. Why did I look that up?* My chest tightened. There was nothing I could do. There was nowhere to hide from this dark reality. Every waking moment pressed upon my heart with a constant sting.

Full of tears and muttering prayers, I looked around me, feeling the love for Henry from other family members. Pelted by painful thoughts, I travailed within myself—*Even though I have them, I don't have any family member like Henry. He is my rock, the one person in the world I trust, the one who knows and understands me, who I love with all my heart, my strength in so many ways. He is my pastor, the father of my son with autism—he holds our family together. He is the only one who can put a smile on my face when I'm melancholic—my lover, my best friend, the one that God hand-picked for me and I for him. How will I ever cope? I cannot imagine or do life without him! This can't be happening!*

Several times I walked down a long hallway to the bathroom just so I could find a private place to bawl. I didn't want to lose it in front of those I was supposed to be strong for—family who did not know the extent of how Henry had been holding me together all of these years.

Back in the waiting room, I reflected on how I saw my father's final days not long ago. Years before then, God had lovingly restored our relationship, and Henry was a big part of helping to heal it. Tears welled up thinking about my dad. *I don't want to say goodbye to another man in my life!*

CUPPED FACE

It wasn't until after Henry and I were married that I truly got to know my father. While planning our wedding, I told Henry, "I wish my dad could give me away, but we haven't spoken in years—I don't even know if he'd want to." I was afraid to reach out, but Henry gently urged me, "Give him the benefit of the doubt. It's important to forgive." He knew my hesitation was rooted in past experiences and heavily influenced by my mother and sister. "Unless you make peace with your dad," he said, "you'll carry resentment into our marriage." I didn't want that. So, I called my dad—and to my surprise, he was overjoyed to walk me down the aisle.

My stepmother GG later told me that giving me away was one of the proudest moments of my father's life. As he led me toward Henry, I trusted his joyful stride and easy conversation. I felt an uncomplicated, genuine love from him. With Henry's encouragement, I had stepped away from my mother's and sister's views and found peace with my father. After the wedding, my memories of him became softer, more tender.

The clearest, and most bittersweet was the last time I saw him. By then, he was in the final stages of dementia. I spotted him across a large room filled with elderly patients, watching TV. When we first saw each other, his face slowly lit up with a wide, crinkled smile, and his eyes sparkled. *He recognizes me!* I chatted with him, and he responded with familiar expressions that made me laugh. He even tossed out a classic Joe Lupone quip and laughed at himself. But soon, I could see he was overstimulated, so we simply sat. I leaned into him as he watched football, both of us content just to be together.

I held his hand and grieved the years lost to misunderstanding, hardship, and distance. Yet at that moment, resting on his shoulder and chest, everything felt restored. My tears turned to healing sobs—I had never experienced my father more humble, gentle, or kind. I was so grateful I made this trip. GG had called just days before, "Honey, this is the last time you'll be able to see him." While packing, I also decided to transfer out of the hospital I had been at for nine years after being slandered by my boss. I longed to hear Dad say, "They don't deserve you. Screw 'em! Get out of there!" I could almost hear it. I lacked the Lupone bravado my brothers had, and now, more than ever, I needed his fire.

Later, I brought out a small photo book I'd made for him. As I turned the pages, he gently nudged me away, he wanted to turn them himself. I smiled as he thoughtfully took in each image—him with Elisha, me with Patrick, and of course, the photo of him walking me down the aisle. I pointed to it and said, "That's a handsome man!" He slowly grinned wide and touched the photo with his fingers. It was clearly precious to him, as it was to me. After a few more pages, he again seemed overstimulated.

We took him outside in his wheelchair for a while, then brought him in for lunch. I helped feed him—he was the only one who needed help. Knowing how much he loved food, I was humbled to be his nurse for one of his final meals. When he was done, I wheeled him to face the door. Though it tore me up inside, I knew it was time to leave.

As I said goodbye, tears flooded my eyes. I hugged him tightly, then cupped his face—my most tender gesture of love. I gazed into his soft eyes and said, "Goodbye Dad. I love you! I love you so much Dad!" *I love you so much Dad!* I held his face taking in the moment and then released my grasp.

He looked up at me with the biggest proudest beaming smile—the same way he looked at me when I was a baby, when I was his "Little Bit" and his whole face filled my view of the world. Time paused while his radiant smile lingered. His squinting resolute eyes seemed to say to my soul—*All this time Elizabeth, and you came for me. I was waiting for you, and I love you. All this time I have loved you! I have never stopped loving you.*

From the look of love written on his face, he might as well have spoken those very words. His long stare of enduring affection will never leave me. I went to the car and bawled like a baby with my husband—he held me and wept with me. Though the grief of knowing it was the last time was terrible, I was thankful I had made it in time to see him before his passing a few weeks later.

BELOVED COMFORTER OF MEN

Close to midnight, Henry's Aunt Lisy and her husband Donny took me to the cafeteria since I hadn't eaten. They kindly bought me a meal and listened as I poured out my grief. I told them how Henry used to say that following Christ meant counting the cost—honestly telling God what you're willing to surrender. In my heart, I was able to surrender everything—except Henry or the kids.

I shared how, during our marriage, I would sometimes cry in Henry's arms just imagining the scenario of losing him. I even prayed that God would take us together, convinced at one point that He had promised me that mercy. Just two weeks earlier, I had one of those moments. Through tears, I had asked Henry, "What if God took you now, after all this healing and love we've built?" He held me and said, "No, Behb. He wouldn't do that. That would be cruel."

As I recounted this to Lisy and Donny, the tears came harder. They were moved by how deeply I loved him. At first, they tried to reassure me, but as I explained the severity of his condition, they understood this could truly be the end. They comforted me as I admitted that while I still hoped for a miracle, I also knew this might be God's will.

What terrified me most was the thought of going on without him. My identity still felt too fragile to survive without his love, his safety, his voice. I feared I'd be angry at God—haunted by Henry's words, "That would be cruel." But I couldn't take the thought of having bitterness towards God, right when I would need Him the most. I couldn't afford to turn away from Him, even in heartbreak.

When we returned to the waiting area, I was grateful to have been heard. I didn't know how I would even grieve without Henry—he was the only one I'd ever trusted enough to be that vulnerable with. Yet, talking to Lisy and Donny showed me I could open up to others too.

The night wore on, and the surgery stretched from one hour to three with no updates. During one of my several trips to grieve in the bathroom, Auntie Carol and Uncle Steve found me shaking in front of the entrance. I clung to Auntie Carol, sobbing, "I can't lose him. He's the love of my life!"

Alone in a stall, I cried out to God, overwhelmed by the weight of what I knew medically and the silence from the OR. Later, Amanda called to me, "Lizzie? Lizzie, are you in here?" Opening the bathroom door, I trembled in her arms and apologized for not being there for her. She held and comforted me saying, "It's ok Lizzie, it's ok." Her soothing strength that night was otherworldly, living up to the meaning of her name, "beloved comforter of men." Being her stepmom had been a sweet journey, a great blessing, and she was the best big sister to Elisha. I remembered how earlier that night in the ER Henry had entrusted her to care for Elisha and me. He knew her strength—and now I did too.

HEARING HIM

As the night stretched on, heavy with dread, I returned once again to my "prayer closet" in the bathroom. I glanced in the mirror at my red puffy eyes. I was losing hope.

I stepped into the stall and locked the door behind me, my hands quivering. I had prayed so many times before—for peace, for strength, for guidance—but never like this. Never for a miracle. Not directly. Not out loud. I had always stopped short, afraid to ask too much. Afraid of what it might mean if heaven stayed silent.

I pressed my forehead against the cool metal wall, trying to steady my breath. What if I asked—and nothing happened? What if I reached for God with everything in me, and He didn't reach back? The thought lodged in my chest like a stone. I wasn't just afraid of losing Henry. There was something deeper, harder to name. What if I asked for the impossible and it didn't come—if the One I had come to love—didn't answer.

But I had no other option. I was at the end of myself. And somehow, in that breaking point, I found the courage to risk it—to ask. Not just for Henry's life, but for something even more fragile—the hope that God would still be who I believed Him to be.

From honest depths, with a tremulous voice and gushing tears, my heart spoke aloud—"Father! His heart is literally in pieces on that table. Is he already with you in heaven? I know you are giving wisdom to the surgeon and touching Henry's body, and I know I've told you many times don't take him, and I am now at the end of myself! I can't control this. I can't do anything about this. This is killing me! You are God and You are the only one who can save him! Heal him, God! Please heal him! You can do anything! Heal him! Heal him, Lord!"

In this moment of desperation, I realized I was totally dependent on God for Henry's survival. No doctor or medical breakthrough could save Henry—only God.

Then, in the middle of my anguish, I heard Him.

His voice broke through the storm in my spirit, declaring three unforgettable truths deep into my heart,

"Don't despair.

He will live.

He will even have a speedy recovery."

I froze, my sobs arrested by His speech. I uttered—"Wha . . . What God? Did You just say that?" *Did I imagine it?* Through broken, shaking breaths I asked, "If that was You, say it again—fifty times more, so, I am sure!" He repeated it once more, gently quelling my doubt. But I knew—His voice was unmistakable. Though fear tried to creep back in, I held onto His words as His will over Henry's life.

Until that moment, the night had been utterly bleak. But now, hope pierced through like light breaking into deep waters. I began to calm down, repeating to myself over and over—*He will live. He will live. He will live!*

TELL THEM

I returned to the waiting area where Henry's family sat quietly—some reclining in chairs, others leaning against walls. Amanda and her boyfriend were out with her mom, while Henry's aunts, Henry's mom, and Vanessa waited in heavy silence. As I settled into my chair, I felt a prompting from God, "Speak it out. What you heard from Me in the bathroom—speak it out to the family." I hesitated, answering Him in my heart, *What if I give them false hope? You haven't told me fifty more times yet.* But the nudge came again, gentle yet firm, "Speak it out—now."

So, I did. I told Bellis, the aunts, and Vanessa what God had spoken to me—"He will live, and don't despair." As the words left my mouth, a weight lifted from the room. The dense anguish that had filled the air seemed to dissolve, replaced by a sense of divine presence. God Himself had stepped into our night, lovingly declaring, "I am here. This is in My hands. There is nothing to fear." I sat there touched that God spoke to me, reassuring us He would see this night through. We began to thank Him. Songs of praise rose from our weary hearts, faith stirred by the hope He had given. I felt God smiling on us, pleased that even in our exhaustion, we chose to worship. Henry's healing would be a miracle, and it would be His alone.

Around the fourth hour of surgery, the charge nurse called to say she'd be out shortly with an update. When she arrived, she handed me a plastic bag with Henry's wedding ring saying, "First thing, I want to give you this." My heart sank—*Was this a sign?* But then she quickly reassured us, "The surgery is going as expected." Relief flooded me. Henry was alive, and there were no immediate complications. It was the first tangible confirmation of what God had spoken.

Bellis and I nestled into a corner of the waiting room, staying awake to pray and sing worship songs while the others slept. Henry's sister Sabrina sent Bellis the song "Defender," and we played it quietly on her phone. We also sang "Raise a Hallelujah," a song of thanksgiving born after God miraculously saved a young child's life.

As the night wore on, I kept thinking about the third thing God told me—"He will even have a speedy recovery." That part was hardest for me to believe, so much so, that I didn't mention it to the family. My mind was filled with the mountain of possible complications. I remembered Henry's words in the ER, "You need to trust God. Even if I survive, my recovery could be long." He had been so lucid, even while drifting in and out of consciousness.

Though God promised me Henry would survive, doubt still crept in. Just nine hours earlier, we were preparing to eat dinner together, and now he was in surgery, his life in the hands of strangers. Exhausted and overwhelmed, I forced myself to stay awake, imagining God in the operating room, guiding the surgeon's hands—and performing His own miraculous work, unseen.

SLEEPLESS

At 3:30 a.m., I called the charge nurse as instructed. She reassured me that the surgery was progressing as expected. Dr. Kazui was focused on repairing Henry's aorta, which required a new graft to hold it together. I had so many questions about the other affected areas from his carotids to his abdomen—but I understood the priority was keeping him alive. Those of us still awake sat in silence and darkness, continuing to pray through the long night.

Sleep was impossible. The ache of the night's fear kept jolting me back into full alertness. Around 6:00 a.m., as the surgery neared completion, I waited anxiously for the next update. By 6:30 a.m. the rest of the family began to stir. Blankets and pillows were scattered everywhere when the pre-op day shift arrived and gently told us we could not wait there anymore. Just then, I received a phone call from the charge nurse who told us Henry was being moved to the ICU, and that we could transition there while his nurse got him settled.

We walked together to the ICU waiting area on the sixth floor, the family base for the next seven days, a space we called "the penthouse." Dr. Kazui would meet us there shortly to talk about the surgery. Surrounded on three sides by windows overlooking Tucson, we all gazed out on the encouraging view. The first light of dawn painted the sky in warm, gentle colors—comforting our eyes with the gift of morning. Henry had made it through the night.

I checked in at the ICU desk to let them know we were waiting. My breaths deepened. Hope began to rise in me and with it, a profound sense of relief. For the first time, I felt a surge of joy.

NINETEEN

Tenuous

Dr. Kazui entered the penthouse visibly exhausted, facing ten anxious family members hanging on his every word. With wide, weary eyes, he explained that Henry's aorta had been successfully repaired with a graft, and that he was doing better than expected. I had many questions, unsure if this would be the last time we'd see the surgeon. But I absorbed the most important truth—the critical repair was complete. The remaining dissection in Henry's abdomen and any complications with other organs would reveal themselves during recovery.

Kazui explained that his main concerns were Henry's blood pressure and whether he could breathe independently once he was removed from the ventilator. "We will be following him closely," he assured us. I was comforted that "he will live" had come to pass. *He is going to be ok*, I repeated, overwhelmed with gratitude. With tears in my eyes, I shook the hands that had worked all night to save him. Though Dr. Kazui shyly resisted, Henry's mother and I embraced him, we couldn't help ourselves.

It took longer than expected—an hour and a half—before I could see Henry. I calmed myself by repeating, *He is alive, he is alive*. I walked alone to his room, as most of his family was hesitant to see him intubated and surrounded by machines. As a nurse, I had cared for countless critical patients, but nothing prepared me to see my own husband like this. His body was swollen, his eyes shut from fluid overload, and I later learned he had gained thirty pounds from life-saving transfusions.

The rhythmic hum of machines droned in my ears as I took in

the sight of my beloved—my Behb—so vulnerable, so dependent on others. I grasped his hand and prayed, tears streaming down my face. This was the beginning of his recovery, one that would require more from all of us than I had imagined. Though I had received a hopeful word earlier, "He will even have a speedy recovery," I couldn't yet believe it. For now, I was so thankful he was alive.

The nurse invited me to sit beside him. For the next hour, I took his hand and wept. His skin was cool, but so familiar that it flooded me with warmth. In those moments, I didn't need to hide in a bathroom or be strong for anyone. I was safe to grieve, to feel, to hold the hand of the man I loved and let the tears fall freely.

BEAUTY OF OUR LIFE

Everything I treasured about Henry surged through me. It's true, you grasp the depth of love most clearly when you nearly lose it. As I sat by his hospital bed, memories of our fifteen-plus years together unfolded like a landscape. I thought of our sweet wedding ceremony, where God parted stormy skies for the exact moments we needed to complete our vows near a lake. With the reception washed away, I treasured our silent dance together under a rain-kissed porch. Early in our marriage, Amanda and I giggled like buddies over our antics, while Henry grinned and playfully rolled his eyes. When I held newborn Elisha in my arms, I cried with gratitude to God, overwhelmed with such a perfect gift, and the beautiful family He had given me with Henry.

I thought of how, as the baby of my family, I have been so tenderly cared for by this firstborn man who has loved me in every way a husband can. Most of all, he has cared for my heart—loving me through every layer of psychological healing, simply by accepting me as I am.

I remembered the season when I was too sick to work during my pregnancy with Elisha, and Henry lost his job in the same two months. We fell behind financially, and when Elisha began showing signs of severe autism, we knew one of us had to stay home. Though I loved being a mom, I struggled to provide the firm structure Elisha needed in the midst of his chaotic inability to communicate. After much prayer, we decided Henry would stay home while I worked full-time as an ER nurse. It was a reversal of traditional roles, but it was what our son—and our marriage—needed.

Through the years, we lived simply and faithfully, pastoring a small church and trusting God for everything, even when we had no medical insurance. We listened for His guidance, and three years before this night, we felt led to purchase coverage. Just a year ago, God impressed upon Henry to upgrade our plan which was timely guidance from a loving Father. Only God could have known the financial protection we would need this very week.

Despite the pressures of parenting a child with special needs and navigating our unconventional roles, our marriage has remained strong and deeply loving. Friends have often remarked on the rare bond we share. We have prayed for coworkers, welcomed others into our home, and always sought God's counsel in every trial. Sitting beside Henry now, I was overwhelmed by the beauty of our life together—and the grace that has carried us through it all.

DON'T LOOK TO ME

Though I know that if God had taken him, He would have drawn me into a deeper intimacy with Himself. I believe He would have brought beauty from ashes, because He is good. But I also know myself. I would have collapsed spiritually and emotionally into a long, dark grief. It would have taken years to recover from the loss of a love so rare, so foundational to my healing.

Ours is a marriage built on mutual respect and trust. We've never had to fight for space or control. Henry looks out for me, and I for him. There's no need to guard or withhold love from each other. That kind of safety is rare, and it's why the fear of losing him was so overwhelming. We've lived out the biblical model of marriage—not as a hierarchy of power, but as a partnership rooted in service and trust. Henry has shown me what it means for a husband to love his wife as Christ loves the church.

Submission, in our marriage, has never meant fear or silence. It's been about giving myself fully—my gifts, my heart, my trust—to someone who has always had my best interest at heart. And because Christ is at the center of our relationship, we've learned to repent quickly, to reconcile, and to seek God's counsel in every disagreement. Watching Henry love his daughter has also shown me what loving fatherhood looks like, another layer of healing for my soul.

From the beginning, Henry has helped me in a healthy way, but he never let me put him on a pedestal. He would tell me, "Don't look to me, look to God. I am just a man, and I will let you down. But God never will. I'm not your source, God is." That truth became real to me that night—I began to understand what it means to truly depend on the Lord. Though I had always relied on Henry, his voice was silenced, his body vulnerable, and I had to trust what God was telling me.

So much of my healing has come through our marriage, but it has always pointed me back to God. Henry has been the arms of Christ to me, but not Christ Himself. That distinction mattered now more than ever. Overnight, I learned that while Henry is a gift, my foundation must be built on the One who never leaves, never falters, and never dies.

AVERSION TO PRACTICALITY

There was another layer to my desperate cry in room nineteen—"I can't do life without you," one rooted not just in love, but in the practical rhythms of our life together. Henry has always been the one to handle the tangible, grown-up parts of living—managing our finances, cooking our meals, driving us everywhere, tipping servers, navigating insurance, making appointments and deciphering legal documents. I relied on him for these things, not out of laziness, this is just how our marriage worked. He found joy in caring for me this way, and I found security in knowing he had it covered while I poured myself into my work. It worked for us, and I never questioned it, until the night I thought I might lose him.

The truth is, after years of isolation in the cult and a childhood lacking foundational parental love, I had developed a deep aversion to the practicalities of life. God, in His mercy, had been restoring me—piece by piece—by allowing me to feel taken care of in every way. At the time, I wasn't yet a fully integrated person. I had many "children" within me—dissociated parts who were content to be cared for and who became overwhelmed by the demands of daily life. Even before we understood the complexity of my psychology, Henry intuitively stepped in. He saw how much I cherished being cared for and how difficult the world could feel for me. With patience and love, he filled in the gaps—not just as a husband, but as a steady presence for the fragmented pieces of me still learning how to live.

MY BEHB

Holding his hand in the ICU, I reflected on the last few years. It takes a strong man to not work in the traditional sense, and Henry carried that weight with grace. Caring for a special needs child, especially in Elisha's early years, took a toll on his health. But recently, we began to dream again. Henry had started doing freelance photography, and we were slowly building toward a shared vision of hiking and eventually backpacking together. We'd been gathering gear, watching trail videos, and even cooking "camp dinners" after evening treks to make it fun for Elisha. We felt momentum—physically, emotionally, spiritually.

This night, this emergency brought all of it to a screeching halt. But on this morning after surgery, I wasn't thinking about our shared goals, I was simply grateful that he made it. All I could think about was how much I wanted him—just him. Not the plans, not the progress, not even the beautiful life we've been building together. I just wanted to walk through whatever life brings with my love by my side.

STEEP ROAD

My focus shifted with resolve towards Henry's recovery. He had always been the one tending to me, now it was my turn to care for him. Every part of me was locked into his healing. There was no time to rest in the miracle of his survival. I knew the road ahead would be steep and as a critical care nurse, I was acutely aware of the risks. I began praying intensely over every vulnerable area of his body.

The dissection had compromised blood flow to his colon and kidney, both potentially fatal if not reversed. Because he required suctioning in the ER, he was at high risk for pneumonia, especially with his history of asthma. And above all, his blood pressure had to remain low to protect the fresh heart graft and prevent further dissection. These weren't abstract concerns—they were vivid, clinical realities I understood all too well. And while I held onto the miracle of his survival, I couldn't yet bring myself to speak the final word I had received—"He will even have a speedy recovery." All of these potential problems were heightened in my mind, and in the doctors' mind, especially during the first several days of recovery.

Henry's family, understandably overwhelmed, didn't want to hear the medical details. Most waited to visit until he was off the ventilator. But I couldn't look away. I was pleading with God, moment by moment, for mercy and healing. My knowledge made it harder to trust, but it also gave me clarity on how to pray. And while my specificity sometimes frustrated others, I believe it helped direct the intercession of Henry's family—prayer warriors who, in time, came to appreciate the focus I brought to our collective hope.

Messages from friends and colleagues poured in, some of whom had been with us in Room 19. My brother Finn called, and the concern in his voice brought me solace. My stepmother GG and stepsister Rebecca even offered to fly out to help, and their support meant more than I could say. In the midst of the medical storm, love from others reminded me I wasn't alone.

DAY ONE POST-SURGERY

Roughly ninety minutes after I arrived in the ICU, Henry began waking far too early from sedation—dangerously alert and disoriented. In a slow, terrifying panic, he reached for his breathing tube with alarming strength. I watched in horror as his blood pressure surged past 200 systolic—an immediate threat to his freshly repaired heart. Alongside the nurses, I helped restrain him, desperate to prevent him from pulling out any critical lines. It took three of us to hold him down until the ICU director arrived. She quickly administered sedation and blood pressure medication. Her calm, confident presence reassured me that Henry was in capable hands. I was stunned by Henry's stupefied power and the fact that he had become a threat to himself. The ICU director would go on to lead cardiovascular ICU rounds each morning, inviting me to join and patiently answering my questions, guiding both my understanding and my prayers.

Over the next few days, the medical team spoke to me with clinical candor, sometimes forgetting that this wasn't just another patient—it was my husband. I heard phrases like "this could kill him," and had to mentally block them out, choosing instead to cling to the quiet promise I'd received—that Henry would have a speedy recovery. My fragile nervous system was hit daily with waves of information, exhaustion, and grief. Scares over potential complications kept me alert, and I had lost my familiar ability to escape. Checking out, like I'd always done, wasn't working now.

Hours later that day, once I felt confident Henry was stable and sedated, I left the hospital briefly to gather clothes for Elisha and myself. Papa had brought Elisha to the hospital, and now we needed to prepare for the days ahead. Though I hated leaving Henry's side, I knew I had to be strong for our son. I hadn't slept for over thirty hours, but with Elisha in the car, I stayed alert, trusting that angels were guiding us safely home. During the drive and once we arrived, I made space for Elisha to talk. I wanted to make sure he was ok, and that he was expressing all that was locked away in that special heart and mind of his. Mostly we took comfort simply being together.

We sat at the kitchen table, stunned that less than 24 hours had passed since Henry was here and everything changed. I reheated the chimichangas he had lovingly made us, his last act of care before the crisis. As I ate, tears streamed down my face. *What if this had been the final meal he ever made for us?* Every item in the house, down to his socks thrown on the floor, his toothbrush tucked neatly upon the vanity, was a reminder of how close we came to losing him. I couldn't bear being home without him, and I felt an urgency to return to his side. We quickly packed our bags and headed back to the hospital. Though Henry's family encouraged me to sleep, I couldn't. Home wasn't home without him.

That night, from the pull-out couch in Henry's ICU room, I stared at Henry's body, dimly lit by monitoring lights. I walked over to hold his hand, my bare feet cooled by the hospital room floor. I prayed over every part of him, recalling the many times we'd seen healing through prayer. Then, gently, God brought back the final word I had tucked away, "He will even have a speedy recovery." I had clung to the first two promises—he will live, don't despair. But now I was being asked to believe for more.

God reminded me of His faithfulness, and I heard in my heart, "Would I preserve Henry's life only to take him a few days later? Daughter—trust Me." My body was tight with exhaustion, running on three hours of sleep in two days, but God wasn't asking for strength— He was asking for surrender. I had already given up control the night before, now He was asking me to do it again. Deep in my spirit I heard him speak, "Lean not on what you know, what all the scans and doctors are telling you and *trust Me.*"

With those words, I felt God closer than ever, calling me to a deeper faith. It reminded me of the Israelites in Exodus, miraculously delivered from Pharaoh's hand, only to struggle with trusting God in the wilderness. He had just delivered Henry from death. Now He asked me to believe Him for the next part of the journey. And I knew I had to say yes.

DAY TWO

I woke the next morning after only a little more sleep, jolted again by the reality before me—Henry, still intubated, still unconscious, recovering from emergency open-heart surgery. I longed to dissociate, to imagine us back home together, but there was no escaping this scene. When the radiology tech arrived for his morning chest x-ray, I asked to see the film and noticed signs of fluid or possible infection in his lungs. It confirmed my growing concern about pneumonia.

Later, the ICU medical director invited me to listen in on rounds. The team was watching for signs that Henry could breathe on his own, a key indicator for when he might be ready to have his breathing tube removed. I mentioned his likely aspiration in the ER, and she agreed pneumonia was a concern to monitor. Though I was told his current fever could be a normal post-operative response, I wasn't convinced. I prayed fervently—for the fever to break, for his lungs to clear, for God to breathe life into him and prepare him to come off the ventilator.

My most urgent prayer came after speaking with Dr. Kazui. He told me that with the aorta graft being so fresh, if Henry's blood pressure were to spike again upon waking, it could be fatal. I carried this knowledge alone, unable to share it with anyone but God. I began asking for very specific prayers from Henry's family and our prayer chains—that God would orchestrate the exact moment for getting him off the vent, that Henry's nervous system would be calmed, and that his body would be ready. Every extra day on the ventilator increased the risk of complications, especially if pneumonia was developing.

The ICU nurses appreciated I was constantly there as a second pair of clinical eyes, and I maintained a good rapport with them, careful with my questions and demeanor, never wanting to come across as controlling. It wasn't easy to stay hands-off, but I remained respectful, knowing it would impact the quality-of-care Henry received. Over time, I developed a deep respect for the ICU staff and their attentiveness to Henry's ever-changing needs.

By late afternoon, I sensed a shift, like the tide turning from waves of prayer. Henry's ventilator settings began to show signs of readiness. I asked the nurse if I could perform mouth care, feeling strongly that it would help prevent pneumonia. As I gently suctioned his mouth, Henry began to stir. The nurse called the doctors, and they decided he might be ready. I felt God's reassurance—this was the moment. As sedation tapered, Henry's eyes opened slowly, his head moving side to side. Unlike the day before, he was calm. His blood pressure rose only slightly. I leaned in, tears in my eyes, whispering, "Behb, you're OK. You're alive! I love you." He heard me. Though restrained, he began to lift his arms—perhaps trying to reach the tube. *Oh no! Not this again!*

Henry grew increasingly restless, his strength returning as he fought to free himself. I hoped it was just the anesthesia wearing off, but I knew Henry—intelligent, strong-willed, and deeply aware of medical risks. If he was trying to pull out his tube, something was wrong. My concern shifted to his mental state. *Is he waking up with stroke symptoms?* The nurse tried to calm him, but he wouldn't stop. My eyes darted to the monitor—*His blood pressure can't spike!* Immediately, I locked eyes with him and spoke with loving firmness—"Behb, I love you. Trust this. The tube has to stay in a little longer. It has to be slow and safe. Trust in God Behb. Trust in God." When I repeated the very words, he had spoken to me in the ER, "Trust in God," he stopped fighting. His eyes stayed on mine, and his body relaxed. It broke my heart to ask him to endure more pain, but I knew it was necessary.

As the anesthesia wore off further, the nurse performed a neurological exam. Henry could squint and show his teeth, but he couldn't move his left hand or leg. My heart sank! The nurse paged the stroke team, and within a minute, ten clinicians feverishly surrounded his bed. They asked him to move his limbs and smile, even with the breathing tube still in place. He showed slight movement on his left side, less than his right. They rushed him to CT to rule out a stroke caused by a brain bleed.

I collapsed into a chair, crying out to God again. Like continuous swells of a mighty storm, the looming threats hadn't ceased! I urgently asked Henry's family to pray that there would be no stroke. God whispered again, "Do not despair." But I didn't know what that meant. Would Henry survive, but be changed? Would he lose the ability to walk or speak? The medical team returned with news—no bleeding in the brain. Without the ability to perform an MRI and rule out a stroke affecting brain tissue, we would only know the extent of any deficits once the tube came out.

Fifteen minutes later, the moment came. The nurse prepared to remove his breathing tube. My heart was in my throat. Would he breathe on his own? Would he show signs of a stroke? When Henry finally spoke, his voice was soft and brief, but it was the sweetest sound I'd ever heard. "Open heart?" he asked. "Yes," I replied, "You're part of the zipper club now, Behb." Relief washed over me—his mind was intact. He could move all his limbs, and though his left side remained slightly weaker, it would improve.

Later, Henry told me the breathing tube was unbearable, but he wasn't trying to pull it out. His frantic movements were just him trying to scratch an itchy nose!

DAY THREE AND MORE

In the days that followed, recovery seemed like it would be slow. We closely monitored his lungs, and antibiotics were started to treat potential pneumonia. When the staff tried to help him stand, he struggled due to thirty pounds of fluid he'd received during surgery and a weakened left side. But God said he would have a speedy recovery.

The third day after surgery, I saw a glimpse of my Henry again.

He looked at me and said, "Hi Behb," in the familiar, affectionate tone I'd heard a thousand times. I smiled, finally able to breathe freely. The anxiety that had gripped me for days began to loosen. That evening, I shared the final word I had received with Henry's family—that he would recover quickly. We had passed through so many threats—no stroke, no pneumonia, no kidney or colon failure. He was breathing, speaking, standing. We were getting him back, whole and healing!

Driving between home and the hospital to bring Henry things he needed, I blasted "Raise a Hallelujah" on the radio, singing along with everything in me. It was my anthem of victory. God had done what only He could do—preserve Henry's life and set him on a path to thrive.

DO YOU HAVE ANY RIGHT?

One night during Henry's recovery, God spoke to me with a piercing clarity, both loving and sobering. In the quiet, He asked, "Do you have any right to demand of Me not to take your husband?" His question struck deep. I've learned that God welcomes honesty, and my heart responded with a pang of protest, "But God . . . You gave him to me!" Yet He repeated the question, undeterred by my emotion, "Do you have any right to demand of Me not to take your husband?" As I looked at Henry resting, I whispered my answer through an outburst of tears, "No." I didn't fully understand why God was confronting me this way in the midst of such vulnerability, but I sensed He was freeing me—calling me to surrender what I was still holding back.

God was revealing the fear I hadn't dared to name—that if He had taken Henry, I might have lost my trust in Him, too. I was terrified not only of losing my husband, but of losing my ability to see God's goodness in the aftermath. This is a tender spot in the life of a Christian, and it reminded me of Job, who lost everything yet did not curse God. Instead, he simply said, "The Lord gives, and the Lord takes away, blessed be the Name of the Lord." I thought of the Bethel church worship leader who lost her young daughter and still declared God's goodness, even when prayers for her child's resurrection went unanswered. These testimonies had always moved me, but now they confronted the part of me that still wanted to cling to what I loved most, as if I knew better than God.

I know that if I had become a widow, God would have been my comfort again, just as He was during my years of isolation. But I had been holding onto Henry, this beautiful gift, as if I couldn't live without him. God, in His mercy, spared Henry's life, perhaps even for my sake. But He was also reminding me that He alone is sovereign, and that His plans are always good, even when they're beyond my understanding. Deep down, I knew this was what Henry meant when he admonished me just before his surgery, "Trust God, because He is good, no matter what."

FORGED IN FIRE

In the quiet hospital nights of Henry's recovery, it felt like we had run a marathon together. We spoke softly, holding hands, marveling at the life we still had. I would walk to his bedside, lean my head against him, and cry. "It's really hard to see you like this," I whispered. "I know," he said gently. "God is good." When I asked if God had been with him during surgery, he said, "Yes. It was really awesome. He was with me the whole time Behb." Though he hadn't seen God, he felt His presence. "I'm so lucky to be alive," he said. "Oh yes," I replied, "you don't even know."

One night, as I sat beside him, Henry began to recall what God had spoken to him during surgery. "If I slay you, will you trust Me?" God had asked. "Yes," Henry had answered. He believed the night was a spiritual battle, a direct attack from the enemy. From the moment he felt the tear in his chest, he said, a *"No!"* rose up within him. When Henry told us in the ER to trust God no matter what, he was also preaching to himself. That night, faith was forged in fire.

With tears in his eyes, Henry told me, "Because I trusted Him, God said He trusts me. God trusts me. But . . . I'm just a man." He described how that night heaven interceded for his life, and how God said to the heavenly witnesses, "Wait—this is not the end." At one point, Henry told God he was ready to go, that he had done all he needed for his family. But God replied, "Yes, but they deserve to be loved more, loved longer."

We began to see that night as a divine crossroads. Though Henry can't recall specific visions, he believes he spoke with God in heaven. The memory fades as soon as it surfaces, but the knowing remains. "I feel like I belong less to myself," he said, "like an edge was taken away."

True to God's word, Henry was discharged home only a week after his brush with death. By day four, Henry began walking—just ten feet at first, each step a struggle. But every day he improved. Watching him, I understood why God moved me as a nurse from the ER to cardiac rehab four years earlier. I saw firsthand how small movements lead to full recovery. After a month at home, Henry joined my rehab program and regained his strength. Nearly five years later, his scans remain clear, and Dr. Kazui still calls him the man with a 5% chance to live. "You are doing well. Enjoy your life," he recently told Henry. And we do. We know God has many years in store for him, and I've received that promise in my spirit for my own peace.

We are forever marked by the love of our Father who saved Henry from sudden death and spared us from unimaginable grief. For months, we called it "the dark night," but now we see it as a night of faith, hope, and miracles. What the enemy meant for evil, God turned for good. It could have been a night of loss—but instead, it became a night of victory. I even wrote a song that we sing in church, and every time I sing it, scenes from that night flood my heart. It was the night faith was born.

"Even in the Darkest Night" by Elizabeth Gonzalez

That night You came
Even in the dark You stayed
The same God so dear to me
You pierced through, faithful and true

Even in the darkest night, You are good
Even when there seems no way, You breakthrough
Even when the answer is bleak, You walk in
Even when it seems all hope is gone
Even when I'm at my end
You begin

Constant faithful One
Rising like the sun
Your steady pulse of life to my soul
Your love it never ends

Even when I fear
Your hands draw me near
You whisper words of hope to my soul
You never let me go

Even in the darkest night, You are good
Even when there seems no way, You breakthrough
Even when the answer is bleak, You walk in
Even when it seems all hope is gone
Even when I'm at my end
You begin

TWENTY

Integration

Eight days after his surgery, I took Henry home and nothing could keep me from staying by his side. Thanks to generous friends like Hannah, Julie and Amanda P. who graciously offered me some of their paid time off as well as Hannah who collected a gift basket of donated funds, I was able to take care of him for an entire month while he recovered. Beloved family members Bellis and Vanessa cleaned and ministered to us, and our Amanda arranged for meals and meal kits to be provided by church members. Learning to prepare healthy food for Henry was good for me since he has always been the one to do the cooking. I also became comfortable driving again, taking Henry to follow-up doctor appointments and going solo to the grocery store. Stretching my wings in aspects of adulthood where I had been taking a backseat for so long strengthened my confidence.

TURNING POINT

Soon after his recovery, Henry and I realized that a monumental shift occurred in my soul the night of his surgery. When God spoke the words of hope that Henry would live, I was already completely undone—stripped of control, defenses, and inner voices that had once helped me cope with life. For the first time, even they were quiet. I stood alone before a sovereign God, raw and helpless, unable to lean on Henry, who had always helped hold me together. I had lost faith in everything—in myself, in my fears, even in the doctors who were at the mercy of God's decision about whether Henry would live. Realizing God was the only One who could save him, I finally let go and surrendered Henry to God.

It wasn't until I reached the end of myself, until I had nothing left but to trust Him, that I could truly hear God. Heavy with desperation, I cried out for a miracle or the strength to survive a great heartbreak. *I needed God to be real!* And He met me—not as a distant deity, but as the Faithful One who speaks truth and keeps His promises. In that moment, I experienced the beginning of a deeper transformation, when my adult voice finally emerged, grounded in surrender and trust.

What I didn't realize then was that this crisis marked the unraveling of my lifelong self-protection. The voices that had once shielded me had no reference to understand or script to respond to this kind of pain. And because they had no answers, they began to fall silent, some even integrating into the whole of who I was becoming. The scattered pieces of my mind settled into place behind my one main voice. For the first time, I responded not from past trauma, but from the present—anchored in faith. That significant night, something shifted in me that could not have happened in any other way.

In the months that followed, I began therapy to process the trauma of nearly losing Henry. There, I received confirmation of what God had already begun to reveal—that I had lived with a non-possession form of dissociative identity disorder (DID), shaped by childhood trauma. Unlike the more commonly portrayed version of DID, mine did not involve distinct personalities taking control, but rather a fragmented chorus of internal voices—dissociative parts of self that had split off to survive. This explained my severe memory loss and skewed sense of identity. But my therapist was stunned. After only a few sessions, I showed signs of beginning to integrate these voices without her intervention. This was because the night of Henry's survival was also my soul's turning point.

In the chrysalis of my life, my liquefication was complete. Nothing that had previously defined me would ever be the same again, and integrating all remaining voices into wholeness would soon follow. God had prepared me for this integration a couple years earlier through the love and friendship of Martha.

MARTHA

When I met Martha as a patient in cardiac rehab in 2017, I sensed immediately that she was safe. Despite the voices within me that rarely agreed about anyone, they all seemed to trust her. Our bond deepened as we shared our fervent love for the Lord and our parallel journeys of healing from childhood trauma. We both found solace in painting, a gift from God that helped us cope as children. Though Martha's trauma was far more severe—rooted in satanic ritualistic abuse (SRA) inflicted by her parents—she never allowed the difference in severity to diminish my pain. "There is nothing to compare dear friend," she would say with compassion, affirming that my healing was just as valuable to God.

Martha's story was harrowing. Chosen by her parents for SRA because of her intelligence and creativity, she developed a full personality disorder. Her husband documented their journey in a book that described how they invited Jesus into each fractured part of her mind, seeking wholeness. As Henry and I read it, we began to understand my own dissociations more clearly. While mine weren't intentionally created like Martha's, they were born to survive repeated trauma—especially the perpetual fear and control I experienced from Em.

Before Martha, I hadn't even recognized these voices as separate. I thought of them as a tangled mess of thoughts, just part of my complicated psychology. But through her, I began to see them as protective, shielding me from pain I wasn't ready to face. Martha helped me understand this fragmentation was not a flaw, but a survival mechanism—an intelligent design from God to help me endure. She told me that God had been good to me, allowing these dissociations to form so I could forget just enough to keep going. Her words reframed my understanding of my own mind. What once felt like chaos began to feel like evidence of God's mercy, His way of helping me live through what I couldn't yet process.

VOICES CARRY

God revealed to Henry and me that while Martha endured a complete personality disorder, my own internal voices were not fully formed personas but fragments—distinct echoes of my psyche with their own perspectives. At one point, I had over 500 of these voices, creating overwhelming chaos. When I placed my faith in Christ, God began a profound healing process—quieting some voices immediately, integrating many more over time, and continuing to restore others throughout our years of marriage. Only since the dark night has He shown me the remaining larger, more distinct pieces. Before my salvation in 2001, I was at the mercy of whichever voice was loudest. At that tenuous time, I believe I was mere weeks from being fully controlled by my dissociations—a complete personality split from which I would not have recovered had God not intervened.

Martha, even with her deep healing and her husband's devoted care, still carried remnants of her personalities until her passing in 2021. Yet, the joy that radiated from her despite such darkness was a powerful testimony to the hope of healing. Her gentle spirit and luminous eyes gave me courage to believe that restoration was possible for me, too. Known for her kindness and thoughtfulness, Martha was a wellspring of grace to everyone she met. And now, I can only imagine the fullness of her healing—completely integrated and whole in the presence of Jesus Himself.

LIFTING THE VEIL

During my friendship with Martha, God began gently unveiling memories I had long suppressed, repetitive traumas buried deep within me. It was as if He waited for the safety of Martha's friendship, knowing she had been healed enough to walk beside me through the process. These memories surfaced in dreams, quiet impressions, tearful moments with the Lord, or even through themes in films.

It was a disorienting time, moving from dissociation to the painful clarity of truth. But God knew I was willing. Healing had been the deepest cry of my heart since salvation, and He was answering that prayer, one He always honors when we seek the truth about our lives from His perspective.

Henry stood with me through every wave of this awakening. With his gift for hearing from God, he offered insight, comfort, and constant prayer. There were moments when the weight of the abuse and neglect I endured felt unbearable, and I would cry out, "Was it really that bad?" Henry never wavered. He held me, prayed over me, and reminded me that God was revealing only what I was ready to face. In His mercy, God never overwhelmed me with a flood of memories. Instead, like restoring a fragile artifact, He revealed each layer of my soul gently with tender care.

Martha understood my desperation to heal. Her joy was contagious, and her testimony gave me hope that healing was not only possible—it was promised. We marveled at how God had preserved our spirits, placed us in loving marriages, and brought us into His care. A few months before Henry's near-death experience, Martha and her husband took us out for dinner and shared how they had partnered with God to bring healing to her dissociated parts. Their Christ-centered approach became a model for us, preparing Henry and me to walk the same path toward my own wholeness.

THEY ARE JUST THOUGHTS

From a young age, I learned to compartmentalize emotions and willfully forget painful memories. But after meeting Martha and beginning therapy, I wondered how my inner pieces were formed. I came to understand that trauma stunts emotional growth, beginning as vague, floaty feelings that, over time, develop voices and distinct identities. Unlike Martha's split personas that could take over and act independently, mine never reached that level of autonomy. Instead, they influenced me internally—voices that spoke to me, but not through me, leaving me feeling tense, breathless and out of sync with my beliefs. These rogue emotions and intrusive thoughts often shocked me, but I came to realize they were parts of my own psyche, shaped by fear and survival.

As a Christian, I feared these voices were demonic remnants from my time in the New Age. I confessed them to Henry—visions, perversions, and disturbing images—and he would ask God about them. God's response was gentle and freeing, "They are just thoughts. They are not who you are." God reminded me to take them captive, as Scripture teaches, and let them go. This acknowledgment brought immense relief. God didn't shame me for having these thoughts—instead, He removed their power and guilt. He also withheld the full truth of their origins until I was ready, knowing that healing would come in stages, not all at once.

Dissociations made me more vulnerable to demonic influence, which is why I longed so deeply for freedom. The torment continued until my voices were fully integrated, as they had been born out of childhood terror. Martha explained how SRA tormentors would deliberately sever hope by saying things like, "Where is Jesus now?" during the creation of alters—ensuring they remained isolated and unreachable. The goal was to keep each piece locked in fear, unable to be healed or be evangelized. But God, in His mercy, had a different plan.

He gave Martha a loving, Spirit-led husband who patiently walked her through deliverance. When I looked into her eyes, I saw the mercy of God—how He had transformed her from a vessel of torment into a woman filled with joy and purpose. As she explained, her healing was not the result of human effort or psychology, but the relentless love of God reaching every part of her. Each alter was met with the gospel, and through that divine love, she was made whole. Her story gave me hope that the same God who healed her could heal me.

HALLMARKS OF DISSOCIATION

Trauma doesn't always come in with a bang from obvious sources like abuse, war, or disaster. Sometimes, it seeps in like fog—quiet, invisible and just suffocating. In truth, everyone has experienced some form of shock—this world is too broken for anyone to escape unscathed. Disappointments, betrayals, illness, loss—these leave marks on all of us. And just as trauma is universal, so is dissociation. Each of us, in some way, develops a lens through which we view the world—a lens shaped by pain, imperfection, and our own flawed responses. These lenses fracture our perception, and though we try to see through the clearest shards, we still can't fully see ourselves or others as we truly are.

Only Jesus Christ, the resurrected Son of God, sees us perfectly. His view is unbroken, unmarred by sin or distortion. Scripture says His way is flawless, His nature unchanging, and His light without shadow. In contrast, we humans approach life from fragmented positions. Our personalities are shaped by the perspectives we adopt—responses to pain, fear, and survival. In a healthy person, these responses become part of a flexible identity. But in someone with dissociation, those responses can become overwhelming, even consuming, leading to spirals of confusion and emotional paralysis.

For me, those spirals were intense. Henry called it my "downward spiral" when voices within me could escalate quickly, creating a cascade of conflicting thoughts and emotions. Unlike someone with fully defined alters like Martha whose entire personality might instantly switch, my shifts were slower but still deeply destabilizing. The sheer number of voices—each with its own fear, judgment, or defense—could leave me breathless and frozen, unsure how to respond or even who I was in the moment.

This was especially true early in our marriage, when visiting Henry's large, close-knit family. Their protectiveness, shaped by past wounds, was understandable, but overwhelming. My dissociations reacted to every perceived judgment. One voice would panic about not being accepted, another would criticize my every word, while another would retreat in defeat. Though I longed to be lighthearted and present, once subjected to a cascade of triggered feelings, I was often paralyzed by internal chaos. I would withdraw to another room, red-faced and tearful, unsure of what was happening inside me.

Henry was the only one who understood the depth of my struggle. He loved me and trusted the vision God had given him of who I would become. I didn't know how to be myself around others, but I knew God had brought Henry into my life to be a spiritual covering—a shield from further harm. In time, I grew to feel at ease with his family, who are truly wonderful. But in those early days, I was anything but at ease. My only refuge was the love I felt from God, from Henry, and from his grandmother Nani, who saw through my fears and made me feel safe.

MEMORY LOSS

It's deeply frustrating to live without access to your memories. When I try to recall, all that comes into my awareness are amorphous remains and hazy impressions. Still, I struggle to tune in, longing to adjust the frequency of my mind—to hear clearly, to remember fully. But no matter how hard I try, the clarity doesn't come. I understand now why I chose to forget—why my brain locked away what was too painful to carry. The mind protects itself from what it cannot endure. And when memories do return, they expand my understanding like a panoramic view replacing a narrow window. Yet even after years of healing, much of my past remains in pieces.

Only God knows the full story of my life. And in His mercy, He reveals it to me with tender imprints and quiet echoes, only as I've been ready to receive it, never uncovering more than I can bear. With the gentleness of a loving Father, His presence has been profoundly intimate, touching the most vulnerable places in my soul. Through this process, I've come to see that He was always with me, even in the darkest times I couldn't remember. He was there in the bathroom, comforting me when my sister locked me away, just as He was there in the bathroom when I cried out for Henry's life. He's been present for every painful tear in between. Even before I knew Him, He was speaking hope into my soul, preparing me for the day I would finally hear Him.

SPACINESS

God revealed that my dissociation began around age three, and I can see the shift in childhood photos—my toddler eyes are bright, but in kindergarten, they're distant. By age six, I had learned to "check out," and memory blocking became my norm. Though I performed well in school, I lived in a fog. When memories began to surface, I grieved for the little girl who had no one to protect her. It's remarkable I could forget so much, but God, in His mercy, designed an intelligent and creative way for my spirit to survive. What served me well as a child became a burden to deal with as an adult.

Only God could untangle the compartments I had created. When I opened my heart to Him, He began to free my spirit. In the midst of grieving, I remembered something I had once read in the Bible—that when we seek God with all our heart, we will find Him. That truth anchored me. My desperation for healing had led me to Him, and He met me with compassion, revealing only what I was ready to face.

During college, my osteopathic physician and mentor, Tasha, prescribed a homeopathic constitutional remedy called "Opium," believing it matched the essence of my dissociative state. She noted that while I was driven, I also seemed mentally sedated. Her insight resonated. At the time, I drew numerous abstract, distorted faces— visual echoes of voices within me. The remedy brought temporary relief, but it wasn't a cure. I quickly reverted to avoidance, and it became clear that no external solution could reach the depths of my fractured soul. Only God could bring the lasting healing I longed for.

THE DISSOCIATIONS

In the season following Henry's longest night, God gave me a deep spiritual understanding that just weeks before I was saved, several of my internal voices had nearly solidified into full personalities. The most dominant of these was what He identified as my "protector." Ironically, this protector mirrored the very person I feared becoming—my sister Em. Whenever I encountered someone who reminded me of her control or volatility, this part of me would rise up in a fury. It was terrifying and uncontrollable, a childlike tyrant desperate for safety and yet, it made sense. What better defense against Em than an inner version of her? As painful as it was to acknowledge, creating this protector was the most intelligent survival strategy I had.

Over time, I came to see this protector as the ugliest part of me—rageful, reactive, and deeply rooted in fear. I had no name for it until God, in His timing, helped me recognize its purpose. It existed to match or outmatch the threat I once lived with, and its strength revealed how powerless I felt growing up. Understanding this piece with compassion became essential to my healing. When I finally voiced my desire to integrate all the parts of myself and become whole, the protector fought hard! Her role had always been to keep the others separate, to lock away the pain. She warned me fiercely, "Trust me! You don't want to know what really happened!" and she enlisted other voices like the doubter, the rebel, and the pessimist to work cooperatively to fight the process.

Though I was afraid to let her go, and as much as she had protected me, I could no longer rely on her. The cost of keeping her as my armor had become too painful. I sensed that God was asking me to lay her down—not in rejection, but in trust. It was time to let Him be my refuge, to allow His strength to replace defenses I had built. So, with trembling faith, I began to release her.

THE TIME IS NOW

During Christmas break of 2019, I felt drawn to read "Brave Surrender" by Kimberly Walker Smith, a worship leader I admired. In it, she described how childhood trauma had fractured her psyche, and how Christian counselors helped her integrate the loudest of her internal voices—one that openly hated and distrusted God. Her story struck a deep chord in me. I trembled with urgency and cried out to God, "I want that! Help me integrate, Jesus—I don't know how!" Suddenly, the protector within me lashed out, insisting, "That's crap, you don't want that!" But instead of yielding to her strong-arming tone, I saw her fear. I ran to Henry, who prayed and received insight from God. The Holy Spirit filled the room with peace, and God gently said of the protector, "She is very tired. She needs to rest."

With my eyes closed and tears streaming, Henry and I spoke to the protector, telling her she could rest now—that Jesus would be my protector, and He was more than capable. Formed when I was six, she responded like a child, reaching out to Jesus, assured by the safety of His presence. In a Spirit-led visualization, I saw Him give her an ice cream cone and take her hand. Together, they walked through a doorway, and she was absorbed into my adult self—joyful, no longer needing to defend me. That moment marked a miraculous integration, one only God could orchestrate.

Afterward, I felt a lightness I had never known. The fear of the bully protector was gone, and for the first time, I didn't fear myself. Though I felt more vulnerable, I also felt safer, able to trust Jesus more deeply. The harsh voice that once sabotaged my closeness with God and others was gone. Martha was the first person I told. She understood the magnitude of what had happened and rejoiced with me. "Oh Lizzie, that is just wonderful. Every time one of my little ones goes to Jesus," she said, "He fills my empty bucketfuls with His love, and I can't stop smiling with His joy!"

This kind of healing could only have come through the Holy

Spirit. No therapy alone could have convinced a protective part to lay down its armor. These pieces weren't just psychological, they were spiritual—rooted in the soul. Only the Captain of our souls could bring them home. Over the next few years, with Henry's spiritual discernment and the Holy Spirit's guidance, the remaining voices were gradually exposed and integrated. It was a process only God could lead, and only my willingness could allow.

Whenever a voice surfaced, I recognized it immediately. It spoke separately from my own voice and felt like a boil that needed to be lanced. I dealt with it right away, not wanting it to retreat into hiding. Plus, I knew the tremendous freedom, healing and release that came from giving it to Jesus! God's compassion met each one like a healing balm, soothing the pain they had carried. As I came to understand their roles—a paranoid piece to calculate risk, a piece projecting negativity to shield me from disappointment, a piece pleading for approval to keep me from self-agency, a perfectionist piece to guard me from judgement—I saw how each had formed to protect me. Through God's tender lens, I finally understood why they existed. And with that compassion, I was able to let them go.

WILLINGNESS TO BE HEALED

Having partnered with God for many years to heal my mind, I believe you must be desperate to transform to be ready for it. It takes a despairing of your own reactions to life—becoming genuinely tired of your own triggers, habitual feelings or patterns of responding. Taking responsibility for your own reactions, you decide to cease blaming others and pray for God to change you.

For much of my life, I worked hard to conceal flustered emotions that suddenly rose within me. Outwardly, I tried to appear composed, but inside, I was overwhelmed by reactions I couldn't fully suppress. These responses felt like live wires—erratic, painful, and impossible to contain. I knew they were childish, yet I couldn't stop them. Only God understood the depth of my suffering and the shame I carried over voices that raged inside me. I lived in fear of being exposed, while experiencing relentless self-criticism and over-analysis. My inner world was a torment, and to say I was stifled in being myself is a gross understatement.

The fact that God has walked me back from that chaos and integrated those dissociative voices into wholeness is the greatest miracle of my life. My healing took time—longer than most—because of the sheer number of pieces that needed to be set free. For someone like me, healing required far more than attending a healing conference or a simple call to forgive everyone and move on. When I heard such advice from other Christians, I often assumed they had grown up in homes where they felt safe and loved. My experience was different. It demanded not only the hand of God but the steady, patient love of God at every step.

Though my healing began with desperate prayers, it was God who led the way. He speaks to all His children about their healing, but there must be a willingness to receive it. My own desire for healing has been fierce since the day I gave Him my heart. I read in the Bible that if we ask anything according to His will, He hears us. And it is absolutely His will that His children know the truth and be set free—the truth about Him, the truth about themselves, and about their lives. Only He could do the delicate work of restoring me and making my heart whole—evangelizing each voice within me to trust Him, and in doing so, making me one.

SEIZURE DISSOCIATIONS

There were moments in my life when new voices emerged, dissociations born from pain too great to face. High school was one such time, when my mother left me with her best friend and I began to drift away mid-conversation, escaping into silence. But the most vivid markers were the seizures—strange, paralyzing episodes that began in childhood. They weren't the kind that left me unconscious, but rather ones that froze me in place, my body overwhelmed by electric waves of anxiety. At the time, I didn't know what was happening. But years later I came to recognize these as psychogenic seizures—my mind's way of buying time, creating space to bury trauma and shape new voices. The first came in fourth grade, after my mother kicked my brother Patrick out of the house. I watched him leave, helpless and heartbroken, and something inside me fractured. Within that week, my body seized at school, and a new voice was born—one that whispered the truth I couldn't yet face—my mother could abandon her children.

Years later, another seizure came during a tense conversation with my brother Finn. It echoed a moment from college, when I had fled a campsite after a fight with my sister, walking for hours in a dissociative haze. When Finn found me after a frantic search, he was furious but deeply concerned. His anger wasn't like Em's—it wasn't about control. It was about care. That night, I realized something new—that being held accountable could feel safe. So, when I froze in front of him months later, unable to speak with a glassy stare, it wasn't manipulation, it was survival. My psyche, overwhelmed by the fear of discord or losing his love, created a diversion. The seizure drew out his concern again, and in that moment, I felt protected. I didn't understand it then, but I see now how my mind crafted these responses to preserve connection—to shield me from the unbearable.

These voices, these dissociations, weren't random. They were shaped in moments of rupture, when love felt conditional, when safety vanished. They became my way of remembering, of preparing for the next time. Each seizure, each split, was a desperate attempt to hold on to something—dignity, safety, love. And though they came from pain, they also carried a strange kind of wisdom—a child's way of surviving what should never have been survived alone.

SOUND MIND

For years, I longed to experience what I had read in the Bible—that God hasn't given us a spirit of fear, but of power, love, and a sound mind. Yet that reality felt far from me, and it frustrated me deeply. Before I had any awareness of my past, I would cry beneath a blanket, the only place I felt safe enough to speak honestly with God. In those moments, I could sense the Holy Spirit holding unstable fissures together in my mind. It's still astonishing to recall, but I felt Him literally filling gaps in my brain—holding me together when I couldn't do it myself. Just as I had once read that all things are held together in Him, I clung to the belief that He was holding me together, too. It was strange, painful, and deeply vulnerable. But He was restoring me, gently and in His perfect timing.

God's patience has been extraordinary. He didn't bring all my pieces together at once, He knew that would have overwhelmed me. When I was born again and His Spirit took residence in my heart, many pieces of me were immediately integrated. But because of the nature of my dissociative mind, much healing remained. Often, He let me understand what He was doing, knowing how much I longed to comprehend each step. Other times, He healed without explanation, because He is loving and doesn't require us to grasp everything in order to be made whole. As the Creator of the mind, He alone knows how to restore it.

What a loving, living God—to heal the very thing I cried out for most—freedom from my own mind. I am a walking miracle. Twenty years ago, I was unrecognizable. My eyes were haunted, my shoulders tense, my thoughts clouded by confusion and fear. I didn't experience a sound mind until these past several years. The healing has taken over two decades, beginning the moment I gave my heart to Him in January 2001. Though I once sought love in all the wrong places, His hand was always upon me. He made a way to reach me, to reveal Himself, and to begin the long, beautiful work of making me whole.

EVERYTHING BECOMES NEW

Caterpillars don't know they're about to transform—they simply respond to a cascade of internal changes. In the same way, I spent the early stages of my life searching for truth and deliverance in all the wrong places, unaware that true freedom would only come through entering the protective chrysalis of God's care.

It was there, in His covering, that I learned to trust Him and exchange my self-made defenses for His. But it never occurred to me that transformation would be heralded with such turmoil.

Like the caterpillar who doesn't know it will become a butterfly, I didn't realize what I was becoming. I couldn't see the change God was working in me. Before He revealed Himself, I didn't even believe freedom from torment was possible. But even when I was surrounded by spiritual darkness, I was never beyond His reach. He pierced through my numbness with the simplicity of the gospel in that single wide trailer. He revealed Himself, personally visiting me, and I knew I belonged to Him and had been set free.

That holy encounter marked the beginning of something I couldn't yet name. I had been set free, yes, but freedom wasn't the end of the story. God was just getting started with a deeper work in me, a quiet unfolding that would take place over time. It was God drawing me into a sacred process, a hidden season where healing would come slowly, layer by layer within the chrysalis of His care.

The chrysalis is designed for transformation. From one angle, it glimmers with promise—from another, it looks like a prison. My years in that dark, secret place were difficult, but they were necessary. God used that time to bring to light what needed healing and to replace what was broken with more of Himself.

I read that anyone who belongs to Christ becomes a new creation—old things pass away, and everything becomes new. This has been my experience. After every trial, He has either brought a new level of healing or revealed more of His nature. He never takes without giving more of Himself in return.

In my caterpillar years, I believed I could reach wholeness on my own. I was vulnerable to a false illusion, manipulated by fear and false promises that I would "get there" if I just kept trying. But once

I found Christ, the lies scattered. I finally knew the truth—I would be healed. God has spoken to my spirit again and again, reminding me not to lose heart, that He is always with me, and that He will never let me go. I've held onto those promises—reminders that I now live by faith in the One who gave Himself for me, and that no one can ever snatch me from His hand. These truths have become the foundation of my joy—an unshakable joy that no one can take away.

PART THREE
Emerging

"Perhaps the butterfly is proof that you can go through a great deal of darkness and still become something beautiful."
—Unknown

TWENTY-ONE

Transformed

Once the butterfly is fully formed inside her protective shell, she must undergo a transitional time to prepare for emergence. The butterfly's final struggle therefore is to break free. With a completely transformed body, she remains encased in her chrysalis which has since morphed into a translucent membrane. Peering through this final veil covering her shape, she knows that her appearance is inevitable; this is no longer just a dream, or merely a hope. Her journey into windswept heights will begin the moment she makes her debut.

She begins pushing against the shell that once held her, not only to escape, but to strengthen and build muscles she will need to fly. Her struggle to emerge is not a flaw—it is the final act of becoming.

Just as the butterfly's emergence from the chrysalis required great effort, my healing—my becoming, took years, marked by countless victories, many of them unexpected. Some were clear blessings from the Father's heart, while others came through the refining fire of trials He allowed. Each one helped me surrender old defenses, see truth from His perspective, and trust Him more deeply. Even during hardships that echoed past traumas, He never left me. The Bible speaks about God being our hiding place, surrounding us with songs of deliverance, and I lived that truth. Through it all, He clothed me in His strength and called me His paladin, honoring the courage it took to persevere and keep saying yes to healing. After a lifetime of feeling powerless, He empowered me with strength I had never known.

To help me bravely emerge from my chrysalis, God rooted me in His Word. I read that those who delight in His ways are like trees planted by flowing waters—bearing fruit in season, never withering. He didn't place me beside stagnant pools, but in the rocky, narrow currents of life's trials, where I had to face hardship instead of dissociating from it. My old nature wanted to retreat, but it was in confronting life through His Word that I began to transform. Without trusting Him, I would have remained bound in fear. "Help!" became my most frequent prayer—and He always came.

Through every season, He has been faithful. Even when I falter, He never gives up on me. Because it's not about how much I love Him, it's always been about how much He loves and believes in me.

BUTTERFLY HOUSE

Not long after Henry's surgery, in the midst of the Covid pandemic, we were suddenly asked by our landlord to vacate our home. The timing was difficult—Henry was still recovering, and we were adjusting his medications. In the past, this kind of upheaval might have felt like the end of the world, but we had seen God's faithfulness. Henry had survived against the odds, and we knew God would carry us through this, too.

Finding a new home wasn't easy. The housing market was intense. Homes sold within hours, and our offers were repeatedly declined. With a looming deadline, we turned to what we knew—we prayed. We included Elisha, wanting him to witness firsthand how faith works in real life. We believed God had something beautiful waiting for us, even in the midst of uncertainty.

During that time, God had already blessed us with our dog Josie, a Cavalier King Charles Spaniel—our dream breed. A coworker, Kristen mentioned her friend in Georgia had a litter, and miraculously, the price was within reach. Even with the cost of a plane ticket for Kristen to retrieve her, it was far less than what we would have paid locally. Josie was a gift, bringing joy and comfort to us, especially after what we'd been through with Henry.

Then came the news—our offer on the butterfly garden house

had been accepted! Elisha and I jumped up and down with joy. It felt like divine provision. This wasn't just a house—it was a symbol of transformation, a place where I would continue to heal. Closing on the "butterfly house" was a victory that affirmed God's goodness and His attention to the desires of our hearts.

Living here has changed me. For most of my life, I only knew how to survive. But this home has helped me look forward to life. It's a daily reminder that God is not finished healing me. We lead worship from our music room, and Henry pastors our small home church. The Spirit of God fills this place—it's our sanctuary, our refuge. Here, I've learned to trust in His goodness instead of bracing for the worst.

The garden has become a renewing space for me. Its beauty calms my nervous system and draws me into God's presence and glory. Like the old hymn "In the Garden" says, "He walks with me, and He talks with me, and He tells me I am His own . . . " I've experienced that firsthand. Sometimes He speaks, sometimes He simply sits with me in the stillness. In tending the garden, I've learned to embrace change, to accept the seasons of life. What once felt like instability now feels like growth. This home, this garden, this season—it's all part of the healing He planned for me.

EMERGENCY ROOM NURSE

For much of my life, I lacked the tools to respond well to challenges. Without a consistent foundation of experience or a trusted family member to guide me, I navigated life awkwardly, reacting from a place of raw emotion. Because my memories were walled off, I couldn't draw from past hardships to gain perspective, so every difficulty felt new and overwhelming. My ability to process setbacks had never developed, and the dissociations kept me from accessing wisdom I needed to respond with resilience.

Oddly enough, the emergency room became a place of calm for me. For the close to two decades I spent in that environment, chaos was externalized; I didn't have to carry it inside. Henry was the one who encouraged me to start my nursing career there because he believed I was up for the challenge. At first, the disorder of the ER mirrored my mind. But quickly, I excelled at triage nursing which taught me how to prioritize true emergencies and discern what mattered most. The crucible of learning ER critical care at a level one trauma center instilled in me how to stay level-headed and cool under pressure.

Over time, those skills helped me triage my own life. What once triggered panic now feels manageable. With the return of my memories and the structure of ER thinking, I've learned to take things in stride. I no longer stumble at every obstacle—I've become someone who can leap over hurdles and keep going.

Since 2016, I've served as both the clinical leader, and now nurse supervisor at an outpatient cardiac and pulmonary rehab, the same place where Henry received care after his surgery. I've often asked God why He made me a leader, and He's shown me it was to redeem my understanding of authority. He's walked with me, teaching me that leadership in His kingdom is rooted in humility and strength through Him. In this role, I'm learning to handle conflict with grace and become the kind of authority figure I never had growing up.

FOUNDATIONAL TRIUMPHS

God has shown me that many of the behaviors and beliefs I once leaned on were simply to help me survive. These patterns—though protective at the time—needed to be gently unraveled, one by one, in the light of His truth. Only He knew the right order and timing for each revelation. As I surrendered them, I began to abide more deeply in His love. Each release became a victory, a marker of His healing hand at work in my life.

At the start of my transformation, it felt like standing before a room filled with tangled reels of ruined film—memories and voices jumbled together with no clear narrative. Into that chaos had settled traits like denial, perfectionism, victimhood, and over-sensitivity. But

God showed me how these were not my identity, they were book-marks pointing to pain I had buried. One by one, He invited me to view them through His lens, and in doing so, He freed me from their grip. Though much of my past was shrouded in confusion, His light has always pierced the darkness. And as I've come to see, He didn't just bring light—He created me to overcome.

OVERCOMING DENIAL

One of the first strongholds God revealed to me was that I was in denial of my suffering, something many trauma survivors can relate to. In the early stages of healing, He repeatedly used the word "injustices" to describe what I had endured. Still dissociated from the full truth, I only had a vague sense of what had happened. Then one day, He spoke clearly to me, "Daughter, I am desperate to heal injustices in the lives of My children." Then He named mine—my sister's abuse, my mother's willful blindness, her neglect, and aban-donment, spiritual manipulation and betrayal, and grooming by a father figure. God knew that before I could fully forgive, I had to be willing to lift the veil of avoidance. Some voices even mocked the process, using humor to deflect. But as more of them were integrated, I stopped negating my experience and began to accept the truth.

In that same moment, God also warned me—"When people suf-fer injustices, they often feel justified to act out in anger when life gets hard." That struck me deeply. I realized how frequently I had responded to stress with a sense of entitlement to my emotions, justifying fight-or-flight reactions because of my past. But God, ever the gentle Shepherd, would meet me in those moments, guiding me back to Himself. When I felt overwhelmed, He would whisper, "Stop. Look to Me. There is no offender here anymore where you felt out of control. I am in control of these waves, and you only need look to Me." Even when circumstances mirrored my past, it taught me how to respond differently, knowing He walks with me, and cares for me deeply. I read that if God is for us, no one can stand against us. That truth has become a cornerstone of my healing—He is for me, not against me.

Because of what I've endured, I understand loneliness, despair, mental-emotional anguish, spiritual deception, and betrayal. I carry a tender heart for others who suffer, and I often find myself moved to tears when hearing their stories. Writing about my own injustices has helped me understand why I remained in spiritual bondage for so long in the cult. But what I discovered was more than just an explanation, it was a revelation of God's deep desire to bless me and set my life in divine order. He has been desperate to heal every injustice and love me as only a true Father can.

SURVIVING ABUSE

Being physically cornered isn't the only way trauma takes root. While I'm grateful I never suffered more than a few minor bruises, trauma doesn't always leave visible marks. It doesn't require a single catastrophic event either. It can build slowly over time through repeated fear, shame, control, and manipulation, especially within families. My abuse wasn't overt violence—it was emotional domination and psychological control. That kind of trauma is harder to identify and easier to hide.

It was God who gently revealed the full scope of what I endured. And modern psychology affirmed what He showed me—that emotional abuse can be just as harmful as physical. Withholding affection, shifting blame, verbal intimidation, jealousy, possessiveness and denying or minimizing abuse all leave deep scars. My fractured mind was evidence of the fear I lived with—fear of Em's mood swings, her confinement tactics, and the absence of any adult willing to protect me. The constant cycle of affection and abuse left me psychologically wounded and deeply confused.

In my healing, God has met me in those memories with boundless compassion. During quiet moments with Him, He has led me into visualizations where He enters the scenes of my past—holding me in the sadness, confronting Em, and freeing me from the places where I once felt trapped and powerless. These encounters have been trans-formative. God has lovingly stepped into my darkest memories and rewritten them—not to erase the past, but to redeem it. What once left me feeling victimized has become a testimony of overcoming, through His presence and healing power.

SURVIVING SHAME

In surviving grooming from Mr. Hg, I had to forgive myself and understand why I was so vulnerable and naïve to his lure. For a long time, the memory throbbed like a hidden boil beneath the surface. I just wanted to ignore it because it was so painful.

People who haven't gone through some kind of sexual manip-ulation or abuse have difficulty understanding how someone can succumb to it—if they were not violently forced and had a choice in the matter. I was not even enticed by him per se, in fact, he did not appeal to me. Still, I had a hard time saying no because he was so insistent, confident and coercive. Over the years, he had become a good listener to me and was an expert at bringing down my defenses. If it weren't for Martin that night, and God—it was certainly a spiritual battle—I wouldn't have received the clarity needed to put an abrupt end to his advances. If, for example, I had sat in the hot tub with him, and he had become insistent or aggressive, I might not have been able to resist his advances due to my own confusion and naïveté.

I understand the guilt and shame that sexual abuse victims feel from blurred lines of right and wrong during or following events. It is not so black and white in the moment with another manipulative predator who knows how to beguile with words. In reflecting on my own experience with this kind of cajoling serpentine persuasion—where I was given a kind of choice in the matter—I came to forgive myself, a step that brought profound freedom.

Many do not even get the opportunity to opt out, and they have suffered unimaginable trauma encapsulated in shame and guilt, even when it was completely out of their control, especially if the horror began in childhood. This is often how the human mind responds to matters of sex—either as something dirty and reprobate or as something wanted and intimate. When it comes to sexual coercion by predators, these lines can blur. Shame is often felt in entertaining, acquiescing to, succumbing to or even wrestling with the suggestion—or agreeing to any part of it.

Though I had been deviously drawn in, I learned to free myself and stop the denial and self-blame. Even in cases of violent exploitation—where victims have no choice—those responses, while normal, are how they cope with the trauma. Seeking healing from it became essential for me, and expressing the shame and guilt was the path to freedom.

SURVIVING NARCISSISM

Healing from the impact of my mother's covert narcissism has required layers of revelation and restoration. Of all the descriptions I've encountered, one explanation resonated most—children of narcissistic parents learn early that love is conditional and transactional. They become performers—striving to earn affection through achievement, perfectionism or emotional caretaking—while abandoning their true selves. This creates a lifelong pattern of people-pleasing and self-betrayal, rooted in the deep pain of being used by the very person who should have offered unconditional love. That betrayal remained buried until I was ready to face it.

Throughout my healing journey, from a dissociative child into an adult transformed by God's love, my mother's impact has remained central to my psychological landscape. The Lord has shone a light upon painful wounds that required immense restoration. For the past decade, I maintained surface-level conversations with her, choosing to honor her as Scripture encourages, while slowly releasing my expectations. With God's help, I've learned to see her more clearly and to suffer fewer disappointments. Each interaction became an opportunity to step further away from her influence and into the truth of who I am in Christ. But nothing brought that truth into sharper focus than my visit with her in November 2024.

After nine years apart, I visited her in a rehab facility following her hip fracture. Though she was initially pleasant, her indifference quickly surfaced.

I helped her as a nurse, assisting with basic care and offering medical insight. But when I gently suggested she should no longer live alone, I recognized a familiar Cecille scowl of entitlement.

Her final words to me when I offered to come back to see her the following Monday—"Well, I don't know what I might have going on then"—made it clear she didn't want to see me again.

In that moment, I knew I was done. The closure I had long needed had arrived.

I spent the rest of that trip with my stepfamily, soaking in their warmth and love. On my last day, I considered visiting my mother again, but the dreary rain outside mirrored the truth I had finally accepted—she never truly loved me. She only loved when it was convenient for her. Here I stood, in the very coastal town she moved to while leaving me as a teenager in high school, and again now, she didn't want to see me again. She had chosen herself over me. The weight of that realization broke something open in me. I no longer blamed myself. Instead, I realized she was never able to give me the love I deserved, and her inability to love me *had nothing to do with me.*

That clarity brought another painful truth—my mother never deserved me. She used me—to support her own image, or for child support money or for whatever benefit she could gain—rather than choosing to love and nurture me. But God held me in the profound hurt that surfaced. He reminded me, "There is nothing more owed. It is Cecille Anne who owes a great debt to her children."

The goal in surviving narcissism is to become your true self—resilient and secure. God has been leading me there every day. My mother deprived me of both a mother and a father, poisoning my relationship with my dad through her narratives. But God, in His goodness, restored that bond before my father passed. And God Himself has been both mother and father to me—showing me my worth, speaking love into my soul, and nurturing me into healing. During the week I confronted the hardest truth about my mother, God gave me a vision of the day I was formed, when God Himself created my inmost being, just as I have read in the Bible. And in the moment of my birth, He showed me He was there—loving me, equipping me, and preparing me to overcome everything I would face.

RECLAIMING AGENCY

When Henry and I began seriously dating, he quickly noticed a pattern in me, one I hadn't yet recognized. I was looking up to him in a way that surrendered my agency, just as I had done with others in my past. Gently but firmly, he said, "This will only work if you stop putting me on a pedestal. God must come first. I'm just a man. I will disappoint you, not because I want to, but because I'm human."

That moment was pivotal. It was the first time someone I loved set a healthy boundary—not to control me, but to protect me. He didn't want to take my agency; he wanted me to keep it. With that, I understood why only God is worthy of my full adoration. People are fallible, but God alone is wholly good. I had read in the Bible that it's better to take refuge in the Lord than to trust in man, and Henry's words brought that truth to life.

Shortly before I first met Henry, I had lunch with Lilith and Ray. When the conversation turned to my weight, I felt Lilith's familiar pull toward control. Years earlier, on the land, a single comment from her had influenced my eating habits so drastically that I swung from underweight to overweight trying to please her.

But this time was different. I had just lost fifteen pounds through discipline and independence, and I was proud of that progress. When she expressed disapproval, I responded calmly, "This is what I've decided, and it's okay for me." For the first time, I didn't let her opinion sway me. It was a small but powerful step away from her control.

Later, when I shared this with Henry, he helped me see how deeply I had given my agency to others, first to my sister, then to my mother. My sister, still a child herself, raised me with control, not care. She didn't want me to think for myself—she wanted obedience. My mother, too, shaped me to fit her ideal, praising what she liked and dismissing the rest. I was raised in a constant state of stress, dependent on their approval, never learning to trust my own voice. That dependency became the foundation for how I related to others.

It was no surprise, then, that I later submitted to two cult leaders. It was all I knew—someone else leading, someone else deciding. My personality developed around that pattern, relying on others to define my choices. But God, in His mercy, began to heal that part of me. He led me from childlike dependency into mature self-determination, rooted in Him.

That piece of me has now been integrated. I no longer hand over my agency—I take responsibility for my emotions and decisions. I've learned to set boundaries and to stand firm in my identity in Christ. My worth is no longer negotiable. It is defined by God alone, and that truth has become the foundation of my freedom.

OVERCOMING REBELLIOUSNESS

In the early days of my walk with God, I struggled with the idea of surrender. Years of being controlled by my sister and mother had left me reflexively resistant to authority, even God's. I remember one moment clearly. Henry felt impressed by God that we should leave the house later than planned. I pushed back, not wanting to be told what to do. But as we drove, we passed a major car accident, one we might have been in had we left earlier. That moment stunned me. God wasn't controlling me—He was protecting me. Over time, He gently exposed the rebellion in me—not as strength, but as a wound, and began to heal it.

Surrendering to God isn't about losing agency. It's about choosing to trust the One who is good. God doesn't manipulate or demand allegiance like people do. He doesn't need followers—He is love itself, entirely self-sufficient. But He longs to free us. True surrender is intelligent and willing—it is giving Him permission to transform us, to align our hearts with His. We still have free will, but the greatest act of love is choosing to yield it to Him. In doing so, we don't lose ourselves, we become more fully who we were created to be.

When God took residence in my heart, my desires began to mirror His. Though I didn't stop wanting things, I did stop needing to please people. My heart turned toward pleasing Him. Obedience became an act of love, not obligation. I read that if we seek God first, everything else will be added, and it has. He has met every need, fulfilled every longing, and become the greatest treasure of my soul.

OVERCOMING VICTIMIZATION

With the awareness that agency was the "linchpin" holding core issues in place, God revealed the next major piece—the victim mentality. When one doesn't have one's own agency, there is no accountability for what happens because there is a lack of self-determination. This means everything that happens is *someone else's fault*. As I reclaimed my own agency, I began taking responsibility for my actions and life outcomes. Good or bad, it all stemmed from my choices, and I gained control over how I responded to circumstances.

I've wrestled with the mindset of victimhood for most of my life, shaped by the entitlement and emotional manipulation of my mother and sister. We were raised to use "I statements," which I later recognized as a subtle form of control—phrases that implied others were responsible for my emotions. I internalized this, believing I had the power to affect how others felt, especially when my sister blamed me for every shift in her mood. It left me hyper-aware of my words and actions, constantly analyzing myself to avoid upsetting others. But

I've come to see that this belief—that I can control someone else's feelings—is a lie.

At the core of my struggle was the need to please my mother, a goal I never achieved. Her narcissistic victimhood shaped my own patterns of self-blame. Even recently, she blamed me for injuring her during years I was in the cult. Before a family reunion I couldn't attend, she refused to pass along my love to our relatives, saying, "They know how you treated me while you were in the cult." I gently reminded her that we now had a relationship, and she could let them know I was doing well. But she refused, because the attention she receives as a victim is something she's unwilling to give up.

This is the destructive nature of the victim mindset—it doesn't just trap the person who holds it, it creates new victims. It distorts every situation through the lens of personal offense and keeps people stuck in cycles of blame. The only way out is to take responsibility for your own feelings and reactions. I've come to recognize this pattern not only in my family but in the world at large. It's everywhere woven into politics, relationships, and identity. Leaders exploit it, and people cling to it because it validates their pain. But it's a trap.

God continues to reveal the remnants of this mindset in me, and I keep surrendering them to Him. He doesn't coddle my victimhood— He calls me into victory. When I was persecuted while working in an emergency room, I could have sunk into old patterns of blame and despair. But instead, God lifted me above it. He showed me that I wasn't a victim, I was a victor. Not because I fought back, but because He fought for me.

Over several months when I worked at a different hospital, I was singled out by my ER Director and two clinical leaders who repeatedly scheduled me to work Sundays—despite knowing that Henry and I were leading a substantial congregation. The pressure escalated, involving even the HR Director and Chief Nursing Officer, until I filed a complaint with the EEOC for religious discrimination. When the EEOC issued a right-to-sue letter, the fallout was swift. All three leaders were terminated within weeks. God proved to me that He was my protector. Where no one had defended me as a child, He showed me that He would always fight for me. My deepest wound—mistrust of women in authority—was met with His justice and care. He reminded me that vengeance belongs to Him, not me, and that my role was to trust and obey under the shelter of His wings.

The day I delivered the legal notice to my boss, I sat on the couch in tears, knowing it would be the hardest thing I'd ever done in a workplace. As I prayed, God gave me a vision of heaven's army—soldiers in radiant armor marching beside me. He instructed me to show her the law she was violating, giving her a chance to change. But she didn't. She doubled down, and her fate was sealed. When the EEOC letter arrived, I watched in awe as God moved. One by one, those who had harassed me were removed, and the hospital finally granted the accommodation I had requested. I knew then, without a doubt, that the Lord had fought for me.

That experience became a turning point. For the first time, someone had championed me, and it was God Himself! He made it clear to my soul that love fights, love protects. Since then, He's called me to face other situations that echoed past trauma. Each time, He has walked with me, helping me respond with courage instead of fear. As I laid down old defenses, He gave me new strength, dignity, and peace. Emotions that once overwhelmed me—anger, anxiety, fear—began to lose their grip as He helped me understand their roots and release them. In their place, He poured out His love and healing. I am no longer a victim. I am a victor.

OVERCOMING PERFECTIONISM

God began revealing several core pieces of my inner life, each one falling like a domino into the next. The one I resisted most was perfectionism. For me, it wasn't just about doing things right—it was about survival. I believed that if I could be perfect, I could avoid the wrath of my sister, the judgment of my mother. But this strategy only turned inward, creating a harsh inner critic I named the "tortured perfectionist." It was a mindset that bullied and judged me, constantly analyzing my words and actions in an attempt to preempt criticism. In trying to protect myself, I became my own oppressor.

This perfectionism made it nearly impossible to feel at ease within myself. God had been speaking to me for years about defensiveness, and while I managed it at work, it often surfaced at home. Henry, with patience, helped me see how I would replay conversations from the ER, obsessing over whether I had upset someone, even when I had simply followed orders. God showed me that this was a core wound, tied to voices of the past. Once those voices were integrated, the perfectionist was exposed, and I could finally begin to heal.

I used to equate criticism with bullying. The tortured perfectionist blurred the lines between the two, making me defensive. But when I began to reclaim my agency, I learned to own my actions. If criticism was valid, I could receive it and grow. If it wasn't, I could thank the person and let it go. That shift was monumental. I no longer had to live under the weight of others' opinions. I could stand in truth, knowing that my worth wasn't tied to perfection. When I valued the world's approval more than God's, I surrendered my agency and undervalued my soul. But God paid the highest price for my freedom—His own life. He didn't call me to perfection, He called me to Himself. He longs to free us from every captivity, to bring us into His kingdom of light. In Him, I found joy, fulfillment, and blessing—not because I'd earned it, but because I am His.

God was never impressed with my achievements, He only wanted my heart. The talents He's given me aren't for impressing the world or proving my worth. Even if I never reach my "full potential" in the world's eyes, if I live with gratitude and contentment, God is pleased. Since the moment He first touched my life in that trailer, He's been gently unraveling me—not to destroy, but to deepen my joy and draw me closer to Him.

Where I once panicked over imperfect details, He's taught me to see beauty in the everyday. In a world full of chaos, He calls me to walk by faith, not by sight—to look for His goodness daily. Perfection will come when I see Him face to face. Until then, He invites me to rest in His perfection, not my own. Life is messy, and I'm learning not to resist it. Like a pine tree bending with the wind, I'm beginning to yield with grace. I no longer chase control. I commit my way to the One who holds all things together, and He brings it to pass.

OVERCOMING SELF-PITY

Self-pity is a natural outgrowth of the victim mentality, it feeds self-absorption and vanity, and without the presence of the Holy Spirit, it can consume a person. For years, I struggled to face the truth of what had happened to me. It was painful to acknowledge how deeply wounded I had become, and how those wounds led me into harmful relationships and cult environments. But God, in His compassion, helped me move from self-pity to genuine compassion for myself and for the little girl who was just trying to survive. I came to understand why I made the choices I did, and with His love, I forgave myself. He knew I needed distance from family members who couldn't take accountability, and in His mercy, He moved me out of California to create that space for healing.

Once I experienced God's empathy, forgiveness became possible—not just for others, but for myself. Because true forgiveness can only happen after receiving it from God. As I understood the depth of what He'd forgiven me for, I no longer felt entitled to withhold it from others. His love has erased every grudge, even the ones I held against myself. Even when old wounds surface, He reminds me, "Was My sacrifice not enough? Do you think punishing yourself adds anything to what I've already done?" His love has replaced the inner bully with peace. There is no condemnation in Christ, and I've learned that even I am not qualified to judge myself.

I had been conditioned to seek understanding through

self-pity—rehearsing my pain in hopes of being seen. But when God embraced my story with His love, it transformed. My testimony became one of overcoming, not wallowing. His compassion was the antidote to my self-pity. It didn't dismiss my pain, it redeemed it. And in that redemption, my story became a reflection of His healing, not merely my suffering.

OVERCOMING DYSFUNCTION

An essential part of my healing has been God helping me understand not just what happened to me, but why I responded the way I did. In unraveling my behaviors, I began to see who I truly was, apart from the survival mechanisms I once relied on. Much of my identity had been shaped by fear and pride, built as armor to protect myself from emotional harm. But God, in His gentleness, didn't shame me for those defenses. Instead, He lovingly revealed their purpose and invited me to lay them down—"This is why you used this, but it's safe to let it go now. I am here to protect and love you."

When I recently saw my mother, I understood more clearly than ever that my deepest trauma was her lack of emotional bonding when I was an infant. That realization explained so much—my dissociation, my disconnection from people and reality. Though it brought anger at first, God held me through it, allowing me to grieve, then gently lifting me into peace. He showed me that grief is necessary, but He doesn't leave us there. Like a loving Father, He comforts, restores, and lifts our spirits.

Now, I know my identity isn't rooted in what I do or say, it's found in who I am in Christ. He has made me new, not just through love, but through the healing power of His sacrifice. Every wall I built, every voice I internalized, was born from stunted growth and forgotten pain. God has been my compassionate guide, helping me understand each layer of my story and the emotions buried within it. He has been zealous to right wrongs, expose lies and mend every wound. This kind of reconciliation with oneself—this deep, soul-level healing—is only possible through the tender mercy of God.

OVERCOMING SENSITIVITY

My oversensitivity to people developed for a reason—to sense micro bits of manipulation, airs of superiority, and deceitful or subversive attempts to communicate disappointment. Namely, I had to be ready to make adjustments based on my sister's moods in a moment's notice. If I heard the smallest nuance of displeasure in her voice, I had to be prepared if she quickly flipped into the blamer, accuser, abuser mode as a young child. From my narcissistic mother, I was additionally sensitive to attention seeking, passive-aggressive tones, emitted lies, manipulation or opportunistic coercion.

Many are oversensitive in a similar way—because they had to tiptoe around others, or because it is a part of a people pleasing mechanism to receive love. Tiptoeing or pleasing people can be a defense to appease an abuser, a narcissist or someone broadcasting low self-esteem. It is actually an attempt to regulate other people's nervous systems in order to remain calm. God has been teaching me healthy boundaries regarding this, switching my old habit of tuning into other's nervous systems and instead remain responsible solely for my own. Because mine has been enough to deal with! Other people's feelings are their own responsibility, no matter how much they may try to make me responsible through passive-aggressive tones, manipulative emotions, or broadcast victimization.

With unresolved trauma, there can also be oversensitivity to sharp sudden sounds, textures, lack of sleep, heat, cold, raised voices, etc. These can even trigger a person into a state of fight or flight, causing immediate aggravation. This is because sensations are the language of the nervous system. If the nervous system stores a burden of traumatic memories, they can loosen in an instant from a sensory experience. In the past, I could immediately move into a fight or flight state when I was stung by a scorpion, got my finger caught in a folding gym, heard the elongated screech of a child or listened to multiple people speaking at once. Inwardly, I hated the sudden flurry of escalated nervous emotion that would rise, creating a kind of internal combustion.

But there is another reason for oversensitivity—even overexplaining things and overthinking, which I have in common with others who have stored trauma in the body. These are symptoms of the soul expressing that it requires understanding, or that it feels misunderstood, or that it needs to prove that it is good to others, in every situation. Overthinking in particular arises from under-feeling and it was a way for me to avoid feeling the discomfort of emotions I wasn't ready to experience. Emotions were very overwhelming, especially because my default pattern was to suppress them.

These over-sensitivities are being healed in me by the Father— through understanding what I had experienced and bringing them to Him. By nature, I will always be a curious overthinker, but not to the obsessive unhealthy extent I used to.

VICTORIES IN MY NERVOUS SYSTEM

I learned that when you begin healing suppressed trauma, your body often continues to react as if the past is still happening. Triggered responses—like surges of emotion, anxiety, or dissociation—weren't something I could think my way out of. Even when I knew my reaction was disproportionate, my nervous system didn't. It still believed I was in danger. After years of trauma, my survival brain had taken over completely. I lived in a constant state of fight, flight, or shutdown, desperate to resolve unmet needs for safety, dignity, and belonging. I didn't know there was any other way to feel.

God led me to discover how trauma was stored in my body and how He wanted to replace my fear with His love. I finally understood why I had always felt uneasy in my own skin. Dissociation, numbness and trying to escape my own experience had become second nature, especially in conflict. I discovered language and tools to understand what was happening inside me. My discomfort wasn't just emotional—it was physiological. My body had been bracing for danger for decades, and I didn't even realize it.

Through body-based practices, Holy Spirit led visualizations and self-attunement—all guided by godly wisdom—I began to release years of stored grief and trauma. I learned to signal safety and connection to my nervous system and ultimately regulate and rewire it. For the first time, I began waking up without fear. I could face the day with confidence. And if and when I did get triggered, I had tools to return to the present moment and reconnect with my body. Nervous system regulation became a way to take off the armor I had worn for so long and finally rest in God's love.

POISED FOR FLIGHT

Reflecting on my journey, I realized I wasn't alone in these struggles. For so long, I felt broken, as if my pain was just in my head. But I came to see that trauma is real, and healing is possible. It took time, compassion, and the right support. God's love and the quiet witness of scripture became a catalyst for true recovery. With God's help, I was able to move from survival to peace, from disconnection to wholeness.

As I stood at the edge of my transformation, I looked back on a life woven with threads of pain and grace. Each moment, from the shadowed corners of my childhood to the desolate trailer in Dragoon, a stitch in God's tapestry of redemption. Though once bound by heartache growing up and the deceptive lures of cults, in His gentle hands, they became the raw material of my chrysalis. In the quiet of that trailer, where isolation once whispered despair, God's love spoke louder, wrapping me in a sacred cocoon of His Word and presence. Like the caterpillar, my old self—fractured, fearful, and lost—had dissolved through years of surrender, rebuilt by His truth into something new. I felt the translucent walls of my chrysalis thinning, my heart stirring with the same gentle flutters I first knew when Jesus became my first love. No longer defined by survival, I was ready to break free, my wings trembling with joy, poised to unfold into the light of His eternal promise.

Strength to Fly

MY OWN BUTTERFLY

After we bought our home, the former owner, Kris, kindly walked us through the garden, pointing out caterpillars that would one day become swallowtails, queens, and monarchs. She showed me hidden spots where chrysalises had formed, and I was captivated.

Not long after we moved in, I went on a chrysalis hunt and discovered a bright green pupa glistening from a pottery bowl nestled in the dirt. I returned to it daily, watching as it turned golden, then translucent, revealing the butterfly inside. One morning, I found her, newly emerged, clinging to the shell of her chrysalis, waiting for her wings to fill with life. Mesmerized, I spent five hours that day watching her journey toward flight.

She moved tentatively at first, slowly opening and closing her wings, exploring her new body. Softly tottering around the garden, she did not attempt to fly. As the hours passed, I noticed she was struggling to find food. It was December, and few flowers remained. Gently, I extended my hand, and to my delight, she climbed onto my finger, tickling my palm with her weightless walking. I carried her to several blossoms until she found one she liked. After feeding, she attempted to fly, falling at first, then trying again—each time with more strength. She stayed in the garden, fluttering around me as if in gratitude, allowing me to photograph her in the golden light. Finally, she perched on a leafy branch, her wings glowing, and then, with a final flutter, she flew away.

That butterfly became the subject of a large oil painting which now hangs in our living room. It retells what God whispered to me that day: "Many don't realize they are already butterflies. They cling to an empty chrysalis—unaware they've been transformed." Like this butterfly, there was a time I didn't know I could fly. I held on to old identities, old fears, old patterns of responding. But God, in His kindness, lifted me in the palm of His hand and led me to the nourishment I needed. Time after time, He has picked me up from where I've fallen and given me the strength to try again.

Watching her lifecycle which mirrored my own, I saw the liquefication, the transformation, the emergence, the hesitation, and finally, the flight. It was meaningful to be reminded that healing is not just about surviving but about becoming. The dark chrysalis of my own life was all part of becoming mariposa. Hope emerged from that hidden place. Only with God's nurturing could I see who I truly am. And like that butterfly, I've learned to trust the One who knows when it's time to fly.

JOHN

The brain cannot feel both fear and love at the same time. Love, in its purest form, deactivates the neural pathways that fuel fear and anxiety, dissolving their effect. In my own life, God has redeemed me from being a body ruled by fear into one that can now receive and experience love in ways I never imagined. His love has rewired my responses, softened my defenses, and brought peace where panic once lived.

I've always been drawn to the apostle John, who called himself "the disciple whom Jesus loved." He was the one who leaned against Jesus' chest during the last supper. John was in love with love incarnate, with the treasure that is Jesus. But his faith wasn't rooted in how much he loved Jesus—it was founded by how much Jesus loved him. He knew the power of being loved by God. That distinction has changed everything for me. It's not about striving to love God more, it's about letting Him love me.

From John, I've learned that healing begins when I stop resisting and let God love me. Jesus said the greatest commandment is to love God with all your heart, soul and strength. I've come to understand that the way to truly love God is to know Him, and to allow Him to love me first. Like any parent, He delights in our response to His affection. My heart, my nearness to Him, is all He's ever wanted.

For years, I exhausted myself, holding up walls built from fear. But in the strength of His regard, I surrendered. I stopped fighting His love. I stopped guarding secrets from myself—I stopped betraying my own experience. When we surrender our pride and defenses, we exchange it for His armor, and He clothes us with garments of salvation and covers us with His righteousness.

I've learned to rest by receiving His love—His affection, His delight in me. That rest required me to lay down my coping mechanisms and trust Him with the process, however long it took. Only God, in His selfless compassion and perfect knowledge, could unravel the knots in my heart and mind. And He has. This healing has not been my work—it has been His.

THE LOVE THAT CARRIES ME

Jesus loves me intensely and unconditionally. And I have allowed His love to impact me and fill me. One of my deepest prayers since receiving salvation has been to feel the fullness of His love. He knew that to answer that prayer, I would need to walk through deep healing with Him. Beyond my willingness to heal, He asked one thing of me—trust. And in countless encounters, He proved Himself trustworthy. For someone with childhood trauma, trusting God did not come easily, but He knew that too. Through revelations of my past, through holding me in my tears, through the tangible touch of His presence and His voice in every trial, I slowly let go of my defenses. I no longer need the identities I created to survive. I only want the breastplate of His righteousness, His eternal goodness, His unfailing kindness, and His humility brought low. I don't need to be anyone other than who I am in Christ. I am returning to the essential me, the one He created from the beginning.

The world teaches the opposite. Culture says to be proud, to seek admiration, to define success by wealth, beauty, and status. But God's ways are not ours, He who exalts himself will be humbled. God doesn't see like us—we look at outward appearances, but the Lord values virtues of the heart—humility, mercy, reverence, faith, and sacrificial love. Jesus taught that earthly treasures perish but encouraged us to store up heavenly treasures that last forever. Henry, while running critical calls on the ambulance, often reflected on how death equalizes all people, rich or poor. In the end, nothing we've achieved or accumulated will matter—only our relationship with God will remain.

Healing into wholeness isn't complicated, but it isn't complete this side of heaven. True transformation comes not from human effort, but from the compassionate hand of an Almighty God. His is a love that no man can take away. It is not earned, and it cannot be lost. And it is the love that carries me, day by day, into the fullness of who He created me to be.

TOOLS FOR EMERGENCE

If a person is truly ready to heal, there is great hope. I wish some-one had told me this years ago, when I had little optimism for love or connection. But for the reader who longs to be restored—even radically transformed—this can become your story. If I were to summarize what I've learned through years of healing from a disso-ciative identity disorder and severe memory loss to becoming a fully integrated, mostly regulated woman who knows the love of the Lord, it would be this—healing is a movement from fear into love. I couldn't orchestrate it on my own, no matter how desperate I was to "get it done." I lived in a body of fear, and though I'd read that there is no fear in love, and that in fact, God's perfect love casts out fear, I couldn't feel that love. Instead, I lived with chronic sadness, anxiety, and fight-or-flight reactions. What I didn't realize was I had tremendous unresolved trauma, and God was walking me through a tender, transformative process.

Despite years of spiritual and psychological language from the New Age, I had to face the truth—I could not fix myself. I was trapped in layers of self-protection I had built to survive, like straitjackets I had wrapped around my own soul. Each layer held embedded pain, distorted beliefs, and behaviors I had no tools to release. Positive thinking and affirmations did nothing for me, in fact, they only deepened my frustration. I had no power to bring about the metamorphosis I desperately longed for! Only God, in His mercy, could unravel what I had bound, and only His love could reach places I had hidden for so long.

1. Lean and Rest

The first step in healing is admitting you cannot heal yourself. For years, I was discouraged by how long it took just to feel mentally sound. In His kindness, the Lord gave me a word picture to help me understand. A coworker's infant daughter with Down syndrome needed cardiac surgery within her first two months of life. God said to me, "You are no more able to heal yourself than this Down syndrome infant is able to perform her own heart surgery, with a toy scalpel." That image arrested me; I was exhausted from striving. God continued, "It's not about you healing yourself. This is My process. My pace is not yours—you cannot make this go any faster. Rest in My care and lean upon Me." His words calmed my frustration and reminded me that healing is not something I can force, it's something I must receive.

My transformation felt slow because of the depth of emotional and mental healing required. In my impatience, He reminded me He is faithful and patient to complete His perfect work in me. From the beginning, He promised to heal me beyond what I could imagine. And He has.

When you begin to trust Him with your trauma, rest is essential. Like Elijah, who collapsed in despair after fleeing Jezebel, God didn't rebuke him—He sent angels to feed him and let him sleep. Then He spoke in a gentle whisper and led him on a slow, 40-day journey to restore him. God designed our minds to heal gradually, releasing trauma in small doses. It's better that way. Healing is overwhelming and impossible without Him. With Him, it becomes an intentional, steady unfolding.

2. Be Willing to Exchange

Healing requires a willingness to let go of the things that keep your fearful, sinful nature in bondage—things that may have once protected you but now only hinder your joy. C.S. Lewis once said, "God has made it a rule for Himself that He won't alter people's character by force. He can and will alter them—but only if the people will let Him." To move from fear into love, the very armor you once relied on must be exchanged for love that only comes from God. This is a process of trust, a delicate unraveling in relationship with Jesus, who is long-suffering and gentle with the soul. God replaces fear with courage, and powerlessness with His strength.

Coping mechanisms are often rooted in pride and pain, built to survive trauma. But God, in His compassion, gently lifts each layer until we no longer want them. He is not afraid of our anger or sorrow that rises up as we release, and He never leaves us shackled to walls we've built. To truly heal, we must be willing to surrender resentment, victimization, and pride. Jesus declared that He is the way, the truth and the life, and to walk with Him means exchanging our ways for His. His ways are higher than ours. And when you surrender your coping habits and pride, when you humble yourself and your ways before Him, He will lift you up.

In the light of His truth, God leads us through necessary seasons of mourning, but He never leaves us there. He transforms resentment into forgiveness, victimhood into victory, and pride into a humble strength. As His children, our sins are forgiven, and we are continually being set free. Often, I take solace in His promise that He will perfect all things which concern me. As He works to heal my life, I am being made new, as a new creation in Christ.

Healing is hard. It takes courage to be vulnerable. But it's far harder to stay bound and constantly feel out of control. Each reaction, each trigger, is a bookmark in your story. And until you read your story with God, you'll relive the worst parts. When you surrender your pain to the One who sees and understands it all, He will completely liberate you.

3. Feel to Heal

While God desires that we understand, with compassion, what happened to us, He will not let us linger in grief forever. With every layer of painful realization in my life, I've known the moment when the emotional weight lifts. At first, the tears seem endless, but soon He replaces sorrow with a cleansing resilience. We may weep with sorrow in the darkest night, but His hope shines brightly in the morning. There's even a divine design in the act of crying—tears flush stress hormones from the body and release endorphins to ease pain. Whether grieving the loss of a loved one, a broken dream, or the ache of unmet childhood needs, God walks us through it all. The Bible says the Lord is near to those who have a broken heart, that He saves those with a contrite spirit. In His care, He has become a shield for me, my glory and the One who lifts up my head—giving me the courage and the strength to carry on.

Jesus Himself wept at the tomb of Lazarus, even while knowing He would raise him from the dead. He understands our emotions. He was well acquainted with grief and sorrows, in fact He carried those to His death on a cross. He came to restore what was broken between God and man, offering Himself as the sacrificial Lamb. We identify with Him in His death because His death became our redemption, and His resurrection our victory. Because He lives in us, He brings light to our stories so we can overcome—not remain victims. To live fully in Christ's resurrection, we must allow Him to put to death what harms us, so that our true selves can be reborn. Simply ask Him, and He will do it, in His perfect timing.

4. Release Stored Trauma

Healing from trauma is not just a mental or emotional journey—it is deeply physical and spiritual. Nervous system regulation helps release stored trauma from the body in small, gradual doses, eventually helping to rewire the survival brain to become well regulated. While I've found somatic, body-based practices to be deeply effective, not all are created equal. Some approaches, particularly those rooted in New Age philosophies, may emphasize energy manipulation, altered states of consciousness, or self-deification. Obviously, I avoided practices that would lead me away from Christ and back into spiritual confusion and vulnerability from which I had been delivered. Other approaches, while grounded in science, may neglect the soul entirely, treating the body as a machine rather than as God's temple.

That's why it was essential for me to find nervous system regulation that was Christ-honoring, rooted in the belief that our bodies are fearfully and wonderfully made and that healing comes through the work of the Holy Spirit. True healing of the soul requires more than technique, and only God can signal unconditional love to the nervous system and bring lasting transformation.

Having grown up with severe memory loss and dissociation from childhood trauma, I lived in a chronic state of fight, flight, or shutdown without knowing why. Through Sarah Jackson's biblically grounded coaching (sarahjacksoncoaching.com), I gained the language to understand what happened to me and how to restore a sense of safety, connection, and dignity to my body, helping me wake up unafraid, and able to live in the moment. While her program was instrumental, I know it was God who ultimately rewired my nervous system. I had prayed fervently for healing, and He answered. When you're ready, releasing stored trauma is liberating; it brings self-awareness, com-passion, and the ability to receive love from God and others. It was a miracle for me to feel secure in my own body, to breathe deeply, and to live with joy.

Some of the most impactful tools for me include self-attunement with prayer, envisioning heaven during quiet time with God, danc-ing to release stored trauma, singing praise and worship, imagining running to complete stored flight responses, practicing body-based techniques and recording "glimmers" or daily moments of beauty. While positive thinking alone doesn't heal trauma, noticing "glim-mers" can reshape the brain's response to life. This practice has helped me replace dread with gratitude. Whether it's a kiss from my dog, laughter with a friend, or the warmth of morning light, I now see God's goodness woven into my days; so, in everything, I give thanks. Gratitude rewires the brain, lowers stress, and strengthens emotional health.

Your identity is not the armor you've worn to survive. That chainmail, forged in trauma, no longer serves you. The real you—free, peaceful, and connected—is waiting to emerge. You are safe to live in your own body—no longer a slave to fear, but a child of God.

5. Attune Gently

Understanding your own story is essential to healing. Without it, you may feel perpetually misunderstood, seek validation from others, numb your pain, or become offended when people don't respond to your emotional reactions as expected. These are not paths to true living. I noticed that when I spoke about my past and felt a flush rise in my body, it was a signal that I still had unresolved emotions and was seeking to be understood. But my story is too much to download to anyone; only Henry knows it in full. While it can be helpful to receive understanding from others, especially those involved in your story, it's not always possible. Compassion for your story grows as you come to know the truth about yourself.

When you have an uncomfortable response, take time to understand your feelings as indicators of needs. Forgive yourself for ways you have coped—denial, achievement, perfectionism, control, dissociations, overthinking, overexplaining or discomfort with touch. These are survival responses. As Sarah Jackson teaches, be exceedingly gentle with yourself—you've been in survival mode for a long time. With God's perspective, get curious about your reactions. Take quiet time with Him and regulate your nervous system to remember—that was then, this is now.

There is no one on earth who can understand you like God can. He has been with you from the very beginning. While friends or spouses may sympathize, only God can fully comprehend your experiences and give you insight into how they shaped you. He will quiet you with His love and He has all the time in eternity to listen. Though He honors your free will, He longs for you to turn to Him. His invitation remains open until your final breath to cast all your care on Him, for He cares for you.

COVERED WITH GOLD

In ancient Japan, broken pottery was not discarded but restored with gold through a method called Kintsugi, a practice that honors flaws and transforms them into beauty. This art form reminds me how God, the original Potter, handles our brokenness. We are all cracked vessels—fractured by our own sins or the wounds inflicted upon us. Yet, in His loving hands, every fissure becomes a place for His glory to shine. He whispers, "Look, daughter, look what I did here. You laid down this pain, and behold, I have made all things new." Just like the butterfly emerging from the cocoon, my life has been gilded by His artistry, each scar now a testament of His redemptive love.

God doesn't discard the damaged—He restores. He holds all things together, and in Him, I was held together when I felt I might fall apart. My mind, fragile and frayed, was steadied by His hand. In that vulnerable place, I cried out, and He answered, lifting me from the miry clay and setting my feet on a rock. He put a new song in my mouth, and now, even when I sing in worship, tears flow freely. Jesus came not for the righteous, but for the broken, the condemned, the poor, the sick, the rejected. He chose flawed, imperfect disciples to walk with Him, just as He chooses us, not because we are whole, but because He longs to make us whole in His love.

RESTORED WITH BEAUTY

The world teaches us to hide our flaws, to mask our brokenness with perfection and performance. It pressures us to become someone we're not, building shells around our hearts to avoid rejection. But God sees through all of it. Unlike the world, He doesn't discard what's cracked—He restores it with beauty. He is the Divine Artist, the One who paints sunsets and galaxies, and He alone understands the intricate design of our hearts. I've learned my only role is to surrender, to stop striving and let Him do the healing. Because without Him, we can do nothing. Even when the process feels painful, He gently continues His work, covering my flaws with His gold, for His strength is made perfect in weakness.

Jesus invites us to rest in Him, calling us to come to Him, lay down our burdens, and receive his abiding peace. Like John leaning on Jesus' chest, we are called to relax into His love. But we often carry burdens He never asked us to bear—expectations, shame, and self-imposed standards. And though we constantly miss the mark, God never does. He is faithful to complete the good work He began in us. As we come to know His goodness, it becomes easier to trust Him—to let Him remove the pain of sin and leave only the beauty of grace.

LIKE A CHILD

There is no encounter more honest than the one we have with the Lord. Unlike the shifting shadows of people shaped by manipulation and control, He is the great I AM—unchanging, trustworthy, and full of perfect love. For someone like me, raised in an environment where trust was dangerous, His authenticity is entirely intoxicating. He is a safe refuge for the wounded, and every tear we cry matters deeply to Him. He has never disappointed me, and He never will because it is impossible for God to lie or deceive. His love is constant because He is love, and so by abiding in His love, we are abiding in God, and He in us. And He is who He is *forever*—a soothing assurance for the soul.

Just as children are honest and unfiltered, Jesus invites us to come to Him with that same childlike trust. He asks us to receive the kingdom of heaven like a child to enter it. And this is also how He wants us to approach our healing. He welcomes our honesty and raw emotions, and He meets us in truth. Many fear His love not because of judgment, but because it is so real, so genuine, so pure. Yet He has always been ready to receive us just as we are. "Whoever calls on the name of the Lord shall be saved" (Romans 10:13 NKJV). No earthly pleasure can fill the void like He can. His love is the wholeness we seek—eternal, unshakable, and more satisfying than anything this fleeting world can offer.

ECHAD

The Father, Son, and Holy Spirit exist in perfect communion—echad, the Hebrew word for oneness—a unity composed of more than one part, just as the Bible says, a husband and wife become one flesh. Made in God's image, we were created for this same kind of communion with Him. He longs to dwell within us so fully that our hearts become His home. He has even called our bodies His temple. If you love Jesus and follow Him, you are a house of God. He desires not just belief, but intimacy—a relationship where we seek Him always, and He fills every empty space with His presence.

For decades, I searched for spiritual connection, believing I'd find enlightenment within myself. But that was a lie. Inside, I only found trauma, confusion, and coping mechanisms. My journey through New Age spirituality and even two cults left me emptier than before. In 2001, I encountered the living God—the God of Abraham, Isaac, and Jacob—and everything changed. In communion with Him, I finally found the love, truth, healing, and purpose I had been craving. Nothing else could satisfy the longing of my heart like a restored relationship with Jesus Christ.

BEAUTY FOR ASHES

Each life is a precious creation, breathed into existence by God. Though we experience joy and connection, we also carry wounds that leave lasting marks. Yet in the hands of our Creator, even sorrow becomes a treasure. He draws victory from pain, offering us jewels from the depths of His goodness. Every trial holds the potential for triumph, and every surrender of anxiety or striving brings freedom. From the ashes of destruction, He calls forth beauty. He gives joy in the midst of mourning, and He gives us the ability to sing His praise in the midst of our most agonizing distress. My life is living proof that His Word is true. He has turned my pain into purpose, my brokenness into splendor.

The journey was long, and the healing came in layers, but over time, the fragments began to settle, and the light grew steadier. Since asking for God's forgiveness through Jesus Christ, I've been fundamentally remade. Like a butterfly emerging from its cocoon, I've transformed into the woman He always intended—joyful, peaceful, and whole. The enemy tried to destroy me, but God has redeemed every wound. He delivered me from all oppression, restored what was lost and has worked all things together for my good because I love Him. His healing has touched every part of me, and I now live in the freedom of His love.

When I first came to Him, I had nothing but a desperate longing for peace and a sound mind. I clung to the promise, "Delight yourself also in the Lord, and He shall give you the desires of your heart"

(Psalm 37:4). I taped it to my trailer wall and hid it in my heart. And He fulfilled it beyond anything I imagined—blessing me with a loving husband, a wonderful son and stepdaughter, a peaceful home, and a career filled with purpose. More than anything, He gave me Himself. Jesus is my greatest treasure. As a survivor of childhood trauma, I never learned to dream, only to survive. But God dreamed for me and gave me a hopeful future. I may never fully grasp the depth of what He's done, but my heart overflows with awe. How did He take the mess I was and turn it into a life full of peace and joy?

ORIENTED

My fervent focus has been to know who I am in God—my identity rooted not in the world, but in the One who created me. It's a beautiful paradox to feel both deeply cherished as the apple of His eye and humbly small before His holiness. His love is beyond comprehension—He knows every hair on my head and every detail of my life. Though I can't fully grasp the depth of His affection this side of heaven, I keep seeking it, drawn by the wonder of His presence. Beneath a prayer shawl, under the shadow of His wings, hidden in stillness, I meet with Him. He reminds me that He will never change His mind about me, and I find the courage to live, to let go, and to receive His love anew.

Intimacy with God is never something to fear. His love is gentle, humble, and free of human agendas. When I sit with Him, I feel the King of the Universe smile upon me, speaking words that hold me together—words that always reflect His truth in Scripture. Especially as someone who was once starved for love, I run to Him without shame. He never withholds affection or gives it in pieces. Again and again, He breathes into my soul, "Daughter, I am never letting you go. I will never leave you. I am always with you." Though I can't explain how He's always near, I've learned to receive the mystery. His presence is warmth in my chest, and His embrace is the safest place I know.

In this life, I may not see Him face to face, but I know who I am—I am a child of God. And as His child, He has left riches for me to discover; I will search Him out and find myself in Him. And I will always long to be near Him. No one else on earth holds this place in my heart. He is always faithful to answer my prayer, "Lord, draw me close to You." In His nearness, I find my identity, my worth, and the love I was created for.

OVERCOME

There is no explanation for the healing I've experienced apart from God—it is a miracle. Buried beneath layers of dissociation, amnesia, and fractured identity, though I was nearly lost to myself, Jesus met me there. He restored my soul and made me a walking wonder of His healing power. In this world it's impossible to avoid trouble. But I take heart that Jesus has overcome the world. Through Him, I became an overcomer. Healing isn't just emotional or mental—it's spiritual. Because we are spirit, soul, and body, true restoration comes only through communion with the One who made us. He alone could reach the deepest places, gently healing pain and breaking chains of sin that once held me captive.

The difference is Jesus—and one cry for help. "O Lord my God, I cried out to You, and You healed me" (Psalm 30:2). He transformed my victimhood into victory, my bitterness into forgiveness, and my fear into joy. Joy is the fruit of healing, and it cannot coexist with pride, fear, or unforgiveness. It is sustained by the Holy Spirit, who reminds me that what Jesus has done for me is finished and eternal. From the moment I first cried out to Him, He promised I would fly one day, and He kept His promise. He formed my chrysalis, carried me through transformation, and lifted me into freedom by His Spirit. He changed my mourning into dancing and filled my heart with gladness. And like the butterfly, my ascent was made possible by the wind of the Holy Spirit.

THE WIND

There's something encouraging about the wind—it both stirs and stills me. Whether it brushes my skin with warmth or kisses my face with winter's chill, it always reminds me of God's gentleness. The wind has always been a comfort, a quiet embrace from the Creator. In its presence, I feel held, calm, and alive. It's as if the breath of God Himself is moving through the air, whispering peace into my soul.

The Holy Spirit is like the wind—unseen yet deeply felt. He moves through the body like a warm, calming love, inviting deeper breaths and quiet trust. I have felt mountain breezes, ocean tides and desert gusts, but none compare to the Spirit of God. By His spirit, we have life. Everything we do and even who we are is immersed in who He is. He never forces His way in but offers freedom—freedom to receive love, to be still, to hope again. His presence is like rain poured on dry land, like a whisper filling you with life.

Since receiving Christ, the Holy Spirit has been my truest companion and the end of all searching for me. His daily reassurance stills my restless heart and reminds me I belong to Him.

Like a butterfly lifted by the wind, my own flight into freedom has only been possible through Him. With the strength of His goodness, He gives me the courage to stretch, to let go, and to soar. Though I trust the wings He's given me, I know it's His breath that carries me.

If you've come to the end of this book hoping for a self-help plan, I offer instead a sacred invitation—to stop striving and return to the One who heals. God is not an idea—He is very real, defined by His Word, full of truth and love. Your soul was made to commune with Him, to feel safe enough to be vulnerable. Without that connection, true healing remains out of reach. Whether you're crawling, dissolving in transformation, or struggling to believe you can fly—call on the name of the Lord and be saved, be healed.

My life is a testimony to His goodness and healing power. If you come to Him, He will show you a love you've never known and a peace that surpasses all understanding. He's been knocking on the door of your heart all your life. If you look back, you'll see the moments He's reached out. He waits now, ready to heal every wound and transform you into something beautiful. He will gild your wings with gold—and the King of Glory Himself will give you strength to fly.

ABOUT THE AUTHOR

Elizabeth Leone Gonzalez is a writer, artist, worship leader, and healthcare professional whose life has been shaped by a profound journey of healing and transformation. Her memoir, *Becoming Mariposa*, chronicles her path from childhood trauma and spiritual searching to emotional restoration and a life anchored in faith.

Elizabeth lives in Tucson, AZ with her husband Henry and their son Elisha, whose presence continues to inspire her journey of love and resilience. She currently serves as the nursing supervisor of a cardiac and pulmonary rehabilitation clinic.

A lifelong artist, Elizabeth still paints, sings and plays the guitar, often collaborating with Henry to write praise and worship songs. Together, they have a small congregation where Henry pastors and Elizabeth leads worship, sharing the joy and intimacy of a life devoted to Christ.

More than anything, Elizabeth desires for her readers to find the wholeness she has discovered through an intimate relationship with Jesus. She has prayed for every person who reads *Becoming Mariposa*, hoping her story will be a light to those navigating pain, confusion, or spiritual longing. Her life is a testament to the truth that beauty can rise from brokenness, and that healing, and even overcoming is possible through the love of God.

Connect with Elizabeth: www.becomingmariposa.info or scan here:

A Personal Request from the Author

Dear Reader,

If this book moved you, taught you something new,
or simply kept you turning the pages,
would you take a moment to leave a review on Amazon?

Your feedback helps other readers discover the book—
and it means the world to me as an author.

Thank you for being part of this journey.

SILVERSMITH
PRESS

Serves new and emerging authors
to help them write, publish, and promote their books.
Are you ready to share your story?

Visit us!
www.silversmithpress.com

www.ingramcontent.com/pod-product-compliance
Lightning Source LLC
Chambersburg PA
CBHW040136270326
41927CB00020B/3411